The Bhils

An Ethno-Historic Analysis

The Bhils
An Ethno-Historic Analysis

Bachchan Kumar

SHARADA

Sharada Publishing House
Delhi-110035
1997

First Published 1997

ISBN 81-85616-47-7

B.L. Bansal
SHARADA PUBLISHING HOUSE
(Publishers on India's Past & Present)
40 Anand Nagar, Inderlok
Delhi-110035 Ph. 5117390

Printed at
Santosh Offset, Delhi-110035

Dedicated to my Mother
Late Mrs. Sudama Dutt

Foreword

The Bhils constitute the largest tribal population in India. Out of 29.8 million scheduled tribe population in India, according to 1971 census, 3.8 million are Bhils. Every seventh tribal is a Bhil.

Dr. Bachchan Kumar has chosen Jhabua district in Madhya Pradesh as his area of study. The Bhils represent 85% of the total population of this area.

Based on his extensive field work, interviews and personal observations, the present study on the Bhils offer us interesting and stimulating fresh insight helpful in unveiling complex mosaic in Indian culture.

Comparing his data from the field with a wide range of ethnographic works published in course of ninteenth and twentieth century, Dr. Kumar has suggested new directions of research on the Bhil population.

On the basis of his in-depth study of a district, the author has reexamined a number of interesting issues relating to the study of the Bhil tribe as a whole.

The origin-myth of the Bhils have been studied in a historical background, focussing the process of the Aryanization of an indigenous tribe of India. The legend which presents Parvati as the sister of the Bhil tribe clearly points to this process.

The author has attempted to uncover the indigenous strata of the Bhil religion on which thick layers of Brahmanical belief system was superimposed in course of centuries.

His analysis of the Bhil life cycle ceremonies centred around birth, marriage and death demonstration that is possible, through a complex process of analysis and comparison to reconstitute the indigenous core of culture hidden under the superimposed layers of Hinduism.

In this ethno-historic analysis of the Bhil tribe Dr. Kumar has offered us a methodology by which the study of process of Sanskritisation could simultaneously unveil foundations of indigenous culture of India.

Prof. Sachchidanand Sahai
Ph.D. Paris
Dean, Faculty of Social Science
and Head, Deptt. of Ancient Indian and Asian Studies,
Magadh University, Bodh-Gaya, Bihar, India

Acknowledgements

I gratefully acknowledge a deept debt of gratitue to Dr. (Mrs.) Kapila Vatsyayan, Academic Director, Indira Gandhi National Centre for the Arts for her patronage and support to my research work.

I express my sincere thanks to Professor Sachchidanand Sahai, Head, Department of Ancient Indian and Asian Studies and Dean, Faculty of Social Sciences, Magadh University, Bodh-Gaya, for his valuable guidance in the preparation of this research work which was originally presented as a Ph. D. thesis.

I am grateful to the library authorities of M. L. Verma Tribal Research Institute, Udaipur, Rajasthan, for allowing me to consult rare books and periodicals and for extending facilities for xeroxing of some of the articles.

To the Asiatic Society, Anthropological Survey of India (Calcutta), Archaeological Survey of India, Sapru House, Central Secretariat, Teen Murti, National Archives of India, Indira Gandhi National Centre for the Arts (New Delhi) and Tribal Research Institute (Bhopal), I extend my sincere thanks for offering me assistance in collecting materials on the Bhils.

I sincerely acknowledge a deep debt of gratitude to the administrative staff, village teachers, *Patwari* and *Tadvis* of Jhabua district for facilitating my field work.

I am beholden to Late Dr. G. D. Sontheimer, Professor and Head, Department of History of Religion and Philosophy, South Asian Institute of the University of Heidelberg, West Germany for his helpful suggestions and criticism.

Mr. Aswini Shankar, Lecturer, Department of History, Deshbandhu College, Mr. B. K. Bhattacharya, Assistant Librarian,

Sahitya Academy Library, (New Delhi) and Mr. Chandra Shekhar Verma, lecturer, Department of English, Magadh University, Bodh-Gaya, offered their valuable suggestions and comments. Mr. Rajendra Taragi, artist, Indira Gandhi National Centre for the Arts has also helped me in drawing the maps of this book.

My wife Mrs. Renu Srivastava remained extremely supportive in the preparation of this book.

Bachchan Kumar

New Delhi

March 15, 1995

Contents

Introduction

Three main considerations inspired me to take up the present study. First, there is no comprehensive study on the Bhils in an ethno-historic perspective. Second, the Bhils constitute the largest tribal group in India. Third, the tradition bound tribal societies, living in almost a closed system before the independence, were exposed to various non-tribal cultural traditions. Due to this exposure most of their customs have completely disappeared. Since the Bhils are very conservative so far as their culture and traditions are concerned, many of their rituals are still in vogue. I propose to document their cultural heritage, before it is completely lost due to their growing contacts with the urbanised social systems.

I have examined various aspects of life-cycle ceremonies—birth, marriage and death as prevalent among the Bhils of Jhabua district. Though, their rituals are quite different from those practised by other tribal and non-tribal groups, I have made an attempt to focus the links between tribals of the different parts of the country, and to understand the traditional culture of this tribe in a limited area of a district.

Aim of the Study

Probably E. B. Taylor was the first ethnologist who pointed out that there are many 'archaic' aspects in culture. He called them 'survivals' and advocated for their systematic study. This concept was further developed by various schools of ethnologists. To some evolutionists, such survivals were the means to trace an earlier, less developed stage in the history of mankind. To some diffusionists, they demonstrated the spread of customs from local points to different areas.

The main aim of this study is to trace out survivals of the Bhil culture by studying certain areas of folk religion, customs and rituals. The subsidiary aims are to introduce aspects of the Bhil culture to a wider range, to demonstrate how they have maintained some time-honoured ceremonies and to point out area of interest for future scholars.

Area of the Study

The area of our study is Jhabua district in Madhya Pradesh. The district lies in the extreme west of the state and is bounded by Banswara district of Rajasthan in North-West, Panch Mahal and Baroda district of Gujarat in the West, Dhulia district of Maharashtra and West Nimar district of Madhya Pradesh in South, Dhar district in the East and Ratlam district in North. The Jhabua district lies in between 22^0 North and 45 ' North latitude and 74^0 East and 38 ' East latitude. The district is situated at 1171 feet above the sea-level.

The district consists of 2 sub divisions, 5 tehsils, 12 blocks and 1760 villages. The two sub-divisions are Jhabua and Alirajpur. The tehsils are Jhabua, Thandla, Petlawad, Alirajpur and Jobat. The sub-division, Jhabua consists of three tehsils: Jhabua, Thandla and Petlawad. Under Alirajpur sub-division, the tehsils are Alirajpur and Jobat. There are three blocks in Jhabua tehsil: Jhabua, Rama and Ranapur; two blocks under Thandla tehsil: Meghnagar and Thandla; one block in Petlawad tehsil, Petlawad; three blocks in Alirajpur tehsil: Alirajpur, Kattiwara and Sondawa and three blocks in Jobat tehsil: Jobat, Udaigarh and Bhabhara.

The terrain is generally hilly and the soil is light, not well suited for cultivation. The vegetation over the hilly terrain has been indiscriminately cut in the past, leaving the hills completely denuded of trees whereby causing considerable soil erosion. The two main rivers of the district are the Mahi and the Anas. The river Narmada only touches the southern fringe.

The forests of this area were once very extensive and valuable but indiscriminate and illicit felling of trees mainly by the tribals has ruined most of them. The important minor forest produce are *kullu* gum, honey, wax, palm, *rosha* oil and *tendu* leaves.

Among the major flora in the forests here are teak (*Tectona grandis*), *mahua* (*Bassia latifolia*), bamboo (*Dendroealamus strictus, bambusa arundinacea* and other varieties), mango (*Mangifera indica*), toddy tree (*Borassus fiabellifer*) and *khajoor* (*Phoenix sylvestria*). There are some good plantations of teak and cashewnut in the area. In the area of Kattiwara, the most important plantations are *mandhar* and *chatyapani*. Among the trees that provide minor forest produce are *temroo* (*Disospyros tomentosa*), *charoli* (*Buchanania latifolia*), *aonla* (*Phyllanthus emblica*) and *bahera* (*Terminalia bellerica*).

The minerals found in this area are soapstone, bassalt, sandstone, granitoidal greiss and limestone. The Soapstone is found in a large quantity while limestone in a small quantity.

In the past, the forests of the area had a rich variety of animals. In the Mughal days, wild elephants abounded in the forest, but they disappeared long ago. In the more recent past, tiger and bison were common, but they too have disappeared. This has been the result of unchecked forest encroachments and indiscriminate hunting. Among the wild animals, which have been reported from the present forests, are panthers (Felic pardus), tigers (*Felis tigris*), hyaena (Hyaena striata), fox (Vulpes bengalensis), bear (Melursus ursinus) and hare (Lepas reficaudatus). Occasionally the wild cock (Ballus sonnerali) is also seen. Pigeons, bhattiars, blue rock pigeons, whistling teals, peacocks and grouse are some of the common birds seen in the forest area.

The pattern of crops is almost the same in the whole area. Though *rabi* and *kharif* are the two main harvesting seasons, the area is predominantly monocropped because of rainfed agriculture and very little availability of irrigation.

The main tribes of the district are the Bhils, the Bhilalas, the Barela, and the Patelia, etc. Of these the Patelias are considered to be more advanced both socially as well as economically. The Bhilalas come next followed by the Barelas. The Bhils are the economically most backward; they rank the lowest in the social hierarchy. The Bhilalas are the off-shoot of the Bhils. They emerged as a result of intermarriage between the Rajputs and the Bhils. The name is supposed to be derived from their act of diversion from the main stream as a result of crossing over i.e., the *Bhil-Adya*, which clearly expresses the contempt of the Bhils towards the newly formed group. But gradually this new group, because of their kinship with a very high caste, achieved a higher social status and started calling themselves as the *Bhilala*, meaning the superior Bhils (*Bhil-ala*). According to 1981 census, Jhabua district has a tribal population of 6,44,149 out of a total population of 7,95,834. In terms of percentage, tribals constitute

80.94 per cent of the district population. The tehsil-wise distribution of tribal population for the years 1961, 1971 and 1981 census of the district is indicated in table no. 1.

Table-1

Tehsil-Wise Percentage of Tribal Population

Sl. No.	Tehsils	% of tribal population		
		1961	1971	1981
1.	Jhabua	87.58	86.81	79.48
2.	Thandla	84.99	85.48	84.19
3.	Petlawad	70.04	70.51	69.28
4.	Alirajpur	84.13	85.18	86.34
5.	Jobat	91.34	90.48	88.60

Source : *Census of India 1961*, 1971 and 1981.

Research Methodology

The present study is based on field work, interviews and personal observations. The Bhils from differents professions, occupations, age-groups and sex were interviewed. People well acquainted with the tribal life-style, customs and rites— *Tadvi, Bhagats* and village teachers were also interviewed.

These interviews have been supplemented by the ethnographic descriptions offered by previous researchers. The following 10 villages— two from each of the five tehsils of the Jhabua district were selected for field work: (1) Surinala (2) Khermal (Jhabua); (3) Bhurighati (4) Kesharpura (Petalawad); (5) Ochaka (6) Munjal (Thandla); (7) Kalyavav (8) Kila Jobat (Jobat); (9) Bada Ondawa and (10) Umrath (Alirajpur).

Crteria of Selecting the Villages

These villages were selected on the basis of location and population. Seven out of ten villages are situated in the interior of the block and away from the tehsil headquarters and three are near the block and tehsil headquarters. The inhabitants of these villages are exclusively Bhils and having not more than 500 population. These villages were selected with the help of geographical map of Jhabua district. It was done with the objective of covering the whole area of the district. While selecting interior villages only those villages were considered which were practising traditional culture.

Design of the Study

The present study was completed in three phases. In the first phase, relevant published source materials were obtained from different libraries and land records from the headquarters of the Jhabua district. In the second phase, a questionnaire was modelled in the pattern of socio-economic study. In the last phase, the information relating to life-cycle ceremonies were obtained through interviews and through participant's observation. The basic data, collected through questionnaire, were analysed by computer.

The ten identified villages have 1030 *taparas* (households) approximately. The sample is generally representative of every third household. In some cases the members of third household could not be interviewed. In all such cases the next household was considered but that was very marginal. Altogether 340 households were interviewed. The socio-economic data were collected in the beginning of the year 1986. The second phase of data relating to life-cycle ceremonies were obtained in the end of the year 1989.

Previous Studies on the Bhil Culture

In his article, 'The Marriage Rites of the Bhils in the Nimar District', Stephen Fuchs offers a study based on the comparative analysis of the Bhils and the Hindu marriage rituals.

S.C.Varma, in his book *The Bhil Kills* (1978), gives an account of crime situation in the Bhil area.

In his paper 'Marriage among the Bhils,' Ram Ahuja describes the marriageable age, different forms of selecting mates, types of marriage, bridal payments, and the distance between villages where marriages have taken place. He also indicates briefly the restrictions imposed by customs on the selection of mates.

S.L.Doshi, in his study *Bhils: Between Societal Self Awareness and Cultural Synthesis* (1971), discusses the circumstances leading to the rise of Bhilism.

N. N. Vyas, in his research paper 'Women in Tribal Society' (1978), examines the inter-relations that exist between husband and wife in the family in a tribal society. His work also highlights the position of tribal women in patrilocal societies which require the wife in her husband's residence.

D. N. Majumdar, in his article 'The Bhils of Gujarat' (1942), opines that from the cultural point of view the Bhils do not appear to be a distinct social group in Gujarat, though they have many non-Hindu elements in their culture. The Bhil women who are credited with freedom and latitude in inter sexual relations, are victims of cruelty, and desertion or divorce is its remedy. The presence of orthodox practices during marriage, e.g. setting up of '*Mandap*' (marriage booth) at the bride's house, lighting a lamp by bride and immediately putting out the lamp by bridegroom, tying up the garments of the couple, are popular among them.

These pioneering researches, though not directly related with the area of my study, have been immensely helpful in understanding the ethnic rituals of Jhabua district.

Scheme of the Present Study

The present study consists of eight chapters. Chapter I offers Demographic and Anthropometric Description of the Bhils, focussing their links with other Indian tribes. Chapter II deals with the origin myths and historical background, outlining their role in shaping the course of events in the areas where they were either the rulers or the ruled.

Chapter III presents the economic profile, focussing the effects of the structural changes in their economy, resulting from the process of transformation of a shifting cultivation system into a settled farming pattern and from the enforcement of the forest laws.

Chapter IV offers an overview of the social and cultural life of the Bhils and the impact of neighbouring cultural traditions on them.

Chapter V determines the core of the Bhils religious practices, taking into account the interaction between the animistic and Hindu elements.

The following three chapters (VI-VIII) discuss the Bhils birth rites, marriage and death rituals.

The concluding part of this book focuses on the cultural traits of the Bhils in the Jhabua District.

1

The Bhils : Demographic and Anthropometric Description

The Bhil population has been distributed along the boundaries of Madhya Pradesh, Gujarat, Rajasthan and Maharashtra. The map of the Bhil region shows that they are spread over within a long irregular triangle of North-Western India. The base of this area is Khandesh, 90 miles North of Bombay, and a narrow apex reaches up along the ridge of the Aravali Hill in Udaipur, which is one of the former princely states forming the Southern boundary of the state of Rajasthan. Throughout this area, the Bhils are spread over 400 miles from North to South at its one extreme, and the aboriginal Bhils of Jhabua at the other. They are also found in negligible number in the state of Karanataka, Andhra Pradesh and Tripura.

According to 1961 census, the Bhil population is the highest in Madhya Pradesh (31.95 per cent) and the lowest in Maharashtra (15.00 per cent). It is significant to note that in Madhya Pradesh, the Bhils constitute only 18.53 per cent of scheduled tribe population. Yet this figure provides the highest proportion of the Bhils in India. The Bhils are a major tribal population in Gujarat and Rajasthan also.

According to 1971 census, out of 29.8 million scheduled tribe population in India, 3.8 million are the Bhils. Thus every seventh member of the scheduled tribe is a Bhil and it forms the largest group among tribal population. Table-2 shows the percentage distribution of the Bhil population in different states of India.

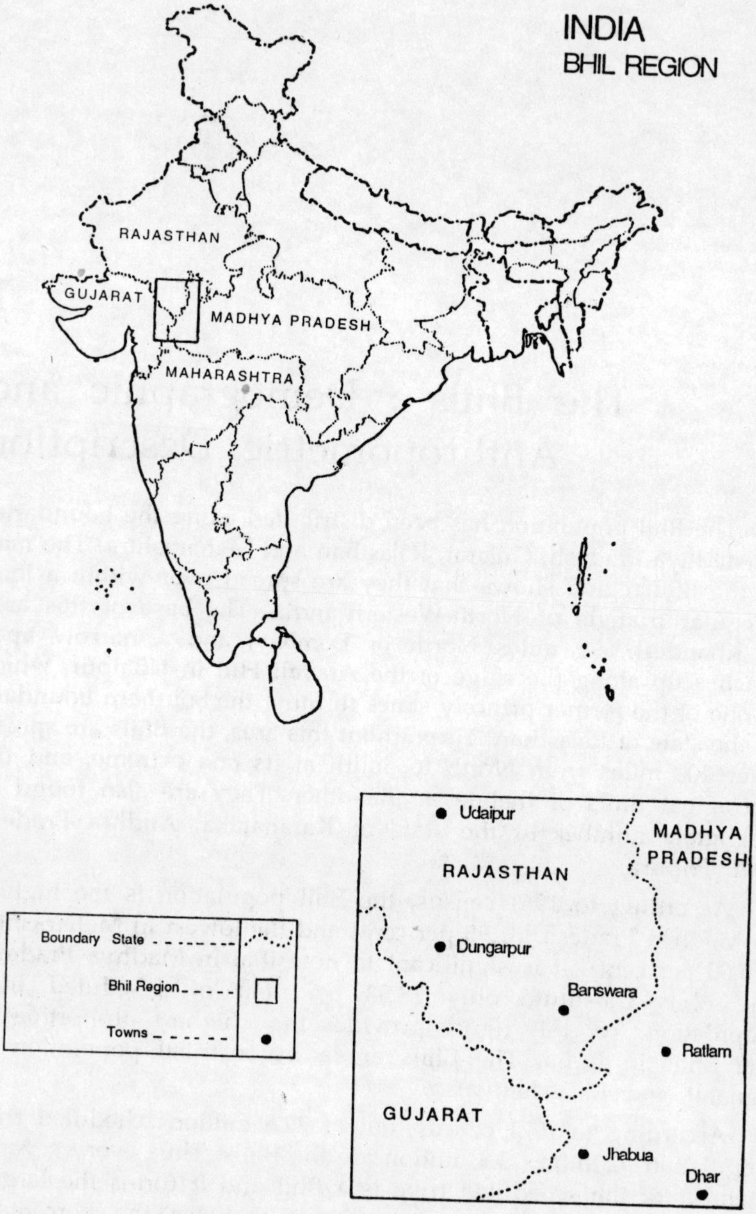
INDIA
BHIL REGION
RAJASTHAN
GUJARAT
MADHYA PRADESH
MAHARASHTRA
Boundary State
Bhil Region
Towns
Udaipur
MADHYA PRADESH
RAJASTHAN
Dungarpur
Banswara
Ratlam
GUJARAT
Jhabua
Dhar

Map 1

BHIL REGION

DISTRICT WITH BHIL AND RELATED TRIBES

TOWN ....

Majority tribal area ....

Boundary. State ....

Boundary District ....

Map 2

Table-2

Statewise Percentage Distribution of Bhil Population in India

State	Percentage to schedule tribe population	Percentage to total Bhil population
Madhya Pradesh	18.53	31.95
Gujarat	40.83	29.33
Rajasthan	38.58	23.70
Maharashtra	23.90	15.00
Karnataka	0.95	0.02
Andhra Pradesh	Negligible	Negligible
Tripura	Negligible	Negligible
India	12.83	100.00

Source : *Census of India,* 1971.

Growth of Bhil Population

During the decade 1951-61, the Bhil population increased from 2.3 million to 3.8 million i.e. an increase of 64.50 per cent. Before 1961 Census, the population under tribal religions category had shown neither any marked stability nor any consistent changing trend. The irregularities in the decade variations of the populations, in the past censuses, are much due to the confusions faced by the state authorities in the classification and naming of 'Tribals'.

Table-3 shows the decade variations in the Bhil population. Though there has been negative growth rates among Scheduled Tribes (1911-31) and nation's population (1911-21), the Bhils have consistently shown a fluctuating positive growth rate- the highest being during the decades 1911-21 and 1951-61. These fluctuations in their growth rate patterns are due to the changes made by the state authorities in the class coverage of 'Tribals'.

Table-3

Growth of Bhil Population in India, 1911-61

Year	Population	Percentage Variation Bhils	India Scheduled Tribes	
1911	10,67,792			
1921	17,95,808	68.18	- 5.05	- 0.31
1931	20,13,177	12.10	- 15.29	-11.00
1941	22,48,152	11.67	6.18	14.23
1951	23,30,278	3.65	6.13	13.34
1961	38,33,331	64.50	32.58	21.49

Source: *Census of India,* 1911-1961

Of the five decades (1911-61), 1911-21 is the only one which registered an actual decrease in India's population (-0.31%). This phenomenal negative rate of growth, under the assumption that the extent of population under enumeration counted at these two Census points of time was the same, suggests that the deaths in the decade were more than births. Evidences are available which show that severe famines and epidemics had spread during the year preceding the Census; the most devastating was the nation-wide influenza epidemic of 1918. Inspite of these rates for India as a whole, the Bhils showed the highest positive rate of 68.18 during this decade. The epidemic might not have spared the Bhil population. They were saved due to the ecological factors and the type of settlement patterns they live in. Ecologically they form a natural region with functionally integrated area- usually the river banks. The availability of plentiful natural resources for everyday basic requirements helps them to face any crisis. Further, their settlement pattern checks the spread of contagious diseases, since they live in hamlets or clusters of four to five huts. These clusters, by and large, are well scattered.

Interestingly the Bhil showed a decline in growth rate for the decade 1921-31 to 1941-51. During these decades Christianity was widely enlarging its followers, and this decline in growth rate is perhaps the result of massive conversion of the Bhils to Christianity. The first phase in 1911-21 witnessed the establishment and intensification of the Christian missionaries in the tribal pockets. It was only during these decades that considerable headway was made in terms of educating and enlightening the tribals, whereas the undercurrent of the acceptance of faith was already created in the subsequent decades

Physical Features

According to Hendley a Bhil is generally very dark; with black hair, straight and long; smooth face with slight moustache (rarely with beard and whiskers); dark eyes with the pelpebral apertures limited in size, making the eye look small. The Iris is grey , and chest has no hair. The face is large, wide and almost round, forehead of fair height, rather more square; vertex of skull, flatter. In some cases, however, the roof of the skull seemed to begin in the centre of the forehead. Thus rendering the facial angle, measured in the ordinary way, appear large, and not affording a correct indication of cranial capacity. Eyelashes and eyebrows ample, bridge of nose broad and sunk, nostril dilated very round, nose slightly retrousse, broad, clubbed at the tip.

Mouth large, lips thick, inexpressive, sensual, giving the impression that they were made merely to cover the teeth, which are large and coarse. The zygoma is very large and silent. Cheeks full. Molar bones flat and prominent. Ears large and prominent and very movable. Jaws evenly hung, massive lower square, large in proportion, angles square, large and widely separated. Expression amiable, but timid. They have dilated large nostril, the movable and prominent ear. To masticate hard and coarse food, their teeth are very large— the incisors are square, broad, fixed vertically in the gums— but are generally flat instead of sharp at the edges, bearing marks like those of the horse, approaching the molar in appearance. Their teeth are very strong and attached to huge jaw which necessitates large muscles. These are accommodated in wide and projecting zygomatic arches.[1]

Becon writes that the Bhils have dark skins, thick lips and broad noses.[2] According to *Encyclopaedia Britannica*, the typical Bhil is small, dark, broadnosed, but well-knit.[3]

Rowney writes that the Bhils are characterised by dark colour, diminutive size, prominent cheek-bones, large nostrils and great personal activity combined with an astonishing power of enduring fatigue.[4]

Kurup narrates about the Bhils of Western Madhya Pradesh. He writes, "they have a complexion varying from olive to copper and busky brown and they possess fine nose and they approach average Indian height."[5]

According to Chakraborti and Mukherji, the colour of the skin varies from light brown to dark brown. The form of the hair is generally smooth and the colour black with occasional reddish tinge. Eye colour generally varies from dark brown to light brown, the common colour being dark brown. Mongolian fold is absent. The brow ridges are moderately developed. Forehead is somewhat retreating in a considerable proportion. Lips are generally thin in the Bhils of Gujarat but thick lips are often met with in those of Madhya Pradesh. Chin is usually oval or round and it is weakly developed. Beard and body hair are scanty.[6]

Psychic Features

Ghurey describes the Bhils character thus: They are in ordinary circumstances— cheerful, hard working folk with a keen sense of self respect, honest, truthful and courageous. Their defects are inordinate life of drink and improvidence. Further they can be readily stirred upon violence and their ignorance and cruelty make them an early prey of misrepresentation.[7]

According to Herbert Risley, the Bhil is the king of the jungle; his arrow flies straight. The Bhil is always ready for the prey. If you are escorted by a Bhil, your life is safe. If you please them, the Bhils are your good friend; otherwise they are ruthless people. The Bhils are very shifty; one buttock bare, the other clothed.[8]

Russel and Hira Lal observe: the typical Bhil is small, dark, broad-nosed and ugly, but well built and active. The hands are somewhat small and the legs fairly developed, those of the women being the best. The Bhil is an excellent woodsman, knows the shortest cuts over the hills, can walk the roughest paths and climb the steepest crags without slipping or feeling distressed.[9] He is often called in old Sanskrit works Venapuka, child of the forest; Pal Indra, Lord of the Pass— these names well describe his character; his country is approached through narrow defiles— Pal or Nal (a causeway). Through these none can pass without his permission. In former days he always levied 'rakhwali' or black-mail, and even now native travellers find him quite ready to assert what he deems his just rights.[10]

According to Venkatachar, the Bhils belong to Pre-Dravidian 'Negroid race'. The typical Bhil has a broad nose, thick lips which are 'opened' and the upper jaw is somewhat strong and prominent. He is dark but owing to much intermixing there are varying shades and darkness among the Bhils of different localities. Their hairs are black but not wooly; straight but not wavy. The eyes are usually black.[11]

Guha opines that physically the Bhils appear to be a mixed type entailing Caucasian and Australoid element and sometimes their features rather suggest a touch of the Mongolian, though their head appears markedly long. The nose shows greater global depression than that of higher caste Rajput.[12]

Rousselet states that the Bhils are generally of the middle height. Their strength and agility are somewhat surprising. Their features are coarse, the nose often flat, and the cheekbones prominent; their black hair hangs down round their head uncared for, a simple twist bound round the temples serving them for a turban.[13]

Anthropometric Measurement

Maj. Hendley took anthropometric data of Maiwar Bhil crops. He found the mean height of 128 males with an average age of 25.89 years was 5 feet and 6. 38 inches. Of 128, the mean length of the upper extremity 31.56 inches (upper arm 13.81 inches, lower 17.75 inches); of the lower extremity, 38.87 inches (thigh 18.71 inches, leg 20.16 inches). The female lower extremities are fairly developed as they are good walker. The measurements of circumference for the neck, upper arm, chest, thigh and knee, in 128 women cases found respectively 11.52, 8.04, 30.25, 15.95, 12.23 inches; the average of pelvis and leg respectively 26.91 and 11.7 inches. The average length of 79 clavicles was 6.71 inches, and mean length of 78 sterna was 6.84 inches.

The skull found dolicho-cephalic. The antero-posterior diameter of 129 heads was 7.21 inches, the lateral 5.66 inches, the depth from vertex to chin in 81 cases 8.05 inches. The ratio of length to breadth was as 100: 79.22.[14]

In 1944, Stephen Fuchs measured 86 Bhils of the Jhabua district and found them to be one of the most primitive groups. He observes that the average Bhils are of medium height. Of them 36 per cent are dolicho-cephalic, 59.3 per cent meso-cephalic, 3.5 per cent brachy-cephalic and most of them have round and oval faces. The chin is normally round or oval and slightly receding.

The forehead is straight retreating and super-orbital ridges are generally well-developed. The nasal measurements showed that 1.2 per cent are leptorrhine, 39.5 per cent mesorrhine, 53.5 per cent platyrrhine and 5.8 per cent hyper-platyrrhine.[15]

Venkatachar measured Bhils of Satpura. He found that the Bhils are of the medium statured (mean stature 1649.52+— 9.23) with long head, (the mean Cephalic index being 72.89+— 0.53). The vault of the cranium is moderately high (mean Auricular height 120.48 +— 0.85) and the face short and narrow, the total facial length being only 110 +— 1.01. The nose is broad at the root, the inter-orbital breadth being 30.30 +— 0.27 and also very wide at the nostrils. It is moderately low as shown by the depth (mean Nasal depth 21.11 +— 0.32), and given an almost chamaerrhine Index (mean Nasal Index 81.38 +— 0.95).[16]

In order to evaluate the developmental sequence of all the bodies, Ranjana and Nath[17] measured 285 male Bhils from the educational institutions of Udaipur in Rajasthan ranging between the age group 7 to 17 years. The variables were collected cross-sectionally and growth achieved by them revealed in table-4.

Table-4

Segmental Growth Rate of Different Parts of the Body

Sl. no.	Characters	Absolute gain (cms.)
1.	Stature	45.8
2.	Sitting Height	22.6
3.	Trunk Height	19.0
4.	Head and Neck Length	3.7
5.	Total Lower Extremity Length	31.2
6.	Thigh Length	14.6
7.	Calf Length	15.6
8.	Foot Length	7.6
9.	Total Upper Extremity Length	25.3
10.	Upper Arm Length	11.9
11.	Fore Arm Length	9.1
12.	Hand Length	5.7

The segmental growth rate of different parts of the Bhils body exhibits distinct growth. In general case, the body of Human beings, it grows up in proportions at different rates, at different times, in different areas and system of the body. It is observed that the Bhil's growth of head and chest region which is most rapid during pre-natal and infancy period begin to slow down with the development of arms and legs expressing a rapid acceleration by the age of 5, while at the age of 6 a child is more or less 2/3 as tall as he would be as an adult due to the fact that the post natal growth in man follows an over all sequence 2-3-4-5, i.e., head and neck dimensions increase by two times, trunk three times, arms four times and the legs five times.

Table-5

Age Group Measurement of Trunk Height, Head and Neck Length

Age Groups (Years)	Measurement	
	Trunk Height (%)	Head and Neck Length (%)
7.0	64.7	35.3
8.0	65.3	34.5
9.0	66.3	33.5
10.0	66.9	33.1
11.0	67.4	32.4
12.0	67.6	32.2
13.0	69.1	30.9
14.0	69.3	31.0
15.0	69.8	30.1
16.0	70.2	29.9
17.0	71.1	30.0

It appears from table-5 that the relative values of head and neck length and trunk height, when obtained in proportion to sitting height reveal that the trunk height increases in its relative proportion from 64.7 per cent at the age of 7 to 70.1 per cent at 17 years. The head and neck length, on the other hand, exhibits a decrease in its proportion from 35.3 per cent at the age of 7 to 30.0 per cent at the age of 17.

Racial Similarities with other Castes

The Bhils have racial similarities with other higher castes. Majumdar has made anthropometric measurements of 187 Bhils of Panch Mahal district of Gujarat in the year 1944. The mean and value data are placed in table 6.

While comparing the above measurements with other well known castes, Majumdar opines that the Bhils are much closer to Pre-Dravidian stock. On the other hand Bhils have longer nose than the Pre-Dravidian tribes and are very close to high castes people of Eastern and Western districts of Uttar Pradesh (India), the *Brahmins* and the *Chattris.*

Table-6

Anthropometric Measurements

Sl. no.	Character	Mean	Value
1.	Stature	162.67	.499
2.	Max. Head Length	181.87	.430
3.	Max. Head Breadth	137.48	.339
4.	Bizygomatic Breadth	131.32	.355
5.	Nasal Length	48.60	.041
6.	Nasal Breadth	37.49	.176
7.	Total Facial Length	112.22	.487
8.	Cephalic Index	75.65	.206
9.	Nasal Index	77.19	.543
10.	Total Facial Index	85.64	.362

The Brahmins of the eastern Uttar Pradesh significantly differ from the Panchmahal Bhils in head length, head breadth, minimum frontal diameter, bigonial breadth, nasal breadth, nasal depth, total facial length, upper facial length and a stature. The Western Uttar Pradesh Brahmins are more strongly differentiated from the Bhils than colleagues in the eastern districts, while significant differences are found between the Rajputs of Uttar Pradesh and Panchmahal Bhils in head length, head breadth, bigonial breadth, nasal breadth, nasal depth, total facial length and upper facial length.

Thus on that basis Majumdar remarks that the more we analyse the data, the more it transpires that the Bhils are racially more distant from the so called Pre-Dravidian groups, while they approach nearer to the higher castes though the nature of the data, it must be admitted, does not warrant any definite conclusion.[18]

Racial Similarities with other Aboriginal Tribes

To establish inter-relationship with the aboriginal tribes, Guha studied Bhils of western ranges of the Vindhya Hill, Munda and Oraon of Chottanagpur, Chenchu of Gantur district of Madras Presidency and Kadar and Nattu Malayan of the upper and lower parts of the hill of Cochin. The study is based on the data collected by P. C. Basu on Munda and Oraon and his own measurement of 50 Bhils of the Tadvi division of pure blood, 23 male Chenchu, 44 Nattu Malayan and 112 male and 31 female Kadars. On comparing the data, he finds close racial similarities among the Bhils, the Chenchu and the Kadar. Considering Auricular height, Bigonial breadth etc. the derived Co-efficient (6.11 +— 0.59) shows close affinities with Chenchu.

On the other hand, derived reduced Co-efficient (18.98 +— 0.27) of Kadar has also shown close racial likeness. The findings by Guha are placed in table 7 and 8.

Table-7

Reduced Co-efficient of Racial Likeness

(Based on 26 Character)

Tribes	Kadar	Bhil	Chenchu
Kadar	-	18.98 +— 0.27	10.30 +— 0.49
Bhil	18.98 +— 0.27	-	6.11 +— 0.59
Chenchu	10.30 +— 0.49	6.11 +— 0.59	-

Table-8

Crude Co-efficient of Racial Likeness

(Based on 26 Character)

Tribes	Kadar	Bhil	Chenchu
Kadar	-	13.09 +— 0.19	3.97 +— 0.19
Bhil	13.09 +— 0.19	-	1.94 +— 0.19
Chenchu	3.97 +— 0.19	1.94 +— 0.19	-

On the basis of the data, Dr. Guha concluded that the aboriginal population of India shows a short, long and moderately

Reduced Co-efficient of Racial Likeness

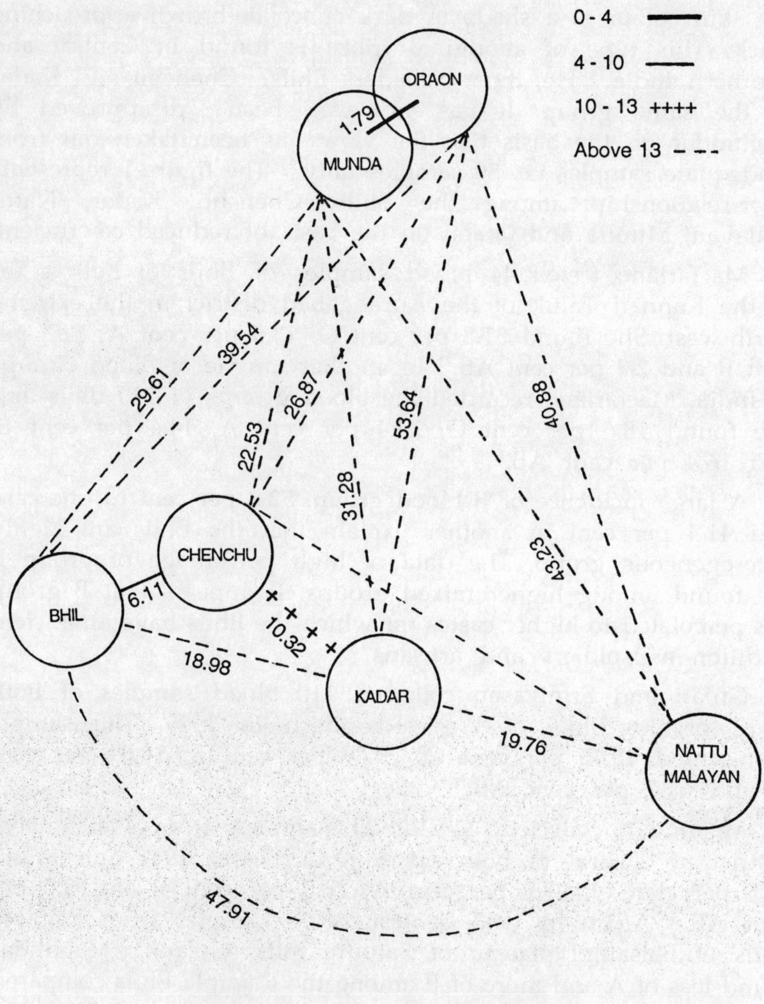

Inter-relationship of Aboriginal Tribes

Fig. 1

high-headed strain with often marked brow-ridges, broad short faces, the mouth slightly inclined forward and small flat nose with the alae extended. The hair varies from wavy to curly and the skin colour is a shade of dark chocolate-brown approaching black. This type of aboriginal tribes is found in Central and Southern India.[19] He, thus, considers Bhils, Chenchu and Kadar of the same group. It has, however, been disapproved by Majumdar on the basis that the view has been taken out from inadequate samples i.e. 50 samples only.[20] The figure-1 represents inter-relationship among the Bhils, Chenchu, Kadar, Nattu Malayan, Munda and Oraon on the basis of reduced co-efficient.

Macfarlane tested 44 blood samples of Bhils of both sexes in the Kannad Taluk of the Aurangabad district in the extreme north-west. She found 31.8 per cent O, 13.6 per cent A, 52.3 per cent B and 2.3 per cent AB.[21] In another sample of Blood Groups in India, Macfarlane recorded the blood groups of 140 Bhils and she found 18.6 per cent O, 23.4 per cent A, 14.4 per cent B, and 16.4 per cent AB.[22]

A large incidence of B blood group, 52.3 per cent in one case and 41.4 per cent in another explain that the Bhils are highly heterogeneous group. The data of high percentage of group B are found among higher mixed groups. It appears that B group has percolated to higher castes for which the Bhils have an ancient tradition as soldiers and artisans.

Gulati and Srinivasan collected 110 blood samples of both sexes of the Bhils of West Khandesh in 1969. The sample represented 45.45 per cent O, 29.09 per cent B, 19.09 per cent A and 6.37 per cent AB.[23]

Majumdar collected 369 blood samples from Panchmahal district of Gujarat of both sexes in December 1941 and found 37.5 per cent O, 27.5 per cent A, 26.0 per cent B and 9.0 per cent AB.[24] Again in 1943 he tested 156 samples from Rajpipla Bhils of Balsamol plateau of Satpura hills (Gujarat). Majumdar found less of A and more of B among the Rajpipla Bhils compared to those of the Panchmahal district but both data are significantly different from those collected by Macfarlane. He disagrees with Macfarlane's estimate of B concentration in Bhils and says that 'we have to seek for reservoirs of group B elsewhere than among the Bhils. The blood-groups of Bhils collected by Uma Basu also depict a percentage analogous to that obtained by Majumdar. The blood group evidence shows that the Bhils might have originally belonged to the original racial stock. There are indications that they have been thoroughly hybridised by contacts with alien races.'[25]

Notes and References

1. T. H. Hendley, "An Account of the Maiwar Bhils", *Journal of the Asiatic Society of Bengal,* Vol. XLIX, no. 4, Calcutta, 1875, pp. 367-368.
2. E. Bacon, *The Encyclopaedia Americana,* Vol. 3, 1969, p. 641.
3. *Encyclopaedia Britannica,* Vol. 3, 1968, p. 494.
4. H. B. Rowney, *The Wild Tribes of India,* London, 1882, p. 29.
5. A. M. Kurup, "Glimpses of Life and Culture of the Tribes of Madhya Pradesh", *Vanyajati,* Vol. X, no. 4, 1962, p. 134.
6. Mukul Chakraborti and Deepak Mukherji, *Indian Tribes,* Calcutta, 1971, p. 97.
7. Govt. of India, *Imperial Gazetteer of India,* Vol. XVII, p. 17.
8. Sir Herbert Risley, *The People of India,* Calcutta, 1908, p. 289.
9. R. V. Russel and Rai Bahadur Hira Lal, *The Tribes and Castes of the Central Provinces of India,* Vol. II, Delhi, 1975, p. 292.
10. T. H. Hendley, op. cit., p. 358.
11. C. S. Venkatachar, "Ethnographic Accounts of the Bhils of Central India", *Census of India 1931,* (Report) Vol. XX, pt. I, Delhi, 1933, p. 246.
12. B. S. Guha, "Racial Affinities of the People of India", *Census of India 1931,* (Ethnographical), Vol. I, Part-III, p. 1.
13. Louis Rousselet, *India and Its Native Princes,* London, 1875, p. 136.
14. T. H. Hendley, op. cit., pp. 366-367.
15. Stephen Fuchs, *Census of India 1941,* Vol. XVI, Holkar State, Part I, pp. 300-303.
16. C. S. Venkatachar, op. cit., p. XLVIII.
17. Ranjna Kumari and Surendra Nath, "Progression of Segmental Growth among Male Bhils of Udaipur", *S. A. P.,* Vol. 6, 1984, pp. 15-22.
18. D. N. Majumdar,"Racial Affiliations of the Bhils of Gujarat", *Journal of the Gujarat Research Society,* Vol. VI, no. 4, 1944, pp. 180-181.
19. B. S. Guha, op. cit., p. 1.
20. D. N. Majumdar, op. cit., p. 180.
21. E. W. E. Macfarlane, "Blood Grouping in the Deccan and Eastern Ghats", *Journal of the Royal Asiatic Society of Bengal,* Vol. VII, pt. 1, pp. 15-24.
22. E. W. E. Macfarlane and Sarkar, "Blood Groups of India", *American Journal of Physical Anthropology,* 1941, Vol. 28, no. 4.
23. R.K. Gulati and S. Srinivasan, "An Analysis of ABC Blood Groups of the Bhils of West Khandesh (Maharashtra)", *The Eastern Anthropologist,* Vol. 26, no. 1, pp. 79-85.
24. D. N. Majumdar, op. cit., pp. 173-174.
25. S.L. Doshi, *Bhils: Between Societal Self-Awareness and Cultural Synthesis,* Delhi, p. 13.

2

Origin Myth and Historical Background

The account of the origin of Bhils is lost in the mist. Though, we do have few glimpses through which their origin can be traced out. These sources are early literatures and mythological traditions. The term 'Bhilla' seems to have occured for the first time in about 600 A.D. It is supposed to be derived from the Dravidian word for a bow which is a characteristic weapon of the tribe known as Bhil. The Bhils seem to be the 'Pygmies' of Ctesias (400 B.C.), and the Poulindai and Phyllitae of Ptolemy (150 A.D.); but the name by which they are at present known can not be traced far back in Sanskrit literature. The Pulinda tribe is mentioned in the Aitareya Brahman and the edicts of Asoka. The Bhils are often mentioned as foes or allies in the history of Anhilvada.[1] In Katha Sarita Sagar, reference has been made to a Bhil Chief oppressing the progress of another king through the Vindhyas.

We have references of Bhils in the epics. The noted author of the Ramayana, Valmiki, started life as a Bhil bandit named Walia. Later he became a sage through the blessings of goddess Saraswati, and his extreme grief over his dark past turned into poetry.[2]

Another reference has been made to a Bhil women, Sabri, making presents of plums (*Ber*) to the hero of the Ramayana, Rama, during the exile.[3]

The *Mahabharata*, tells us about the famous archer, Eklavya, who was a Bhil. Eklavya approached Dronacharya, the preceptor of the Pandavas, to learn the art of archery but his candidature could not be accepted. Later he made an idol of Dronacharya and treating it as his Guru, practised the art of archery. He became a prominent archer. Knowing this, Dronacharya came to him and asked for forefinger of his right hand as Guru Dakshina, which he gladly offerred.[4]

Another tragic event occured with the Bhils in the Mahabharata. By mistake Jaratha, a Bhil hits an arrow to Krishna fatally, though he has taken aim to shoot a deer. A curse is said to have thereafter descended on the Bhils so that they are not able to handle the bow with the forefinger of their hand.[5]

Major Hendley interpreted this story in a different way. In fighting against the royal Krishna, the Bhils were condemned to lose the forefinger of their right hand, that they might never enter into conflict with the friends of the hero. Hence, it is said, they never used the forefinger in drawing the bow.[6]

The Muhammadan annals and early annals of the British India mention about the turbulent Bhils issuing out now and again from their mountain fastnesses and committing great depredations on the plains both in Northern India and in Western India and of measures taken from time to time either to suppress or conciliate them.[7]

A mythological story tells about the deluge and how the Bhil tribe originated. The story reads as follows : "A Dhobi who used to wash his clothes in a river was one day warned by a fish of the approach of a great deluge. The fish informed him that as he had always fed those of his species he had come to give him this warning and to urge him to prepare a large box which would enable him to escape. The Dhobi prepared a box and got into it with his sister and a cock. After the deluge, Rama sent out his message to inquire into the state of affairs. The messenger heard the crowing of the cock and so discovered the box. Rama then had the box brought before him and asked the man who he was and how he had escaped. The Dhobi told his tale. Rama then made him face in turn to north, east and west and swear that the woman with him was his sister. The Dhobi remained firm in asserting that she was his sister. Rama then turned him towards the south, upon which the Dhobi contradicted his statement and said she was his wife. Rama then asked who told him the way of escaping. On hearing at once had the fish's tongue cut out, and since then that kind of fish has been tongueless. Rama then told the Dhobi to set about repopulating the world, and he, therefore, married his sister by whom he had seven sons and seven daughters. Rama presented the first born son with a horse,· but the recipient of this gift, being unable to ride, left the horse on the plain and went into the forest to cut wood, he and his descendants becoming foresters started the Bhil tribe."[8]

The Puranic tradition traces the origins of the Bhils from the thigh of Vena, son of Anga, a descendant of Manu Swayambhuva. Vena was childless and the sage, therefore, rubbed his thigh and produced 'a man like a charred log, with flat face, and extremly short'. He was told to sit down (Nishada). He did so and since then they were known as Nishada, from whom sprang the Nishadas dwelling on the Vindhya mountains, distinguished by their wicked deeds.[9]

According to *Bhagawata Purana,* the king Vena, son of Anga was a tyrant who ruled his subjects with an iron rod. He ordered the people to worship him and not to perform Vedic 'yajna'. He also mishandled Rishis and Sadhus. On this act, they became annoyed and cursed him to die. Raja Vena had no successor, hence he prayed the Rishis for a son. In turn, the Rishis created the Nishada from his body, who was black like a crow and possessed a flat nose and blood-red eyes. His descendants lived in the forest.[10]

The most common legendary account tells that Mahadeva (Siva), sick and unhappy, was one day reclining in a shady forest, when a beautiful woman appeared, the first sight of whom effected a complete cure of all his maladies. The intercourse between the god and this stranger resulted in the birth of many children. One of the sons, who was from infancy distinguished alike by his ugliness and vicious habits, slew the favourite bull of his father, for which crime the angry deity cursed him and expelled him from the haunts of men to dwell in the forests and mountains. His descendants have since been called Bhils or outcastes.[11]

Luard records another story : "Once five men went to see Mahadeva. Parvati, seeing them approaching, said to her spouse 'here come five of my brothers to ask *Dhapa* (dowary) consequent on my marriage with you'. Mahadeva gave them a feast and then explained that except for his bull *Nandi* and his *Kamandala* he had nothing to give. They, therefore, went home. In order to give them something, however, Mahadeva placed a silver stool (*Pat*) in their way, but they were incapable to seeing this. Parvati noticing how they had missed the gift sent for them and told them what had happened, pointing out that as they were not able to see the stool, there was little hope of their prospering, but she would do what she could, and so informed them that they may be very careful of the Nandi whose hump was full of wealth untold. On reaching home one of the five suggested slaying the Nandi and obtaining the wealth, the others demurred, but he prevailed. No wealth was found in the hump and the five were dismayed. Parvati now appeared and told them that they should have yoked the bull to the plough and thus gained wealth from mother earth, but that as they were so foolish as to slay the sacred animal she would never look on their faces again, and left in high displeasure. For thus killing the sacred animal the Bhils have ever lived a miserable existence, and been of no caste."[12]

This story recognizes the great Parvati, wife of Mahadeva, a sister of the Bhils. Another myth relates Mahadeva and his consort Parvati as parents of Bhils which seems to be not much popular among all the Bhils. This myth is popular in the northern parts of the Bhils' country in Rajputana and the surrounding districts.[13]

The Bhils of Rajasthan consider themselves the offsprings of Rajputs. According to them king of Dhar had two sons, Masar and Damor who migrated from Dhar to the neighbouring place where they practised agriculture. One day, one of them put a bullock's tail in his mouth, On conduct, he was outcasted and declared polluted. Consequently both brothers were banished. The Bhils of that region established matrimonial relations with two brothers and their descendants gradually came within the sphere of the Bhil Tribes. Their branches are called : Herat, Tejat, Nebat, Khetal, Ratnat, Amrat, Metat, Jagat, Rangat and Nikyat.

The Bhils of Deopura, Mandava, Amarpura (Rajasthan) trace their origin to the Sisodiya Rajputs. They were outcasted as once they killed a cow.

There is another story about the origin of the Bhils of Nimar District (C. P.). According to the story, the ancestor of the Bhils was Varya, a great thief and highway man. Through his robberies he had amassed great wealth and many wives. One day he began to get tired of his unlawful life. He asked his wives what he had to expect as a punishment for his crimes. They told him that he probably would go to hell and suffer severely. He then asked how they themselves would fare, for it was for them that he was robbing. They replied laughingly that they never had asked as to the source of his income and that they had no part in his crimes. Varya found their replies very distressing and set out to the jungle to do penance for his sins. One day, Mahadeo and Parvati (the consort of Mahadev) passed through the same jungle on their pilgrimage to Kashi (Benares). Varya saw the gods and approached with the desire to be absolved of his sins. When he fell down before Mahadeo, to touch his feet, the god harshly ordered him to be off, for he knew that the Bhil was a great robber. But Varya followed the divine couple a long way on their pilgrimage imploring them to pardon him. At last Parvati's heart melted and she begged Mahadeo to forgive the penitent Bhil's sins. Mahadeo replied that Varya belonged to a caste, which nobody could rely upon. Today these Bhils might be sorry and repent for their crimes, but to-morrow they would return to their evil life and be worse than before. To forgive them would be weakness. But as Varya continued to ask for pardon, in order to get rid of him, Mahadeo told him angrily to stay where he was and to walk for penance round an Achar tree (*Buchanania latifolia*), till he himself bade him stop. Mahadeo thought that the Bhils would soon get tired of walking around the tree and go away.

After a lapse of twelve years, on their return from Kashi, Mahadeo and Parvati passed through the same jungle. When they reached the spot, where they had left the Bhil walking around the tree, Parvati reminded Mahadeo of him and wanted to see whether he was still doing penance. Mahadeo had passed on for he had not the least doubt that the Bhil had returned to his old metier. But to please his wife, Mahadeo looked for the tree of the Bhil's penance. When the divine couple approached the tree they saw to their great astonishment a deep ditch running right round the tree. Looking down to the bottom of the ditch they perceived Varya, the Bhil, still walking round. During the twelve years of his penance the ground under his never— resting feet had given way and sunk 300 hath (600 feet). Mahadeo, moved by the sincerety of the Bhil's repentance caught him by the scalp lock and lifted him out of the ditch. He forgave him his sins and bade him settle in the country which is the district of Nimar.[14]

According to a local traditional account of the Bhils of Gantali (Rajasthan), they were earlier settlers on earth. They claim their origin in the era of 'Satyug' when Ninama and Maira Bhils were born as twins. The god were surprised at the smell of human flesh in their vicinity. They hailed the birth of Bhil twins with mixed feelings and decided to test the bravery of the twins. The work was entrusted to fairy named Kakai to ask them for their head and eyes. Kakai accordingly went to them and demanded the Maira's head and Ninama's eyes. Without any hesitation, they offerred their head and eyes. Kakai went to heaven with the offerings given by the Bhil brothers. The god became pleased and asked the fairy to re-set the head and eyes of the two brothers and give them life. Since then the Bhils have been living in the world.

There is yet another account prevalent amongst the Bhils describing their origin from a Rajput clan. Moti Chauhan ruled the Dhar state (M.P.). His eldest son Maira, being displeased, migrated to the region of 'vagar'. He had twelve wives and a number of children. His sons entered into matrimonial alliance with the Bhils and as generations passed their descendants came to be considered as Bhils.[15]

According to Major Erskine, the Bhils are among the oldest inhabitants of the country and said to have entered India from the north and north-east several hundred years before the Christian era, and to have been driven to their present fastness at the time of the Hindu invasion.[16] Col. Tod describes them as the aboriginal people of India, The *Vanaputras* (the children of the forest).[17]

Historical Background

We have very little source material about the earliest inhabitants of India. Among the few traces they have left behind are some rude stone circles, upright slabs, earthen pots, agate knives and rough flint-axes which have been unearthed from the valley of Narmada. It is impossible to identify the people who made these implements. It is, however, significant that these rude implements have been found from those places which are presently occupied by the Bhils, whose ancestors might have been the builders of these remains. However, there is no written record in support of this view.[18]

Pre-Historic Period

Though the Bhil worships Shiva and Parvati and many rounded stones smeared with red paint, and practises animal sacrifices to the local goddesses, he has not left some of the old practices of building cairns, cromlechs, dolmens or stone plateforms or of depositing images of horses for the use of the souls of the dead for shortening their journey to heaven. The ancestors of Bhils in the pre-Aryan and pre-Dravidian times left megalithic monuments which corroborate the pre-historic origin of this tribe.[19] Megalithic structures are not common in Gujarat but Major J. W. Watson offers description of one such monument at Palanpur, which points to the existence of Dolmen like structure in the Bhil area commonly noticed in the Neolithic age throughout the world. The pillars of the porch in this structure are about four feet high and the great capstone is some ten feet long by six feet broad while the capstone of the inner chamber is somewhat less. In the centre is placed a 'Palia' or monument stone, but is without any inscription. The structure resembles, on the one hand, the dolmen and other megalithic monuments of the Palaeolithic age and on the other hand the crude differentiation between the outer chamber and inner chamber is a forerunner of the inner and outer *mandapa* of all Hindu temples. The monument occurs in an area from which the Bhils have been driven into the hills, so it would not be incorrect to assume that they were original people responsible for the construction of this structure.[20]

Recent excavations and archaeological findings in different parts of, what is now the Bhil region, have proved that man lived along the rivers Mahi and Sabarmati and also Gambhiri, and its tributaries Berach and Wagen at least 1,00,000 years ago. This man was a nomad, maintained himself on wild fruits, roots and the flesh of animals. It is still not known when this man became stabilized and took to farming. The area near Ahar (now part of Udaipur City) was chosen by man as his stable habitat some 4,000 years ago. This man in all probability was the Bhil.[21]

Rima Hoja uses the word 'Totality' for Bhils and relates them to the Late Stone Age (Mesolithic) traditions since the Bhils use iron and practise the slash-and-burn agriculture. Their life style, thus, has been that of hunter-gatherers in an advanced sense of word.[22]

The tribes, which entered India by the North-east and North-west passes, have been broadly divided into three categories- the Tibeto-Burman, the Kolarian and the Dravidian. The Bhils are placed in the Kolarian group. However, Thompson has ruled out the possibilities that the Bhils belong to the Kolarian tribes.[23]

At the time of the Aryan invasion of Rajputana, the Bhils were in possession of Maiwar or Jodhpur.[24] From where they were driven to the Aravali and Vindhya hills under pressure from the invaders. From there, they spread over Gujarat, Central India, Kotah, Dungarpur, Banswara, Danta, Ider, Devaliya, Partapgarh and the localities of big Jamindars like Jawas, Juda, Panarwa etc.[25] Their present settlement in the hill tracts of Aravali and Vindhya was chosen for its strategic suitability.

Early-Historic Period

About 1400 B.C. Krishna is supposed to have founded a kingdom in Gujarat after a fierce struggle with its inhabitants, many of whom were probably the Bhils. In fact, Viratnagar, a town in Gujarat, was at that time governed by Shridoshra, a Bhil queen, according to the local traditions.

In 850 B.C. Dhanji was the king of Malwa. He is generally considered to be a Bhil. This view is supported from the fact that the name Dhanji is very common among the hillmen even at the present day. Evidently at that early period the Bhil race was very powerful in Malwa. The descendants of Dhanji ruled for 387 years. His successor is said to have shaken off, in 730 B.C., the yoke of the sovereign of Delhi.

After a long interval of more than 1200 years the scene shifts from Malwa back again to Gujarat, and one of the three Bhil women mentioned in history is brought to notice, in 696 A.D., in the following account: Rani Rupsundri, the wife of Jayashekar, king of Punchasar, fled into the forest when the capital was beseiged. A kind hearted Bhil woman gave her shelter and food. In this woman's hut, Rupsundri gave birth to a son who became the famous vanraj. The Queen and her child remained with their humble benefactress for six years.[26]

The 'Harsh Puran' mentions the Bhils as semi-civilized

aboriginals and their relations with Lord Krishna and his kinsmen. It is believed in the local lore that a Bhil's arrow ultimately killed the lord and they were the people who had snatched the ladies of the royal family of yadavas while being escorted to Mathura by Arjun, Pandava, inspite of his famous bow *Gandiva*.[27]

The Bhil Kings have been mentioned in the *Mahabharata* as rulers in Rajputana, Malwa and Central India.[28]

From the time of Mahabharata to 325 B.C. when Alexander invaded India, historic records mentions nothing about any part of Rajasthan. In 200 B.C. Menander, a Greek invader, attacked Madhyamika Nagari (known in Pali literature as Majjhma or Majjhimika Nagari meaning a town in the middle of Mathura and Ujjain). This town located around Chittor (known as Shivi Janpada) was well known for its riches. The Shivi Janpada was under the Bhils domination. Near the small village Nagari, at a distance of 9 Kms. from Chittorgarh, finely dressed stones bearing exquisite carving lie strewn over a large area to tell the glory of its past. But nothing could be said about the life led by the people living in vast expances of the forest in the surrounding region.[29]

The First Phase of Bhil Rajput Co-operation (7th to 13th century A.D.)

About 626 A.D. Nagaditya, the ruler of Edur and the fourth in the dynasty of Guhilots, founded Nagda (near Eklingji) in Udaipur district with the co-operation of Bhils. At that time, Edur was governed by a chief of savage race. His name was Mandalica. Somehow, getting tired of their snobbery or ostentations superiority, the Bhils assailed Nangaditya while hunting and deprived him of the life of Edur. Shiladitya, the successor of the assasinated ruler retired to Nagda and in order to improve the prosperity in his domain and his relations with the Bhils he developed certain saltmines in his region. Among the eary Guhilots in this region Bappa Rawal has been most important and well known. Bappa Rawal is a corrupt form of *Vap-raj-kul*(father of royal dynasty). The local legend and the Bhil lore state that Bappa was bread and brought up among the Bhils. Becoming their leader at a very early age he was given *Tika* of blood from the thumb by the Bhil Chief of Ogana. Since then the tradition of *Tikka* has been continuing for the coronation of Rajput ruler.

The region around Chittorgarh was by this time appropriated by Mauryas of unknown origin who originally constructed the fort of Chittorgarh at the capital. During 725 A.D. to 738 A.D. Arabs, under the leadership of Junaid ravaged this region, and Man Maurya succumbed against them. But Bappa with the co-operation of the Bhils, was at last successful in driving the foreigners out and gain hold over Chittorgarh. There is little in the historical accounts about life and social status of the Bhils and their relations with other segments of the society during the next six centuries. But it is certain that the Bhils were in no way despised. They had their Chiefs ruling over certain areas like other Rajputs and intermarriages were frequent. Instances occasionally occured in which the children of a Rajput by a Bhil wife was recognised as Rajputs.

In 951 A.D. the capital of Maiwar was shifted from Nagda to Ahar, and the latter continued to be the capital of Maiwar in spite of being invested by Vakpati Raj Munj, the Parmar king of Malwa some time between 974 to 993 A.D. The region around Chittorgarh including the fort was lost not to be regained from the hold of Parmars and later from the Chalukyas of Gujarat for another two centuries. In 1174 A. D. Rawal Samant Singh revolted against the Chalukya authority, but the Gujrat forces in turn uprooted him altogather. The fugitive ruler like his ancestor 540 years before again sought the shelter and co-operation from the Bhils. After killing Chaurasimal, the oppressor of the Bhils, he founded the kingdom of Wagar with its capital at Baroda, later shifted to Dungarpur.

In Maiwar, Kirtipal Chauhan of Nadaul (in Pali District) taking advantage of the unsettled political conditions spread his sway. But Rawal Kumar Singh, the younger brother of Samant Singh, husbanded the local co-operation and could easily reinstall Guhilot authority in the region.[30]

In the eleventh century Maiwar was held by the hillmen. The chief's name was Ashawhom Karan, the Gujarati king, defeated and slew at Ashawal, the site of the present city of Ahmedabad.

From the history of Udaipur it appears that in the eleventh century, a great part of Maiwar and the Norh-west parts of central India was under the Bhils. In 1134 A.D. the king of Udaipur invaded their country and annexed part of their territory. Some of the predatory Rajput chiefs too, bent on plunder and territorial expansion, entered the hills with the purpose of subduing the inhabitants. To this end they are said to have broken their caste rules by taking in marriage Bhil women. The intermarriage explains Rajput features so marked in many of the present day Bhils. The intermixture of the Rajputs and Bhils has produced new castes, such as the Garasias, Bhilalas etc., who claim to be socially superior to the hillbills.

About 1190 A.D. the king of Abu, Jethsi Parmar had a daughter, Ichani Kumari. The Gujarat king, Bhimdeo II, wished to marry this princess and sent an ambassdor to the Abu king with a request for his daughter's hand. Jethsi Parmar could not, however entertain the proposal, as his daughter had been already betrothed to the son of the Ajmer king. Bhimdev, greatly annoyed, declared war against Abu and took the fort on the summit of the hill. It may be mentioned here that, at present, the Parmar is a name of Bhil clan in Maiwar.[31]

About 1224 A.D. after Nagda was invested by Shamsuddin Altamash, the Slave king of Delhi, the capital of Maiwar was shifted from Ahar to Chittorgarh which was sacked in 1303 by Ala-ud-din Khilji.[32]

The First Phase of Social Degradation of Bhils (14th to 16th century A.D.)

Rawal Vir Singh Deo of Wagar with an intention of shifting his capital to a more secured and inaccessible site, treacherously killed Dungaria, the Bhil Chief of the region and founded Dungarpur. It is believed that being afraid of the curse of Dhanna and Kali the two devoted wives of Dungaria, who followed their husband to funeral pyre, Vir Singh named his capital after Dungariya. Two shrines of Dhanna and Kali are still there on the hill adjacent to the southern flank of the town known as 'Dhanna mata-na-magra' i.e. the hill of mother Dhanna. An annual fair is held there.

The story of this stark treachery must have spread far and wide. So the Bhils of Maiwar did not co-operate with Rana Hammir Singh who after regaining Chittorgarh in 1326 A.D. was trying to ensure his sway over the region. The ruler could win over only few by awarding jagirs and promising rewards. But others organised resistence in their hilly strong holds in Magra and Bhomat region. They were subdued only after much diplomatic persuation accompanied with desperate fight and perdition.

The time that followed was that of large scale subjugation of the Bhils, ousting them away from the better lands and administering a cruel blow on their economy. In 1341 A.D. with the active support of Maha Rana Hammir, Devi Singh Hada subdued the Meenas,[33] aboriginals of Haroti plateau and carved out their state of Bundi.

During the Muslim rule, the hill tracts of Rajputana were under the control of Bhils. In the year 1388, Kanad Dev Chauhan of Jalore, defeated by Muslim, fled to the hills. He subsequently defeated the Bhils and declared himself ruler. His son became the Rao of Merpur. The Rajputs of the plains considered Rao and his father as low and stopped all marital relations with them. From the intermarriages between this new Rajput dynasty and the local Bhils, originated the sub-caste of Girasias.[34]

Rao Ran Mal of Mandore while acting as the regent of Maharana Mokal from 1420 to 1428 A.D. during his operations against the Bhils of Bhomat openly beheaded the *gameti* or the Bhil headman of the Pal of Pai (in Kotra tehsil of Udaipur district). As a resulted so much was the Bhil antagonism that the assains, Chacha, Mera and Mehpa Panwar were given shelter by the Bhils who not only guaranteed their safety but also created a small fortress named Rata Kot, the Red Fort for them. All efforts of the state forces to capture them were rendered abortive by the Bhil resistance. Ultimately Rao Ran Mal himself went to the house of the Gameti, the savage he had despised and killed and begged pardon of his widow. The Bhils remaining true to their discipline, not harming one who sought their asylum, pardonned him and withdrew their support to the assasins. About the same time the Bhils of Wagar also revolted and Maharawal Gopinath gained the fame of crushing the unruly-savages.

This was the period when the Bhils were robbed of their good lands. Their good qualities of truthfulness, unadulterated simplicity and non-diplomatic ways were exploited for ignoble ends. Their blood was also considered as having some magical effects to provide strength to the fortresses and edifices constructed by the rulers. Under the foundations of majority of the 32 forts and numerous other constructions of Maharana Kumbha (1433-1468 A.D.) and Dam of Gaip constructed by Maharwal Gopi Nath lie burried the head or whole of the body of one or more Bhils. These unfortunate beings were either killed by force or offered themselves for the bane in the hope that the ruler will be making the life of their descendants more comfortable than what they could do in their life time.

There emerged two new states named Banswara and Deolia in the year 1530 and 1561 A.D respectively. The capitals were founded after killing the Bhil chiefs by means which were decidedly not in keeping with the Rajput intrepidity and fortitude, and then named after the 'slain savage' as a diplomatic compensation or as recognition of his mystical right over the land. The traditional hearsay and the bardic records present numerous other examples when the Rajput Chieftains, uprooted from their established domains by superior forces, and given shelter by the Bhils repaid that hospitality with treachery.

True, the Bhils were cruely oppressed by the Rajput, especially at the time when Marathas were occupying Central India and operating even in Maiwar. They were flogged, hanged, behaded, gunned down and burnt to death on the least pretext. Even the Bhil women and children were not spared.

But the Bhils were oppressive in their turn. It is evident from the statement of Mann : 'Kokni (a Hindu caste) immigrants from the plain were permitted to settle in the domains of Bhil Rajas. These Koknis introduced permanent cultivation in the hills. The Bhils levied taxes from the Kokni settlers. The relation between the two was rulers and subjects. Koknis mercilessly oppressed by Bhil Raja who come with their bowmen, take possession of Kokni's crops and cattle, demand supplies of food and on occasions even abduct Kokni girls.'

The Second Phase of Bhil Rajput Co-operation (16th to 17th century A.D.)

Shortly before the final sack of Chittorgarh, Maharana Udai Singh and the royal family migrated to Rajpipala and took shelter with the Bhils. In spite of ravaging and severe attrocities on them by the Mughal forces under Hussain Kuli Khan the Bhils could keep the Rajputs safe. But it was Maharana Pratap who gave the Bhils their due place, equal to that of the Rajput. Maharana Pratap had the wisdom of mobilising the Bhils, with all respect and affection. They in turn became his devoted friends and followers. Among them he was affectionately known as 'kika' meaning 'son' in the Bhil dialect. He improved their economic and social position and used their skill to strengthen his impoverished army.

In the famous battle of Haldighati against the Mughal forces headed by Man Singh of Amer on 21st June 1576 A.D., the Bhil foot-men took their positions on the hills and hillocks of the *Ghati* (valley) with their short swords, bows and arrows and poured their blood for the defense of the country.

The Bhil loyalty and assistance were never found wanting during the next 10 years when during frequent Mughal invasion, Maharana Pratap had to resort on guerilla war fare. In fact, in the defence and resistance organised in the rugged defiles of the hill, the Bhils proved better than their Rajput counterparts. They not only fought bravely but also conveyed messages and often looted the Mughal supplies. During 11 years before his death in 1597 A.D., when Maharana Pratap regained most of the lost territories, he rewarded the Bhils and gave them jagirs. The Bhil co-operation continued during the reign of Maharana Amar Singh I and the Bhil foot-men numbering in thousands were involved in the guerilla fight against the Mughal forces, which continued for almost 15 years till a treaty was concluded in 1615 A.D.

The Second Phase of Social Degradation of the Bhils (15th to 17th century A.D.)

During this phase the lot of the Bhils was materially not improved but they were awakened by the happenings of Maiwar. In 1583 A.D., the Bhils of Khandu in Banswara revolted. When Maharawal Man Singh arrested and insulted the *Gameti*, the latter was bold enough to kill the ruler.

In 1677 A.D. an entirely new phase appears in this history, in the attempt made by the Emperor Auranzeb to pervert the whole of his Hindu subjects to the Muhammadan faith. With this subject in view, colonies of the followers of the prophet were placed among the hillmen some of whom eventually embraced Islam.

The Bhils of Bhomat also contacted the Mughal emperor Akbar when he was on his way to seek asylum from Shambhaji. In 1679 A.D. when Auranzeb invaded Maiwar, the royal family was shifted to Nenwara in Bhomat and the Bhil Chieftains of Panarwa,

Merpur, Juda and Jawas alongwith 50,000 Bhils foot-men had joined the forces of Maharana Raj Singh.

Thus during this brief intermission of about 125 years the social and economic status of the Bhils was considerably regenerated in Maiwar. But in Kanthal and Wagar regions under the States of Deolia, Dungarpur and Banswara the age-old despising and destitution continued.

The Dark Age (18th to 19th century A.D.)

The age of Mughal invasions was over. After the death of Auranzeb in 1707 A.D. the authority at Delhi was too feeble to launch any organised military operation on any part of Rajasthan. The services of the Bhils seem to have been forgotten. Hateful despising alongwith serious effort to keep them in perpetual privation became the way of the 'others' in the society. Rajputs began to regard the Bhils as inferior, monkey-like people more akin to wild beast and vermin than men. The rulers occasionally put them to forced labour, abducted their women for inhuman molestation or using them as kepts or concubines and imparted them rough justice in which the victims might be whipped or have their eyes gouged out or be decapitated.

When the new ruler ascended the throne his first 'heroic act' was to pillage and burn down one or more of the *Pals* of the Bhils. They were punished not only by keeping them into forced labour but their Chiefs were cruely executed and their bodies were kept hanging for several days in the small fortress.[35]

About 1767 Alia Bai, the widow of the king of Malwa was queen over the kingdom that formerly belonged to Dhanji. In ruling the Bhils, she first tried gentle measures but these failing, she had recourse to a rigorous policy. She, however, continued to allow them their claim to levy a small duty on goods passing through the hills.

Under the Mughals the Bhils were probably never sorely oppressed, except during the reign of the Emperor Taghluk. Under the Marathas, however, they suffered terribly. Sir William Hunter writes that during eighteenth century the Marathas failed to bring the Bhils to order, treated them as outlaws and permitted their lowest officers to take their lives without trial. Torture was freely used. They were exposed to the sun with slit nose and ears shaved from head.[36]

In Khandesh during the disturbed period of the wars of Scindhia and Holker about 1800 A.D., the British betook themselves to highway robbery and lived in bandit either in mountains or in village close to them. Within a short time they became so bold as to appear in bands of hundreds and attack towns, carrying of either cattle or hostages from whom they demanded handsome ransoms.[37] Bhils were hereditary and professional plunderers and has described them as the 'soldiers of the night'.

From 1804 to 1817 the Pindaris, following the example of the lawlessness of the Marathas, plundered the hillmen and laid waste their village. Parties of two thousand or more horsemen rode rapidly from place to place and carried off all the cattle and property they could find. Their excursions were characterised by horrible atrocities. Terror and anarchy filled the land and the inhabitants were driven to choose between throwing in their lot with the Pindari free booters or of going into exile. Many chose the former and became robbers and plunderers.[38]

The turbulent Bhils of Rajasthan and Madhya Pradesh revolted against the British occupation of their lands. Since then, the Bhils occasionally rose against their hated oppressors. In 1817, Bhils of Khandesh mobalised 800 strong peasants against the British imperialists over the issue of the encroachment of their agricultural lands. Again in 1819 the Bhils rose against the colonial expansionists and burnt down several military outposts and ravaged the neighbouring plains. But the imperialist rulers took punitive action and killed many of them, and subjected others to severe punishment with their superior arms. With occasional lull, they again rose under their leader like Sewaram, who was a blacksmith by profession. K. Gough remarks that this sort of revolt occured with the tribal peasant "were deprived of their livelihood, evicted from their homestead or squeezed in their tribal territories."[39]

The Age of British Protection

It was in the midst of such troublous times as these that all the Bhils in 1818 came under the protection of the British. Although possessing only bows and arrows as their national weapons of warfare, they have never been entirely conquered. Their numbers have again and again been decimated by sword, famine and disease, yet there are still two millions of them left as a witness to their vitality.[40]

In 1820 Bhil Agency was set up with its headquarters at Kannar and yeoman's service was done by some of the British Military officers in reclaiming the wild and recalcitrant Bhils.[41]

In 1823 A.D. Colonel Tod appropriated, *Bolai*, the money which the Bhils collected for safe conduct of travellers through the forest region of Magra and Bhomat, but inspite of the severe operation of the British Army from Neemuch, the Bhil revolt could not be quelled till the position was restored.

In 1836 the Bhils in different regions of Banswara became very 'unruly' and Maharawal Bhawani Singh had to carry a large scale operation to bring them under control, and large scale uprising in Bhomat (Maiwar) against the local rulers in 1839 could be quelled with much difficulty and again with the assistance of British forces. The necessity of repeated intervention by the British Army instigated them to adopt the policy of recruiting local troops to help to enforce order among their own people. Thus, the Maiwar Bhil Crops was organised in 1840-44 under a British commandant at Kherwara and his deputy at Kotra, with the object of weaning a semi savage race from predatory habits, giving it honourable employment and assisting the Darbar in preserving law and order.

During the mutiny of 1857, the Bhil troops stood by the British Government and checked the outburst created by Tantya Tope in Banswara in December 1858. The then ruler of the State, Laxman Singh, had to seek refuge in the forest when Tantya Tope came with his followers. The army of Bhil troops controlled the situation and the leader had to march towards Maiwar.

Due to deep-rooted hatred among Bhils against Banswara rulers, a set of uprisings occured in different parts of the state to disturb law and order. The first recorded sporadic revolt of the Bhils of Banswara took place in 1844 during the regime of Laxman Singh. The bordering state of Malwa used to pay a fixed tribute to the Bhils of Banswara as consideration for their promise not to plunder Malwa and disturb its peaceful existence. The State of Malwa after entering into a treaty with the British Government, ceased to pay the prescribed tribute to the Bhils.

This they resented vehemently. A gang of about 5000 Bhils attacked the Mokheri village on the border of Malwa, but the uprising was suppressed by the military forces of the Western Malwa Agent.

Yet another uprising of the Bhils of Banswara took place in 1872-73 during the period of the same ruler. Dhula Bhil Rawat of Sodalpur village denied the claim of the Government to exact the revenue of Rs. 2000/- from his village. When compelled, he collected a number of Bhils from the neighbourhood villages and stood against the state. The Political Agent interfered in the matter and a compromise was effected between the ruler and Dhula.

Another outburst was engineered in 1873-74 against the state by the Bhils of Shergarh village who carried out constant depredations in the 'Elakas' or regions of Panch Mahal and Rewa-Khanta. The absence of control over the Bhils loomed as a grave problem for the ruler of the state. His position became embarrassing for he failed to establish law and order in his state. The Political Agent of Maiwar handled the situation and assured the state that he would spare the services of Major Kanked for controlling the Bhils.[42]

There arose an uprising in the region of South Rajasthan in 1881 for re-asserting tribal authority. There were different causes of this uprising.

After the war of independence and the invasion of Marathas the economy of the state was completely ruined. The State nobles usurped Khalsa land and subjected the Bhils to various oppressions. In the area of the effective control of Rajput Chiefs the Bhils had to pay 1/4 of the agriculture produce. Non-payment of land revenue invited extreme action of the attachment of entire villages by the Rajput *Jagirdars*. They used to impound the cattles and even took liberty to carry away the women and children. They were given freedom when every Head of the family paid Rs. 5/-. Another nefarious practice to which the Bhils were subjected by the Maharana and his Jagirdar was forced labour.

Another cause of the uprising was the arbitrary system of collection of Land Revenue. There were two systems, the Batai and Kankut, in vogue. Both were based on estimation which was weighed in favour of state or the *Jagirdar*. The revenue officers mostly belonged to Bania class which not only hated but also maltreated and exploited the Bhils. The Bhils were reduced to a state of destitution and they had to sell their children to meet the excessive demands of the state officials. The appeals of the tribals to the Maharana against higher estimation of Land Revenue and misbehaviour of the revenue officials went unheeded. Among the other form of exploitation was the business of money lending. It was carried out mostly by *Banias* and *Pathans*. The Pathans charged exorbitant interest and took recourse to violence for recovery of loans. This was naturally resented by the tribals.

The tribals keep their born right on forest. They never felt any difficulty in utilizing the forest in which they lived. Forests were divided among the villages and clans which had the exclusive right of hunting, grazing, and cutting of teak. Forest trees like Mango and Mahua were never cut and collection of fruits or their cutting by outsiders led to feuds. The Maharana of Maiwar leased out some forest tracts in the tribal areas and the lessee indiscriminately felled trees, especially Mangos and Mahua, which outraged the feelings of the tribals. Besides tribals were not allowed to distill liquor from the Mahua tree owned by them. This restriction had an adverse effect on their social and religious life.[43]

The enumeration of men and women during the 1881 Census created apprehension in the minds of the Bhils. Some lower level persons in the charge of Census made light hearted remarks that after the Census young spouse of old man shall be given to young and old man shall have old lady as his match. Lean and thin women married to fat man shall withdraw and shall be handed over to lanky fellow and the fat man shall, in exchange, have fat lady as his wife. This was a serious matter and threatened the harmony and social cohesion of the tribe. It was sufficient provocation for the Bhils to take up arms against the Maharana of Maiwar.

According to Kaviraj Shymaldas the immediate cause which sparked off the 1881 uprising was a quarrel between a mounted man of Durbar and headman of Paduna village over an evidence in a land dispute which resulted in the killing of the Sowar. But the oral tradition and folk songs suggest that the immediate cause of the flare up was an attempt by a liquor vendor to outrage the modesty of a tribal girl named Ratni of Village Barapal. Having failed in his design the vendor conspired with the Police

Inspector to arrest the girl. This was most atrocious action which provoked the Bhils to give a call for a fight with the regime. The Bhils attacked the Police outpost of Barapal and killed 17 persons including the Police Inspector. The native troops were despatched by Maharana Sajjan Singh. Meanwhile the revolt had spread out to other parts of the Bhils region. Everywhere the tribals came out with bows and arrows and killed a few state officials and policemen. Several Police outposts were set on fire. The road communication between Udaipur and Gujrat was blocked. Within a period of three weeks from the start of this uprising, the situation had so worsened that the British Political Agent had to intervene and persuade Maharana to reach an agreement with the tribals. Negotiations were held at Rishabdeo and an agreement containing 21 points was reached.

The agreement conceded to the Bhils most of their rights hitherto enjoyed by them without any interference by the Maharana. The Census operation was stopped. The Mahua was exempted from customs duty. Likewise no duty was imposed on opium. The most significant part of the agreement was that the number of police outposts was not to be increased and the policemen posted at Chokis were to be withdrawn.[44]

A series of movements took place amongst the Bhils like Lasodia (1890-1900), Gulia, Viswanath, Mavji against the economic distress and social oppressions. The Bhils of the Panch Mahal and Naikdas organised movements under their tribal leaders. They believed their leaders as incarnation of the supreme deity (Parmeswar or Siva among the Naikdas, and Vishnu among the Bhils). They were convinced that their leaders would deliver them from rapacious colonial rulers and establish an independent, ethical kingdom for the tribals, which the Naikdas named 'Dharmaraj' (kingdom of virtue). These movements were participated by about ten thousands.[45]

Another movement (1900-1912) occured amongst the Bhils under the leadership of Govindgiri.[46] He hailed from Bedsa village of Dungarpur district and belonged to semi nomadic Banjara community. He was born on 30th December, 1858. He did not have much formal education.

It was a religious movement flared up with the objective of converting the tribals to Hinduism. Govind Giri's religious sermons were quite simple. He told his followers to worship

Rama, adorn *Rudraksha Mala,* perform *havan* and lead a moral life, speak truth, avoid sexity, and not to steal. They should abstain from meat and wine and should take daily bath and wear clean cloths. Through this process he wanted to sanskritise the Bhils and bring them at level with other sections of the Hindu society. The followers of the movement were described as Bhagats. With the introduction of new faith, he became more popular day by day and declared himself as an incarnation of God. His main mission was to elevate the socio-economic conditions of the Bhils.

By the year 1903 the movement reached its zenith, when Govind Giri went to Mangarh hill and performed a big *havan* and hoisted religious banners. Thereafter this ritual continued uninterrupted till 1907.

The rapid rise of the influence of Govind Giri seems to have turned the history of Bhils. When Giri reached Mangarh in the first week of December, 1908 for his annual ritual he started collecting armed Bhils. It is alleged that he began to plan nothing less than a Bhil state of which he would be the head. The present day followers of Govind Giri deny this charge. They, however, admit that Govind Giri exhorted the people not to render forced labour, not to pay exorbitant land revenue and other levies. From the point of view of colonial administration and princely states, it was a political movement. The rulers of native states of Banswara, Sant Rampur, Devgarh Baria and Dungarpur approached the Political Agent to dispach the Maiwar Bhil Corps to deal with the situation. The Bhil Corps were moved to Mangarh hills with machine guns and artillary under the command of Colonel Sherton to help the native troops. It is said that nearly one and half lakh Bhils had gathered on Mangarh hills.

Events were moving quite fast in a fluid situation. Some Bhils raided the Police outpost of Mogagadda and Khedpa Gaddi Station of Sant Rampur, killed one Inspector and took many policemen as hostages. On the way to Mangarh hills, the Bhils established outposts at various points and nobody was allowed to escape.

Now the Bhils and the native troops were poised against each other. The native troops and Maiwar Bhils Corp were on the eastern side and the Bhils were on the western side. A small valley divided the two sides. Soon after camps were established, Colonel Sherton started negotiations with the aides of Govind

Giri with a view to persuade the Bhils to withdraw peacefully from the hills. He offered on behalf of the native rulers to reduce land revenue and also not to subject the Bhils to forced labour and other levies. But Govind Giri did not accept any settlement. Even warning by Colonel Sherton of dire consequences had no effect. This led to skirmishes between the two sides. Colonel Sherton ordered to fire warning shots in the air. Naturally it did not hit any body and Bhils in retaliation started shooting arrows and gunfire on the native troops. Finally, Colonel Sherton ordered machine guns and artillary fire. The ill-equipped Bhils were no match to superior fire power of the native troops and in a few minutes nearly one and half thousand people were indiscriminately shot down on December 7, 1908. But the shrewd Bhil potent escaped unhurt and hide in a cave. Other followers of the guru were fled ahead long towards South West. They were not chased by the native troops.

Govind Giri was put on trial and sentenced to death. But this was converted into life imprisonment, part of which he served in Ahmedabad Jail. After the victory of allied forces in the first world war, he was released on parole. He settled in Idar for some time and then was again imprisoned to serve the remaining period of the sentence for his alleged involvement in the Home Rule Movement. He remained in Jail for three years. On his release, he worked with Thakkar Bappa at Dohad but soon left him. In prison he had become addicted to hemp smoking. He died in Kmoi village near Jhalod as a forlorn man. However his religious mission still survive, but, now it has been given the colour of social reform.[47]

Notes and References

1. *The Imperial Gazetteer of India,* Vol. VIII, Oxford, 1908, p. 101.
2. Kamladevi Chattopadhyaya, 'The Bhils of Gujarat and Rajasthan' (in) *Tribalism in India,* New Delhi, 1978, p. 56.
3. *Valmiki Ramayana, Ayodhya Kanda,* Chapter 50, Sloka 50, and *Aranya Kanda,* Chapter 74, Slokas 17-18.
4. W. Crook, *The Tribes and Castes of the North Western India,* Vol. II, Delhi, 1974, p. 47.
5. Kamladevi Chattopadhyaya, op. cit., p. 56.
6. T. H. Hendley, op. cit., p. 368.
7. Sarat Chandra Ray, "The Black Bhils of Jaisamand Lake in Rajputana (with plates)", *The Journal of the Bihar and Orissa Research Society,* March-June 1924, p. 1.

8. C. E. Luard, *Jungle Tribes of Malwa*, Lucknow, 1909, p. 17, and W. Koppers, "Bhagwan the Supreme deity of the Bhils", *Anthropos*, Vol. XXXV, p. 289.
9. C. S. Venkatachar, "An Ethnographic Account of the Bhils of Central India", *Census of India 1931*, Vol. I, Part III (Appendix 1), Section A, p. 240.
10. *Bhagwata Purana*, Skanda 4, Chapter 14, Sloka 45.
11. James Hastings (Ed.), *Encyclopaedia of Religion and Ethics*, Vol. II, New York, 1909, p. 554.
12. C. E. Luard, op. cit. pp. 17-18.
13. W. Koppers, op. cit., p. 282.
14. Stephen Fuchs, "The Marriage Rites of the Bhils in the Nimar District, C. P.", *Man in India*, Vol. XXII, Nos. 2 & 3, 1942, pp. 106-107.
15. S. L. Doshi, *op. cit.*, pp. 7-8.
16. Major K. D. Erskine, *India District Gazetteers, Rajputana*, Udaipur, 1908, p. 228.
17. Col. James Tod, *Annals and Antiquities of Rajasthan*, London, 1950, p. 181.
18. Chas S. Thompson, *Rudiments of the Bhili Language*, 1895, p. V.
19. P. G. Shah, "The Original Inhabitants of Gujarat", *Journal of the Gujarat Research Society*, p. 27.
20. Major J. W. Watson, *Indian Antiquary*, February 1874, pp. 53-54.
21. D. N. Chaturvedi, "The Bhils of Rajasthan through Ages", (in) *The Tribe*, Vol. V, no. 3, 1968 p. 39.
22. Rima Hooja, "Prehistoric Hunter-Gatherers: Forerunners of the 'Tribal' Tradition", *Tribal Movement*, Ram Pande (Ed.), 1984, p. 28.
23. Chas S. Thompson, *op. cit.*, p. V.
24. H. B. Rowney, *The Wild Tribes of India*, London, 1882 (reprint 1990), p. 24.
25. A.V. Thakkar, *Tribes of India*, p. 209.
26. Chas S. Thompson, *op. cit.*, pp. VI-VII.
27. D. N. Chaturvedi, op. cit., p. 40.
28. D. N. Majumdar, "The Bhils of Gujarat", *Journal of the Gujarat Research Society*, Vol. IV, No. 4, 1942, p. 222.
29. D. N.Chaturvedi, op. cit., p. 40.
30. Ibid., pp. 41-42.
31. Chas S. Thompson, *op. cit.*, pp. VII-VIII.
32. D. N. Chaturvedi, op. cit., p. 43.
33. There are many similarities in the manner and customs of Bhils and Meenas and hence some persons make no distinction between these two tribes. A.W.T. Webb writes: "Whatever may be the origin of the Meenas that is uncertain, their only affinity to the Bhils perhaps is the fact that they were among the earliest inhabitants of Rajputana." Shashi writes "Meena word is used for Bhils Tribe" (S.S. Shashi,*The Tribal Women of India*, Sandeep Prakashan, Delhi, 1978, p. 55).

34. R.S. Mann, "Bhils is Historical Perspective and in Relationship with Non-Tribal", *Rajasthan Bhils,* N. N. Vyas, R. S. Mann and N. D. Chaudhary (Jointly edited), 1978, p. 20.
35. D. N. Chaturvedi, op. cit., pp. 45-47.
36. R. V. Rusell and Rai Bahadur Hira Lal, *op. cit.,* p. 282.
37. *Ibid.,* pp. 282-283.
38. Chas S. Thompson, *op. cit.,* p. ix.
39. Madan C. Paul, *Dimension of Tribal Movement in India* (A study of Udayachal in Assam valley), New Delhi, 1989, pp. 45-46.
40. *Ibid.,* p. 48.
41. G. Ahmed Khan, "The Bhils of Khandesh", *Man in India,* 1935, p. 137.
42. S. L. Doshi, *op. cit.,* pp. 16-17.
43. Roop Singh, "Anatomy of Three Tribal Movements in Rajasthan", *The Eastern Anthropologist,* Vol. XXXVI, no. 2, pp. 118-120.
44. Kavi Shyamaldas, *Veer Vinod,* Vol. II, no. 3, pp. 2217-2228.
45. Madan C. Paul, *op. cit.,* p. 48.
46. *Ibid.,* p. 47.
47. Roop Singh, op. cit., p. 121.

3

The Economic Profile of the Bhils

The economic structure of the Bhils of Jhabua is, like others, undergoing change. Formerly Bhils were using the pattern of *dajia* or the *Jhum* cultivation. About thirty years ago, shifting cultivation was restored to plough cultivation. With the enforcement of forest laws, the land which a Bhil holds is generally small in size and of low fertility which cannot produce enough food. Money as a medium of exchange plays vital role in Bhils' economy. To fulfill day to day expenditure and social needs they run for debt. The debt has both good and bad results. On the credit side, it increases facility of contacts with the outside world, a command over a wider range of necessities and a greater simplification of the daily rounds of economic exchange. The disadvantages have, however, been greater. They have developed a tendency to overlook the economic and monetary sides of any issue and have begun to get into debt by spending disproportionate sums of money on marriage and other social ceremonies; some of them still indulge in drinks on which a considerable part of income is lost, inspite of the prohibition laws which are not enforced rigidly.

To pay off these debts they sell their lands and consequently become poor, on this set up a vicious circle of poverty and want, disease and ignorance which they can never escape. They lack the spirit and vigour to the independent identity to retain and expand their property. They obtain money as advance loans from the forest contractors, with the promise to work exclusively for them during the next season. Moreover, they have to go for the contractor's work whenever the latter wants, leaving their own agricultural operations and thus falling into further difficulties. The result is that some of the landless Bhils have become landless serfs. In this way the old economic independence of the Bhils is gone. Whenever they try to continue to be dependent on the land, Bhils do not get enough to eat. He has to go to the clutches of *sahukar*, the forest contractors or the big landlord.

The Bhil economy, in general, is an outcome of certain historical processes which have influenced them through the course of centuries. Before the establishment of stable government under the Marathas and Rajputs, the Bhils remained lawless and independent, fond of fighting, shy, excitable and restless. Believing themselves doomed to be thieves and plunderers, they were confirmed in their destiny by the oppression and cruelty of their rulers. They were treated as a wild animals and ruthlessly killed whenever encountered; if caught red-handed committing serious crimes, they were impaled on the spot or burned to death.[1] After the establishment of law and order which India experienced during the British rule compelled a majority of them to adopt a settled or semi-settled life and practise agriculture. At present their principal occupation is agriculture. They also work as labourer on farms, factories and road constructions. Their economy is from hand to mouth, with very little savings for a rainy day, which is always around the corner in the form of failure of crops, diseases of cattle or serious illnesses in the family. If a Bhil has enough to eat today he will not work for tomorrow.[2]

According to Watson, the Bhils of Jhabua are an industrious class cultivating the ground, selling grass, fire wood and jungle produce and thus earning a decent livelihood.[3]

The Bhils Village

The landscape against which a Bhil dwells in a series of hills covered with different shades of green. Within the shades of greenery their houses are situated. The villages situated in these valleys present a scattered pattern of settlements, where the house are located far apart from one another. Thus sometimes, a village may occupy an area of 2 to 3 square miles. Probably the main reasons for such scattered locations of the houses are the fear of the neighbour being a witch, the dread of some potential infection, the requirements of safety against fire and the over-consciousness of the Bhils regarding their womenfolks.

The Bhil houses are rectangular buildings, raised above the ground on a layer of earth and stones, with mud walls. The roof rises at an inclination of about 45 degrees from the two long sides. The houses are made of bamboo thatch, mud and cow-dung plaster. All the walls are blind except the front one, which has a small door. Some houses have entrances from behind also, though these are strictly private, leading to the kitchen-cum-sleeping rooms, no person who is not intimate with the household, can enter a house through such a rear door. The proper entrance is the front door, which generally remains open but is closed from inside by an obstructing bamboo door at night and padlocked from outside when the inmates go out.

The Bhil erect a bamboo stand for water *mohali* just adjacent to the hut, generally at the back of it. Water for cooking and drinking purposes is kept on it. Water is taken out of the earthen pot with the help of a wooden cup named *dovi* or *tumbi* and drunk with the help of palms. *Dovi* or *tumbi* is not permitted to be defiled by touching the mouth. A thatched cattle-shed *mandva* is also erected in front of the house. In the dry season, hay and grass are piled over this shed.

Soil and Rainfall

Jhabua district has a peculiar geological formation which contributes to drought and scarcity conditions every year. It covers an area of 6782 square kilometers marked by numerous ridges, steep escarpments, hills and hillocks and very narrow valleys. Soil depth in this region varies from 5 to 10 centimeters and the nature of the soil is *murramy*. Black soil is found only in patches. The vegetation over the hilly terrain has been indiscriminately cut leaving the hill completely denuded of trees thereby causing considerable soil erosion. The soil is therefore highly infertile. Rains are erratic and not evenly spread. In the five years the maximum average rainfall of the district was 1033.7 milimeters in 1981 and the minimum 611.8 milimeters in 1982. The tehsilwise average rainfall records from 1980 to 1984 is given in table-9.

Table-9

Tehsilwise Rain Records of Jhabua District

(fig. in milimeters)

Sl. no.	Name of Tehsil	Total rainfall (from 1st June to 30th September) 1980	1981	1982	1983	1984
1.	Jhabua	720.9	1025.0	417.6	846.8	754.3
2.	Thandla	699.4	904.1	673.4	856.0	763.0
3.	Petlawad	967.0	934.5	867.0	1302.0	957.0
4.	Jobat	643.8	1200.4	665.8	872.0	643.6
5.	Alirajpur	694.0	1104.5	435.0	912.9	642.6
	Average	745.4	1033.7	611.8	957.9	752.1

Source : Land Record Section, Collectorate, Jhabua (M.P.)

The district has about 2800 square kilometers of forest area out of a total area of 6782 square kilometeres. Thus 41.29 per cent of the total area is under forest. Forest in earlier days provided a secondary means of subsistance to the tribals particularly during famine and scarcity. But the tribals' traditional right to forest has been curtailed and forest policy has been regulated. The forests are exploited for timber, raw material for pulp, bidi and chemical industries.

Occupation

The largest concentration of the Bhils of Jhabua district depend on agriculture. Thus the main occupation of Bhils in the district is agriculture. According to 1981 census, out of total workforce of 3,33,145 as many as 83.1 per cent depend on cultivation. 7.65 per cent are agriculture labourers. Since the landholdings are small and marginal and the land is infertile there is not much distinction between cultivators and agricultural labourers. The cultivators also engage themselves as agricultural labourers as and when they get wage employment. Workers engaged in household industries, manufacturing, processing, servicing and repairing constitute only 1.28 per cent. The percentage distribution of the workforce in the district is given in table-10.

Table-10

Percentage Distribution of Workforce

Sl. No.	Category of Workers	% of the Workers
1.	Cultivators	83.01
2.	Agricultural labourers	7.05
3.	Household industry, manufacturing, processing, servicing and repairs	1.28
4.	Other workers	8.66

Secondary Source of Income

Since the soil of Jhabua is not fertile, people have to depend on other sources of livelihood. The other sources of income are: forestry, labourer, artisanship, service men. The wage earners constitute 90 per cent of the respondents.

The participation of women and children in the family income is as important as that of men in the area. Besides assisting the male adult in agriculture and household work, they participate as a labourer in mining, quarrying, livestock and forestry.

The number of workers per thousand in Jhabua is 561 which is higher than any other district of Madhya Pradesh. The number of male workers per thousand is 598 in the district which is lower than the State figure of 602 but the number of female workers per thousand, which is 523, exceeds the State figure by 83, the figure for them being 440.[4]

Landholdings

In Jhabua district, majority of the families possess land for cultivation. Only 6.17 per cent respondents are landless. The lands possess by Bhils are of three categories: the cultivable, non-cultivable, pasture and grazing land. The size of the landholdings is shown in table-11.

Table-11

Landholdings: Cultivable and Non-Cultivable Land

(in acres)

	Landless	1- 2.5	>2.5- 5	>5-10	>10-20
No.	21	98	86	99	36
%	6.17	28.83	25.29	29.12	10.59

The above table indicates that the majority of the respondents fall under the category holding 1 to 10 acres of land. 28.83 per cent of respondents have 1 to 2.5 acres, 25.29 per cent have 2.5 to 5 acres, 29.12 per cent have 5 to 10 acres and 10.59 per cent have above 10 to 20 acres. Considering the low productivity of land, drought and famine, the respondents can be placed in the category of marginal and small farmers.

Table-12

Households Holding Non-Cultivable Lands

(in acres)

Size of Non-cultivable landholdings	No. of households	%
0.5 - 1	66	94.28
> 1 - 2.5	2	2.86
> 2.5 - 5.0	2	2.86
Total	70	100.00

Table-12 depicts that the 70 respondents possess non-cultivable lands. Majority of the respondents have 0.5 to 1 acre of non-cultivable lands which constitute 98.28 per cent.

Table-13

Size of Pasture and Grazing Lands

(in acres)

Sl no.	Size of Land	No. of Households	%
1.	0.5 - 1	40	95.23
2.	1 - 2.5	2	4.77
Total		42	100.00

The Bhils face a lot of problems during drought. To meet the requirements of fodders at the time of drought they leave their land pasture. Out of 340 repondents only 42 i.e. 12.35 have left their land pasture for grazing their cattles.

Only marginal number of respondents have pasture and grazing lands. The size of such landholdings is also nominal as table-13 indicates.

System of Manure

The manure used for fertility of soil is organic. It is composed of the dung of all the farm animals. The system is to collect the dung at a distance of 30 to 50 yards from the hut in a corner of one of the fields. In course of time the collected dung which is mixed with the refuse from houses decomposes and becomes manure. The dung heap is taken to the fields by bullock carts. The quantity of organic manure added to the soil largely depends upon the strength of cattle a man possesses. Generally an average family produces about 5 to 10 carts load of manure annually.

Now, chemical fertilizers supplied by the Block office are chiefly used by the Bhils throughout the district. The chemical fertilizers used by them are ammonium sulphate, super phosphate, green manure, urea and C.A.N. Few of them avoid to use chemical fertilizer only because they have the view that it mitigate the fertility of the soil. Some have reported that they have lost their crops while using it. It happend only due to unproportionate use of fertilizers.

Source of Irrigation

In the hilly region of Jhabua district where water level is very low and the land uneven, people wholly depend upon rain. Nevertheless, wherever possible, the land is irrigated through wells or tanks. Since the district has seasonal river, the canal irrigation is not found. The assistance for irrigation well and pumpset has been provided but it has not been fruitful in some of the area because of water level is very low and many of the wells often dry up. The irrigation system through pump set is useful in some of the villages. The device of Persian wheel has been introduced and are being used.

Agricultural Implements

The Bhils are agricultural people, though their techniques are crude and clumsy as compared to the other agricultural communities of the country. They carry on their farming with wooden ploughs and a pair of bullocks. The plough has two parts : *ken* and *hamada*. They make their own agricultural implements. Their tools are made up of wood and iron. Most of the tools are indigenous. The implements used by the Bhils are weeders, axes, sickles, crow-bars, rakes (*dharias*), hoes, etc. Ropes are used as an important agricultural implement.

The plough is made of Babul wood (*Acacia arabica*) as it lasts long. It consists of three wooden pieces. It is a 4 feet long wooden piece fixed by a wooden shaft (*hal*) measuring about 7 to 8 feet in length. At one of its end is fixed a wooden nail. The lower end of the *hal* is slightly curved, and to it is fixed the iron rod.

The plough is attached to the *dhora* a wooden framework of the length of about 5 feet and is tied to the bullocks. At both ends of the *dhora* are fixed two wooden rods. The Hal falls on the central node and the bullocks draw the plough.

The levelling of the fields is done by the *hamada,* a kind of wooden tool. It is a flat, smooth piece of wood measuring 10-12 feet in length. At about two feet from each side holes are made in which the *ken* is fixed vertically and the ropes of the bullocks are tied to it. Five or six men stand on the *ken* when it is drawn by a pair of bullocks.

Principal Crops

Two principal crops i.e. the Kharif or monsoon crops and Rabi or dry weather crops are grown in the villages of the district. Kharif crops cover an area of about four times as large as the Rabi crops. This is due to insufficiency of irrigation and partly to the fact that Bhils are content to have only grain sufficient for their living. Among the dry weather crops they may grow grams when the rains have been heavy enough to keep the ground moist till November. The villagers produce these crops for two purposes i.e consumption and obtaining cash. The principal Kharif (monsoon) crops and their sowing and harvesting period are shown in table-14.

Table-14

Food Crops and their Sowing and Harvesting Period

Sl.no.	Crops	Month of sowing	Month of harvesting
1.	Maize	June - July	Sept. - Oct.
2.	Jowar	June - July	Sept. - Oct.
3.	Rice	July	October
4.	Kodra (Paspalum sroviculatum)	June - July	Sept. - Oct.
5.	Kuri (Panicum miliaceum)	June - July	Sept. - Oct.
6.	Batti (P. crusgalli)	June - July	Sept. - Oct.
7.	Urad (Phaseolous rariatus)	July	October
8.	Mung (P. Mungo)	July	October

In the villages of Jhabua district, mostly five different crops are grown as a cash crop. The cash crops and their showing and harvesting period are mentioned in table-15.

Table-15

Cash Crops and Their Sowing and Harvesting Period

Sl. no.	Crops	Month of sowing	Month of harvesting
1.	Til (Sesamum Indicum)	August	November
2.	Jute (Cropelaria juncea)	November	February
3.	Sugarcane	March	Jan.- Feb.
4.	Ground Nut	August	February
5.	Cotton	August	Feb.- April

In Rabi (dry-weather) crops, Wheat and Grams are cultivated as food crops while Mustard and Cumin seed are used as cash crops for generating money for daily use and other articles. Food crops and cash crops and their sowing and harvesting period is placed in table-16.

Table-16

Food and Cash Crops and their Sowing and Harvesting Period

Sl. no. Crops	Month of sowing	Month of harvesting
Food Crops		
1. Wheat	November	March
2. Gram	November	February
Cash Crops		
3. Sarson (Mustard)	November	February
4. Zira (Cumin seed)	November	March

In the village Ochaka and Khermal, of monsoon crops, maize is by far the most important one as more than half of the cultivated land is utilized for growing it. The inferior millets such as Kuri, Kodra, Batti and Khulat are grown by all as these require little labour and water. Ochaka and Khermal agriculturists do not grow cash crops during Kharif cultivation. It is because of that they are not conscious of the market economy. They are satisfied in producing whatever they require for the year. They do not have to import foodgrains in the village in normal years. From amongst dry weather crops they grow grams only. The land is suitable for a wheat crop also but idleness keeps them away from arduous tasks. They do only because of that lack of initial investment.

Agricultural System

A Bhil ploughman is busy with agriculture throughout the year except during a few months of summer when the fields remain dry. The Bhil cultivator has divided the whole year into two distinct divisions : one for crops of monsoon and the other for crops of dry weather.

In the month of June, the Bhil farmer makes full preparations to till the land for the maize crop which is staple food. It does not involve hard labour. After the first shower of rains the land is ploughed once or twice and after the second shower, it is reploughed and pressed; and when it has retained sufficient water, the maize seed is sown.

Hindu ideas as to propitious days have become general, with some modifications, in the observances followed. Thus the day *adhatij* is considered the proper time for commencing operation. Before sowing a cultivator sets a stone up at the top of the field and anoints it with red lead breaking a coconut over it. This stone represents Ganesh. Twice or thrice in the rains a solemn worship is held called *jatar.* No work is ever done on the day of *Amawasya* (i.e. dark moon night). The day of *Amawasya* is considered as an inauspicious day because it brings destruction of the crops.[5]

The evil eye is averted from crops. To avert the evil eyes two sticks are planted in the ground with a piece of conspicuous coloured cloth tied to them, or heaps of stones are raised and white washed. The onlooker's gaze thus falls first on these objects.

After the reaping is completed, the evil spirits are appeased by the offering of a cock and liquor. If this is not done they may, annoyed at the removal of the grain, visit the threshing floor with disaster.

Before a well is sunk a stone is set up and anointed with red lead and propitiated with offerings, the stone standing in this case for the water-deity of the locality.

Most of the Bhil cultivation being done on the indifferent soils of the tract is regulated entirely by the rain fall as it is not possible, as in richer soils, to commence operations before the rain has actually fallen in sufficient quantity to moisten the soil thoroughly.

Like others, Bhils have some common proverbs relating to the crop seasons, but their application refers to the better classes of soil and not in reality to tie conditions on the most jungle covered tracts. If there is rain under the *Magha nakshatra* (February), the wheat crop will be above the average. If the rains under *Uttara nakshatra* even the dogs will scorn bread. If *til* is shown in *Sawan* (July) the plants will flourish, and yield much blossom and good seed. Wheat sown in *Aghan* (December) yields bumper crops. But it yields poor when it is shown in *paus* (January).

Among the Bhils of Malwa, it is customary on the day when they begin their autumnal sowing to perform the mock marriage of two wooden dolls. This ceremony is performed before the commencement of rains. As soon as the rains commence the dolls are thrown into a stream to float away. These dolls represent the deities who control the rains.[6]

Income and Expenditure

A survey of Kathiwar block conducted in 1966 reveals that the cultivation was the main source of income of the villagers. The average annual income derived from it was Rs. 541.81. The other sources of income were forestry, poultry, milk, etc. Table-17 represents the annual average sources of income.

Table-17

Average Annual Sources of Income

Sl no.	Source	Average annual income in Rs.
1.	Agriculture	541.81
2.	Forests	94.80
3.	Livestock (Poultry)	1.80
4.	Milk	40.06
5.	Others	95.41
	Total	773.88

Source : *Bulletin of the Tribal Research and Development stitute,* Bhopal Vol. VII, no. 1 & 2, June & December 1969, p.

The income derived from agriculture constitutes 70.01 per cent of the total yearly income of a household. As compared to this income derived from the forest produce is very low, forming only 12.25 per cent, and it is only 1/6 of the income from agriculture. As a matter of fact the income from the forest produce should be higher than the above figures because the major part of the block is covered by the forest but it is such an irregular source of income that it is difficult for the individual to keep an account of it. The contribution to the average income from forest as given in table-17 can be considered as an under-estimate.

Income from milk products is 5.18 per cent which is reasonable but the income from livestock and poultry is also very low, forming only 00.23 per cent of the total. The factors responsible to giving a low figure of income from forest, seem to be applicable here also. Income from other sources forms 12.33 per cent.[7]

The data collected from Petlawad Block reveal that the total average expenditure of a family is Rs. 1219.15. Their main source of expenditure was on food and other intoxicants. The itemwise annual expenditure is given in table-18.

Table-18

Average Annual Source of Expenditure

Sl. No.	Items	Average Annual Expenditure
1.	Food	948.48
2.	Betel, tobacco & Other intoxicants	119.84
3.	Fuel & Light	73.64
4.	Clothing	67.67
5.	Others	9.52
	Total:	Rs. 1219.15

Source : *Bulletin of the Tribal Research and Development Institute*, Bhopal, Vol. VII, Nos. 1 & 2, June & December 1969.

The average annual expenditure on a single item i.e. food, exceeds the total average annual income. The average annual income per household is Rs. 773.88 and the average annual expenditure on food is Rs. 948.48. The expenditure on other items is negligible as compared with the expenditure on food.[8]

Indebtedness

Like other tribals, indebtedness is a general phenomenon among the Bhils of Jhabua. Out of 340 respondents 50 have borrowed high amount from moneylenders. The moneylenders are generally the local *banias* and the dealers of fair price shops. Most of the respondents did not consider the amount from *banias* as debt as it was a regular affairs. If we consider this aspect of the debtors' perception the amount of households would swell to almost 100 per cent.

Loans from moneylenders have been taken for agricultural inputs, paying of *dhapa* (bride price), social obligations, festivals and repayment of previous debt. It can be seen that the loans from the different sources are not only taken for capital investment in agriculture but also to previous loans.

The rate of interest varies from area to area and person to person. In the village Surinala the loan varies from 25 per cent to 50 per cent. In the village Ochaka it is upto 100 per cent. In some of the anterior areas like village Bhurighati it has extended upto 250 per cent.

Market

Only negligible number of villages, falling generally on road or which are easily accessible by the trader, have shops. They deal in commodities of day-to day use. In every Block office of the district have a number of shops. In every Block there held a weekly market from where the Bhils purchase their commodities of daily requirements.

The main commodities brought by the tribals to the markets are grains, vegetables, forest produce like *mahua, doli,* honey, gum, *charoli* and fuel etc. The forest produce are generally bartered for grains. In livestock they bring goat, fowls and eggs. A few of the tribals bring *ghee* (purified butter) also.

The commodities purchased by the tribals are salt, spices, edible oils, tobacco, kerosene, clothes, potteries, grains, liquor etc. Pottery at the Jhabua market is exchanged for fuel. Ornaments made of alluminium, bead necklaces and bangles are purchased by women. Arrows, *daranta* (a big sickle used as an agricultural implement and a weapon) and agricultural implements (iron) are also purchased from the weekly markets.

Migration Pattern

The rate of migration is very high; out of 340 respondents families 275 families migrate for employment during the lean season. The migrant households constitute 80.88 per cent. The reason for migration are low wages and seasonal employment. The migration pattern suggests that in majority of cases the respondents migrate outside the state. The number of such migrants is 198 which is 72 per cent of the migrant household. 34 households have migrated within the State but outside the district. In the case of 43 households we find migration within the district. Only 15.64 per cent migration takes place within the district. Out-migration in large numbers suggests the uniformly poor employment potential in the district. Table-19 indicates the duration of migration in different categories. The period of migration in most of the cases is 3 to 6 months.

Table-19

Place and Duration of Migration (in %)

Place	Within the District	Outside the District	Within the State	Outside the State	Total no. Migrants households	
No.	43	12	22	198	275	
%	15.64	4.36	8.00	72.00	100.00	
Duration	1 months>	1-3 months>	3-6 months>	6-8 months>	8 months	Total
No.	14	119	129	11	2	275
%	5.09	43.27	46.91	4.00	0.73	100.00

Livestock

Livestock plays important role in the Bhils economy. The livestock consists of a pair of bullocks for agriculture, a few she-buffaloes and cows for milk, sheep, goats and a few hens. Few of them rear ducks and pigs. The dogs are among the commonest pets and these keep away wild animals from picking up the babies and livestock or drive away any that may stay into their domain. The dog is also the watchman's assistance in the fields.

Notes and References

1. M.M. Khan, *Census of India 1891,* His Highness the Nizam's Dominion, Vol. 23, part2, p. 218.
2. S. L. Doshi, *op. cit.,* p. 54.
3. J. F. Watson (ed.), *The People of India : The Races and the Tribes of Hindustan,* Vol. VII, Delhi, 1987, p. 356.
4. F. Bahadur (ed.), *Bulletin of the Tribal Research and Development Institute,* Bhopal, Vol. VII, no. 1 & 2, 1969, p. 48.
5. C. E. Luard, *op. cit.,* p. 33.
6. Sir James George Frazer, *Aftermath : A Supplement to the Golden Bough,* London, 1963, p. 351.
7. F. Bahadur (ed.), *op. cit.,* p. 49.
8. *Ibid.,* p. 49.

4

Social and Cultural Life

As in all tribal societies, among the Bhils too, the family is the basis of their social life. The Bhil family serve several functions important for the individual as well as the society. It gives fulfilment to the effective and sexual urges of males and females; it provides protection and nurture to the young in the years of childhood; it provides elementary education for the young generation in basic knowledge and social habits and customs; it fosters the cooperative union of labour between man and woman and their dependents.

The Bhils live in family group each occupying a separate dwelling. The father is the head of the family and he is responsible for the maintainance of law and order in the family. Late marriage is in vogue. Usually child marriage is discouraged and one can frequently find men and women of 20 to 25 still unmarried.

The primitive Bhil family is based on individualism and seldom represents the joint family system, for when a grown up son marries and after the first issue the male member, if he is not the only son, sets up a separate family with his wife and children. Except in the case when a Bhil has no male issue, married daughters are always separated but when a married daughter or sister dies leaving children behind they are looked after and brought up at his place till they reach the age of eight or ten. In some cases a man may be found to live in one family with his sons and grand-children.

Table-20

Size of the Family

No. of family Members	1 - 5 (Small)	6 - 10 (Medium)	11 - 15 (Large)	16 - 20 (Very Large)	Total
No.	89	188	53	10	340
%	26.18	55.29	15.59	2.94	100.00

It appears from table-20 that out of 340 respondents, 26.18 per cent belong to small family size. High percentage i.e. 55.29 found in medium size family. The size of large family is less i.e. 15.59. The very large size family represents very less percentage i.e. 2.94. The high percentage of medium family represents only due to increase in the number of dependents, old mother and father as well as nephews. Large family represents joint family.

The Bhils observe strict clan exogamy, but tribe as a whole is endogamous. They are patrilineal. The property of the family is equally divided among all the heir. The Bhil family is patrilocal. After the marriage, the bride comes to reside in the parental home of the bridegroom.

Widow re-marriage is commonly practised and if there is no one to look after her sons and daughters, she takes them with her to the new husband. A younger brother can keep the widow of his elder brother but not vice verse.

Polygamy is permitted, but its practice is mainly determined by the financial condition of a man. The marriage of a second or third wife is attended with the same ceremonies as in the case of the first, provided she is not a widow. According to Luard, the Census of 1901 showed 1,024 wives to every 1,000 husbands. Thus that the custom is not general.[1] Out of 340 respondents, 34 respondents i.e. 10% have more than one wife. This cases have been found in the well to do family i.e. village Tadvi and its related family. No cases of polyandry has been found. Thus polyandry is not in vogue among the Bhils.

Motherkin exists, though rarely among the Bhils. A father in the absence of a son often gives his daughter on the condition that son-in-law should remain with him and his children should inherit the grandfather's property. The son-in-law, commonly known as "Gharjamai" thus lives in the wife's home.

Family among the Bhils is the smallest unit of social organisation. The kiths and kins live side by side forming a group known as *kutum*. The *kutum* is represented by one person. All the members of the *kutum* are expected to help mutually at the time of births, marriages, death, family feuds, quarrels and ritual performance etc. Thus, the *kutum* offers all the possible support to the family including economic assistance.

Role of Women in Bhil Society

The role of women in the Bhil society is very important. They play an important role in almost all walk of life. Like the women of any other tribes or castes, the Bhil women of Jhabua pass through three important stages; maidenhood, wifehood and motherhood. As an unmarried daughter she is reared in her parental house where socialisation occur with the norms of the Bhil culture. In her childhood a tribal girl has to assist her mother in domestic affairs. At the age of seven or eight she nurse her young brothers and sisters during the absence of her mother. By the time she reaches the age of 12 or 13 she is able to do all the household work with full responsibility.

A Bhil woman works in home as well as in the field with her husband. She collects wood from the forest and grazes the cattle. She is a more industrious and hard working than man. She milks the cows and buffaloes and performs the labours of the dairy, moulds cow-dung into cakes and brings water for domestic use in earthen jars from the neighbouring step-well, pond or tank. The boys and girls occupy themselves with grazing while the men-folk take to agricultural, pastoral forest, and other manual duties.

The unmarried girl is considered vary sacred. They symbolise fertility and thus because of the symbolisation possesses enormous powers. At the time of crops she is always given the first raw grains, for it results in prosperous yields. During marriage celebrations, she welcomes the bridegroom, carries an earthen pitcher over her head. She also ties turban over the head of bridegroom. She also ties and unties the garments of the newly wedded couple during the marriage rites.

The position of the wife conforms to the form of marriage. In the villages, where most of the families are polygamous, a wife is not very happy nor does she enjoy a high status. In a house where there are two or more wives, the position and status are accorded to the wife in relation to the degree of preference she gets from her husband. However, she be the senior-most, she enjoys a better say in family affairs relating to rites and ceremonies and other social matters.

Kinship

The kinship terms of the Bhils include both descriptive and classificatory terms. There is no particular term for grand father, he is being described as the 'older father' or the 'aged father'. Grandmother is also described similarly. Paternal male mother is also described similarly. Paternal male cousins are described as the 'sons of father's brother', and the paternal female cousins are described as the 'daughters of father's brother'.

To exemplify the classificatory terms it may be mentioned that one term, *kaka,* is used to address all male persons of father's age. All women of mother's age are similarly addressed by *jiji* (mother's sister).

The prevalent systems of marriage have influenced the kinship terminology of the Bhils. Thus, due to the custom of marrying either of the cross-cousins, the same term, *mamo,* is used for the father's sister's husband, the mother's brother and the wife's father. Similarly the wife's mother, the mother's brother's wife and the father's sister are addressed by the same term *fuisi.* On account of junior levirate and junior sororate, the step father is called *kaka* and the step mother, *jiji.*

The relations between the in-laws, *vevais,* is very important. For a man, his son's wife's father, latter's brothers and other relatives stand as *vevam* and vice versa. On occasions of joy or sorrow they are the first to increase or share them. Whenever there is a marriage ceremony at one of these people's places, the other party is invited with much respect. They exchange gifts at these occasions and in hours of need they help each other.

There is a large number of joking relationship among the Bhils, of which special mention may be made of that between a woman and her husband's younger brother and husband's sisters. There is also joking relationship between two cross-cousins and between two *vevais.*

They also observe a few avoidance rules the most rigid one being between a woman and her husband's elder brother. She should not speak to him, nor can she utter his name, and even she is not allowed to look at him. Similarly but less rigorous avoidances are there between a woman and her husband's father, and between a man and his wife's mother.

Kinship Taboos

Husband and wife are not permitted by custom to mention each other's name, as such mention, it is believed, would bring famine or other calamity to the settlement. The husband and wife in calling or referring to each other generally use their children's name, such as "so and so's father" and "so and so's mother". The expressions *gharwalo* (master of the house) and *gharwali* (mistress of the house) are also used. The wife of a younger brother calls her husband's elder brother jethji but must not take his name, nor must she takes the name of her husband's father.

A Bhil woman is required to draw her veil over her face in the presence of all persons related to her as *sasura,* and *jeth* in the classifactory sense, such as the husband's father, husband's father's brother, husband's elder brother, husband's mother's brother, husband's mother's sister's husband and husband's father's sister's husband.

Kinship Salutation

A Bhils woman has to fall at the feet without touching them in saluting the following relations of her husband, namely, her husband's father, father's brother, elder brother, mother's brother, mother's sister's husband, father's sister's husband.

The general rule as to salutations among the Bhils is to fall at the feet of those who might be called "superior" relations and embrace those who may be said to be "equals" in kinship status.

These rules as to salutations appear to be more strict in the case of women than of men. Particular duties and functions belong to certain kin on occasions of birth, marriage, and death.

Caste Subdivision

The Bhils of Jhabua form a compact group, which, although not cut of from communication with other sections of the tribe in the neighbouring areas have been considered as a major tribal group. It has not, any local designation. They are said to be no higher or lower caste groups in the Bhil tribe as met with in this district.

The Hindu Bhils do not admit outsiders into the caste but the Muhammadans admit a man of any but the impure castes. A simple ceremony is solemnised in which the neophyte must be shaved and circumcised and the *Kazi* gives holy water to drink and teaches him the profession of belief in Islam. If a man is not circumcised, the *tadvi* or Muhammadan Bhil will not bury his body.[2]

According to Luard, 122 septs have been found in Jhabua state. Each sept is represented by a totem. It is customary that they will not destroy or injury any object of which he belongs. The Bhils revere the object which he belongs.[3]

As regards outcasting the institution is entirely an important from Hindu custom, and the low status of the tribe as a whole practically precludes the admission of outsiders. A ceremony has, however, now been devised for such admissions. The person desirous of entering the Bhil caste has to prepare for a ceremony. It is known as *tirth*. This consists of mixing cowdung with Ganges or other sacred water in a dish. The *tirth* is then given to the chief man of a *panchayat.* The chief man sips this mixture which is then passed round to other members of the panchayat. Rice boiled in goat's blood is then handed round and partaken of in the same way. The ceremony concludes by a gift of a few rupees which are placed in the dish of the *tirth* and are perquisite of the chief man. This same ceremony applies in cases where a Bhil is re-admitted into the caste after having been outcasted.

Leadership

For seeking advice on their family affairs and at the times of disputes, people approach the *Tadvi* or the *Patel,* the Kotwal, the *Mafidar* and the *Baragarya Patel.*

The *Tadvi* or the *Patel*: The same person is designated as *Tadvi* among the Bhils and as Patel among the Bhilalas. He is the Headman of the village. During the times of Princely States, he used to bring people together for paying the land revenue. He himself was not empowered to collect it but now it is the Patel who collects the revenue.

The *Kotwal* : Being indirect contact with the villagers and working as mediator between the villagers and the officials, the Kotwal has been enjoying a very good position. On certain occasions he wields a greater influence on the people than the Tadvi. So far as leadership is concerned, the Kotwal's position is secondary. He receives remuneration from the village people. Payment depends upon the economic condition of the payer. The usual rate has been 8 seers of maize or *samree* (an inferior millet) per plough.

The *Mafidar* : Persons who helped the management of the State in some way or served the people were given rent free land and were known as *Mafidar*. The *Mafidar* used to help the Patel in the discharge of his duties. He enjoys nearly a parallel position in the village.

The *Baragarya Patel*: Above the village Patels, there have been *Baragarya Patels*. Their jurisdiction, as the designation indicates, has been an area of 12 villages but this rule was never stuck to and there are *Baragarya Patels* who exercise influence over more than 12 villages.

Pujari and *Badwa* are considered as socio-religious leaders. They do not enjoy the status enjoyed by the persons mentioned above.

The Panchayat

As elsewhere, the statutory Panchayats, known as the Gram Panchayats, have also been organised by the Government in this area. Though all the Blocks of the Jhabua district have been divided by the Government in the administrative units, the traditional Panchayats still exercise effective control over the people. It consists of the Tadvi, or the Patel, the Kotwal, the Mafidar, occasionally the Pujari and a few other elders of the village. Now the members of the Gram Panchayat are also invited in the sittings of the Panchayat.

During the times of Princely States, few cases were settled by this Panchayat. At the instance of only major cases, the traditional Panchayat used to settle the breach of the rules of marriage. All the other cases were taken to the court of law headed by the *Makavisdar* (equivalent to Tahsildar, exercising the powers of a third class magistrate). For cases pertaining to the rules of the caste or tribe, the Kamavisdar used to invite the *Patel* and a few other leaders and ask them to take their own decisions, reserving, of course, his right to give the final verdict even with amendments, if necessary. In such cases he generally used to agree with the village leaders. The Bhils of Jhabua have no laws of its own, but in certain special cases the customs of the tribe are taken into consideration, as in the disputes among Bhils and other ignorant classes, the procedure adopted is of a summary nature, through their Panchayats, especially in matrimonial cases. The Patel in any way had no rights to impose fine upon the parties in terms of money. In cases of absconsion the amount fixed as bride price was given by the culprit to the parents of the girl. After a decision was taken *chhak* was performed for lifting the tension. Liquor was called and the parties offered it to each other, thus expressing their friendly spirit among the members present there. This method of settling disputed exists even today.

To indicate the breaking of other kinds of disputes a piece of wood is held on either side by both the parties and on an order from the leader they break that piece of wood with a jerk. As the broken piece of wood can not be joint together again, the dispute thus ended is supposed to remain broken for ever.

After the abolition of zamindari, the types of cases coming to the traditional Panchayat for settlement have increased. The cases now settled by this Panchayat are pertaining to petty quarrels, petty thefts and those pertaining to breach of rules of the tribe.

Fine imposed by this Panchayat range from Rs. 10.00 to Rs. 15.00. The amount below Rs. 10.00 is consumed on the spot in liquor and tobacco but when it exceeds Rs. 10.00, a sum of Rs. 5.00 is deposited with the Panchayat.

Persons challenging the decision of the Panchayat are ex-communicated and are accepted back in the tribe only after purificatory rites known as *chokha karna* (meaning, making pure).

For settling bigger issues or on the advice of the Patel, people go to the Baragarya Patel. Since people belonging to the higher castes are negligible in number, cases of dispute between these and the tribals are not known. Thus, it is the traditional Panchayat which exercises control over the people and the statutory Panchayat has no significant role to play.

All the functionaries mentioned above are hereditary. They are changeable only in cases of invalids or issueless deaths when usually the posts are given to the nearest relatives of the deceased or invalids.

Customs

Marriages among the Bhils are settled between the father of the two families. At betrothal "Dapa" is contracted which is an amount ranging between Rs.100 to 1000 payable to the girl's father by the other side in exchange for the bride, on a ceremony, after the marriage. The bridegroom proceeds on foot accompanied by the marriage party consisting of both men and women to his father-in-law's place where marriage takes place with the traditional Hindu rites with the course some local and tribal changes. The widow is not allowed to leave the precints of the house for one year of her husband's death and after this period she may marry again.

Rules of Inheritance

The Bhils determine inheritance. Of the property, half goes to the youngest son, who is responsible for the payment of all expenses incurred on his father's *nukta* (the feast given after his death, usually on the 12th day after). He has also to make provision for his sisters. The other half is divided between the elder sons. If they all live together, a very rare occurence, they share equally in the property. In the case of the deceased being a *Tadvi,* his position is assumed not necessary by the eldest son, but by the most fit, who is chosen by the *Panches.* He then becomes entitled to the usual rights pertaining to the position, as well as its responsibilities, such as entertaining strangers of position, etc. In the case of a Tadvi dying childless, his successor is chosen in the family. A widow is mistress of her husband's property for life, provided she conducts herself properly. It is not uncommon, however, to divide the property in order to prevent disagreeable quarrels. A daughter can under no circumstances inherit her father's property. Only those who are *sagotra* (of the dead man's sept) can inherit.

Food and Drink

Due to wide spread poverty, Bhils consume low variety of grains. The grains consumed by them are broadly divided into two categories- the *chhota dhan* and *mota dhan*. The *chhota dhan* includes *Samli, Bhudli, Kuri, Gujra, Baotra, Kodra, and batti*. The grains which belong to *mota dhan* category are *Makka* (maize) and *Jowar*.

Rabdi is a treat for a Bhil. It is a thick gruel of maize flour without milk or sugar, but the way of a Bhil eats it shows the satisfaction he derives out of it. The maize is consumed in different ways. The one way of consuming maize is that the corns are roasted and eaten as such. In the other way, the housewife prepares flour from maize almost every day by handmill. The food is prepared with flour as *Roti* (bread), *Pania* (a kind of cake prepared on the green leaves of *Tendua* and heated directly on the fire) or *Rabdi*. Jowar flour is also used in preparing *Roti* (bread) or a thick gruel.

Among the pulses, *urad*, and *tuar* are used. *Urad* is more commonly used than *tuar*. The pulse is boiled in water with a pinch of salt and used. Gram is an occasional substitute for these cereals. *Mahua*, mango (*Mangifera indica*) and some jungle roots and fruits *ber* and *gular* are used whenever available.

Milk and milk products are not very uncommon, but their availability depends upon the economic status of the family. Normally, goats and cows are kept by family households. Milk is ordinarily used after boiling, but sometimes, curd, *chhach* (butter milk) and *ghee* (clarified butter) are also prepared. Milk is also sold, but this is a rare phenomenon and happens only in village nearer the urban areas.

The flesh of certain animals are not eaten, viz., monkeys, duck, tortoises, snakes, lizards, rats, crane(*saras*), crocodile, jackals, peacocks etc. But goat, pork, sheep, hares, buffaloes (male and female), deer, nilgais, fish, and fowls are eaten.

Tobacco is in common use and form an important part of Bhil life. Its offering is symbolic of esteem and regards for the recipents. The *bidi* is usually smoke by male members. Chewing of tobacco is not very common, smoking being prevalent, but *pan* (betel-nut) is taken only on ceremonious and festive occasions.

Liquor plays a vital role in the Bhil life, especially during festivals and socio-religious ceremonies. Toddy acts as an intoxicant and is also a vital food item during the leaner days. It is tapped during the spring and summer seasons from the palm trees surrounding the habitations. They are grown and owned by the Bhils and form a precious part of belongings. Liquor is purchased from the liquors of the area. Sometimes, illicit distillation from *mahua* flowers for home comsumption is also done.

Dress and Ornament

The dress of a Bhil woman mainly consists of a petticoat (*ghaghara*) in red and black colours, a bodice (*kanchli*) and a piece of cloth used both as waist-cloth and as head dress (*odni*). The petticoat or ghaghara covers half the body up to the waist. It is skirt-like and is made of red and black coloured khadi or some other coarse cloth with a number of plaits and it hangs from the waist to the ankles. The female way of wearing a ghaghara is to keep the left hand side shorter than the other, the ends being tucked in; the longer end is taken to the back from between the legs and is tucked up there in such a way that the lower side is once more stretched and tucked at the front, known as *Kachhado*. The decent way of wearing this cloth is that the shorter side must cover the whole thigh. The woman who keeps the thigh open is regarded as an immoral woman or a woman who runs after many persons. The *kanchli* or bodice is so worn that it keeps the breasts almost half-exposed and it has to be tied at the back with two strings. The *odni* is used to cover the head or it is fastened to the petticoat, on which it hangs on the right-hand side, while the remaining portion of the cloth is used to cover the head and the bosom.

Luard[4] has mentioned the dress of the Bhils of Alirajpur. The dress of males consists of a piece of cloth (about a span wide and a yard long) which passes between the fork and is fastened loosely to a cord tied round the waist so that during movements the end flaps like a tail. The *pagri* or turban is a long narrow piece of cloth twined like a string and fastened to the head, so as to leave the crown exposed. When out visiting, a *chaddar* or cloth is thrown over the right or left shoulder : they either go bare-footed or wear sandals, consisting of a piece of leather for a sole fastened to the foot with string or bark.

The possession of clothes for a Bhil is just a necessary to protect him from the cold and sun. Bhils are so poor that he cannot have more than one pair of clothes. It is only when the crops are ready and the grain is sold then the clothes are purchased. These serve him for at least one whole year. Before this period, they use the available rags and bits of cloth which they had previously purchased and preserved.

The hair style of the Bhils is unique. Men oil and comb their hair with a parting in the centre, fashionable young bloods apply collyrium to their eyes. The hair is usually worn long falling at the sides, but the rest is hidden in the turban. On the other hand female also oil and comb their hair which is twisted in the form of a knot, resting on the nape of the neck. They indulge in collyrium which is applied thick round the eyes, while a circle or dot or red powder is applied to the centre of the forehead. Generally Bhils shave their beards except the moustaches. The Bhil women apply oil and occasionally wash their hair with milk or curd. After washing, they part their hair in the middle. Sometimes they tie the hair at the back in a bun and sometimes they leave the pig tails dangling down at the back with a silken tassel to each of them. This lends colour and beauty.

The Bhils are also very fond of ornaments for their personal adornment. Both men and women invariably wear earrings and finger rings made of white metal or brass. Those who can afford it wear rings made of silver or gold. Ornaments are considered to enhance the beauty of the wearer; they are also a sign of wealth. The young people occasionally display a certain amount of coquetry in their dress, especially the women.

The Bhils of Rajasthan are also very fond of ornaments made of bronze, aluminium or nickel and silver. They wear *murkis* in ear lobes, *hansli* round their neck and *kada* round their wrists. They are very fond of silver buttons, which they use with their Jackets. There are very few Bhils of village Kailashpuri who use silver *murkis* and silver *kadas* and there is no one possessing gold ornaments. The Bhil women wear a number of ornaments, some of which are considered very essential. *Bor* made of silver on the head, *ognies* and *karnphool* in the ears, *vesar* in the nose, bangles of ivory, coconut shell or lac on the heads and *paijanias* on the ankles are commonly worn and possessed by all the women. There are other ornaments too viz, *Jhalar, gujri, thusi, timania, bazuband, hathphool, langar, tanka, anwla and nevris.* All these ornaments are worn by the women at the time of festive occasions.[5]

Tattooing

The tattooing is customary among the members of both the sexes and especially among the females. Tatooing is carried out in the weekly market (*hat*) and more often when big tairs are held. This operation is generally performed at ten to twelve years of age on girls, on the cheeks, forehead, arm below the elbows, chin and wrists.

Men are tattoed between the ages of 8 and 9, on arms, wrists and chests. Man operates tattoo on men and woman among the girls. The object of tattooing is said to be this. After each individual is asked whether he has been pricked by thorns in the jungle, the presentation of these tattoo marks is considered an affirmative answer, without this they would have to be pricked with thorns in after life.

Design are numerous and are made to the fancy of the person operated on. Boys are in the habit of burning marks on each other on the back and wrist, in either five or seven distinct places. This is done with a piece of smoldering cloth or the match of a matchlock. The custom is called *dhamla* and appears to have the same object as tattooing. Females are never branded in this way.[6]

Dance and Music

The Bhils are fine dancers. Probably no primitive tribe of aboriginal India ever equalled the Bhils in the presentation of dramatic performances. On ceremonial occasions the dancers are adorned with paints and are elaborately costumed and masked to represent legendary beings, or sometimes animals. The dances are electrifying in their vividness, realism and dramatic power. The germs of dancing have so impregnated their blood that their dances have become part and parcel of their life. All the men and women, boys and girls dance with the same perfection. They give him an incentive to work, a stimulus to face the hard realities of life and thereby soften his heart. And what else is happiness but a similarly complete integration of the whole personality with its environment. It needs no demonstration to convince that the happy person is not the one who has no troubles to face but the one who can face troubles without losing that integration of personality which is the essence of happiness. And the Bhils have reduced it to a fine art.

On ceremonial occasions, these displays deal with mythological subject matter, supernatural 'siezures' and miraculous restorations but they are nevertheless more social than religious. Bhairon Puja and Bhinyavad are characteristic examples. One description will illustrate the vividness of these displays. Bhinyavad is a folk dance of the tribe in which Amba, the incarnation of Kali is surrounded by her devotees who dance around Devi Amba and worship her. The devil Bhinyavad (Bhasmasura) who wants to kidnap Amba appears on the scene. Bhinyavad unheedful of the warnings of the devotees chased Amba. Angry Budia-Lord-Shiva arrives and a fight ensues between Bhinyavad and Budia. Bhinyavad is defeated and killed. They make a brave show. With extremely slow movements they begin to dance, just as if they are imitating a slow motion picture. After much vigor and valour, they begin to quicken their movements, twisting their arms and hands all to the booming rhythm of the toms-toms. The men use dance sticks and swords, kick at the earth a lot; their energy is amazing, for they dance with agility and determination hour after hour. During Bhagoria fair, men and women of different ages forms separate circle and dances on the sound of traditional musical instruments like drums and flutes through out the day. They jerked their bodies up and down.

The Bhils of Maiwar perform a special dance under which men and women of different ages formed two concentric circles, women within men, for dancing round and round in solemn rhythm. The dance began with a series of choruses, each homogenous group singing one after the other. After a while with more and more excitement they quickened the rhythm of their singing and jerked their bodies violently up and down in a slanting style, to and fro, with every syllable. In contrast with other dances they, became more and more excited as the dances gained intensity and went on for a couple of hours without any halt or hesitation lending no monotony to the spectacle.[7]

The Bhils of Gujarat[8] perform a number of dances at the time of social functions. The chief forms of dances are Ghoor, Antiya, Vana, and Dharva.

In Ghoor dance which is meant for female only, the partaking members take their hands interlocking each other and form a circle. Then the dance is performed with graceful rythmic movement in a circular motion.

In Antiya dance, males only take part. They stand alternatively with sticks in their hands and a set of drums are played. The sticks strike against each other to keep tune. This is an active dance with a gradual increment of movement and later on the whirling movements become faster as the dance reaches its climax.

In Vana dance, males and females form a circle and drummers accompanied with 'Thali' players stand in the middle of the circle and dancers move in circular motion.

Musical Instruments

The Bhils tribe of Jhabua district have a large number of musical instruments, the drum being predominant. On this, three main notes are used, for joy, grief, and fear. Other instruments are the tom-tom, cymbals, small and large-sized bamboo flutes, a mouthpiece string which is held tight and vibrated with the nails (*Tengari*), a small *tambut* made from a coconut sheel and horse's hair attached to a small stick (*mandol*), and a bronze *thali* (plate) beaten with a stick.

Traditional Weapons

The Bhils are brave fighters. They are skilled in archery. The wood of the Dhaman (*Grewia vestita*) or bamboo is used for the bow. The string is either of a thin and long bamboo strip tied at both the ends with threads made from the 'movasy' plant or a strong rope. The *Khari* wood or bamboo is used for the arrows. The metallic pointed part of the arrow (bilkhi) is made of iron and is very neatly tied, feathers are tied and glued to the other end of the arrow so as to guide the arrow's flight correctly. Six types of arrows have been used in the different parts of Jhabua district. They are 1. Ghadiyal 2. Jamni 3. Bhalka 4. Tavadia 5. Kanyali 6. Bitla.

The swords and *dharias* (shield) are used as weapons for offence as well as defence. The *phalia* is a favourite for committing homocide. Some of the Bhils are also experts in throwing stones or missiles from string and there are stories wherein the Bhils have badly hurt their enemies by using only slings and stones. Some Bhils have been able to get arms licences and they, have with them muzzle and breach-loading guns. They also prepare traps for catching birds and small jungle games.

Festivals

The main festivals which are held by the tribals in the course of their cultural life in Jhabua are : 1. *Wavni* 2. *Divasa* 3. *Nawai* 4. *Desarya* 5. *Duyari* and 6. *Holi*.

1. *Wavni* (Sowing) : Before sowing is started, the deity of the earth (field) is propitiated. The *Puja* is performed in the following manner in the area of Kathiwara. The plough is fixed in the middle of the field, vermillion is smeared on the yoke and a coconut is cracked. Then liquor is poured on the first furrow with the belief that the deity will be pleased to receive the offerings and good crops will follow. Both men and women participate in the worship. No specific date is fixed for this ceremony and it is performed before the cultivator starts sowing.

2. *Divasa* : The festival is celebrated either in the last days of *Asadha* (July) or in the early days of *Shravana* (August) when the maize crop is about one foot high. The *Pujari* (priest) collects subscription from the tribal families in the form either of money or of commodity and brings liquor, a goat, milk, rice, a coconut, vermillion, incense and an earthen lamp. The village folk gather at the place of *Badadeo* (the deity of the village-Gramdeota). Then *pujari* burns fire and cooks sweet pudding of rice. He worships the deity and sacrifices the goat. Drops of liquor are sprinkled on the deity and the offerings are distributed to the participants.

The festival is celebrated in order to please the *Gramdeota* so that he may protect the village from calamities.

3. *Nawai* : As soon as the new crops come up, Nawai is performed. New crops are mixed with old and vegetables available at the time are cooked together. Pulse of beans, known locally as *Chawla*, is also cooked.

This preparation is offered to the ancestral spirits first. No one can partake of the new crop before *Nawai*. The cooked food served on two leaf plates and an earthen lamp (of ghee) is placed there. Liquor is also served in the name of the ancestors and after this the participants partake of it. *Nawai* is the day of ancestor worship.

4. *Desarya* : It is not their own traditional festival. Desarya fair is held in the month of *Aswin* (according to the Hindu calendar). This fair is in existence from the times of Princely States and is popular throughout the district. A buffaloe is used to be

sacrificed on this day. This event is known as *Meghraj Ki Bali*. On that occasion, the worshippers of the Meghraj (the deity of rains) worship the deity.

The animal sacrifice worship has been stopped with the abolition of the zamindari and it is believed that Meghraj is infuriated because of this. It is also believed that the scarcity of rains is due to his anger.

But the fair is held even today. With their *mandar* (a big drum) and flutes they keep on dancing all the way. Dancing goes on throughout the day in the market and in the evening the people return home. It is followed the next day too.

Amongst the Bhils of Malwa, a district of north-western India, during the *Naoratras* (the nine days' fast which precedes the festival of Desarya), a certain grain called *jowar* is planted in seven small baskets, which are then arranged thus, two to the north in the names of *Camunda-mata* and Kachumar, two to the east in the names of *Dharm-raj* and *Sharda*, one to the south in the name of Rani Kajla, and two to the west in the names of *Manora* and *Devi-mata*. They are spirinkled with water until they germinate. Music and dancing are performed round them. The *Badwas* or witch-finders present on these occasions become possessed and prophesy. On the Desarya day the baskets are carried with music and singing to the nearest stream and floated down. The person at whose these baskets were prepared is obliged to remain bare-headed from the commencement of the ceremony. After the baskets have been floated down the stream his relatives present him with a turban and he puts it on as a sign that all is completed.[9]

5. *Diyari* : It is celebrated in the month of Kartik (October-November). On the fourteen day of the month, the tribals cook *ghat* (maize-mash) and pulse. On the fifteenth day, they prepare sweet dishes of maize flour and decorate their houses in night by lighting earthern lamps with oil. Village temples and Shrines are also decorated and lighted lamps are placed all around.

On the day followed Diyari, the bullocks are worshipped and offered good fodder, a few bread and salt. The body of the bullock is painted with different hues and the horns with a special of red or green colour. It is free to move in the village. It is free to enter any body's field and destroy the crop — no one has the right to drive it away — for it has full freedom on that

This day is known as *Badi-diyari* and is followed by *Chhoti diyari* on a day chosen by the people.

For the tribals, *Diyari* is the day of worship of the bullocks which plough their fields.

6. *Holi* : Holi is celebrated at the end of Phalguna (March). Fire walking is the most important event during Holi. People making promises to gods at the time of their difficulties do this during Holi. Fire is made of wood and after offering it a cock and a coconut, they walk on it twice without the slightest trouble.

A special performance takes place in Holi. A man is blackened with charcoal and dressed in a blanket and is called Budelya, another man dressed as a woman being called Raiyi. These two dance while one sing obscence songs, much liquor is drunk and practically all present gradually become inebriated.

The Bhils of Malwa celebrate a festival when a rainy season is to be arrived. On the *Akhataj* day, they perform the mock marriage of two wooden dolls. All the ceremonies are carried out, grain being given as *dahej.* As soon as the rains commence, the two dolls are thrown into a stream to float away. These dolls represent the deities who control the rain.[10]

Fairs

The most important fairs of the Bhils are 1. Singhasan Mata Ka Mela and 2. Bhagoria Mela.

1. **Singhasan Mata Ka Mela**: At the time of rains, five *Badwas* from different villages gather together at the abode of *Singhasan Mata.* They keep fast for a few days during which period they take only a preparation of milk and *kola* (pumpkin). At nights, they remain near the Mata and keep singing throughout the night. On the fifteenth day of the first fortnight of Bhadrapada (September), the worship is performed. People coming from the nearby villages bring goats with them. These goats are sacrificed and the offerings are taken away by those who bring them. It is believed that this worship brings good rains.

2. **Bhagoria Mela** : Bhagoria is a Bhil word means run away with the would be life partner. It starts a week before Holi. It is held at the market places on the market day. It is one of the main attractions in the lives of the Bhils; it is actually a mass *Svayambara* (wedding) where the young people choose their

life partners. *Bhagoria* is the venue of the run away marriages. The unmarried boys and girls come to the fair with great expectation of finding out a mate. On mutual approval the girl absconds with the boy she likes. Sometimes, the boy and the girl have an earlier liaison and only absconsion takes place at Bhagoria. The Boys and girls who are unable to find out a mate try other Bhagoria.

On the day of *Bhagoria* the men put on their best clothes, carrying bows and arrows reach at the *hat.* They join the dance in a circle. Dancing is always performed in two groups, men in one group and women in the other. The movemnets are rhythmic and in many cases accompanied by the beat of sticks in time to the somewhat monotonous chant to which the dance is performed. The musical instruments like Drums and flutes are played. The boys and girls keep dancing throughout the day with their flutes and drums.

In the *hat,* if a boy is enamoured of a girl, he follows her and applies *gulal* (red powder) on her face. If the girl returns the compliment, then it signifies that she too likes him and is willing to be his wife. If she does not apply the *gulal* in return, her unwillingness is indicated. But the boy generally does not get discouraged by such refusals. He goes on following her and tries to apply the *gulal* as many times as he can. He may ultimately succeed. Once the acceptance is signified, they start moving together in the market.

But all the boys are not equally fortunate. There are many who come to the market and try to win the favour of some sweet maiden whom they had never seen before. They try their level best; success may or may not follow, for there may be many more like them who might be interested in the same girl. At such critical moments, the services of middlemen are made use of. These middlemen are known as *Bhangadyas*. The *Bhangadya* assists their clients in making approaches to the girls and may even sing praises of their clients before the youthful blonde.

Once the selection is made and the proposal accepted, there are mainly three ways by which the young couple may be accepted as husband and wife by the society.

After the exchange of *gulal,* the boy and girl roam about the hat, eating various delicacies, swinging in the merry-go-round, joking and laughing and when they find themselves away from prying eyes, they slip away in the remote areas, forest or any of his relatives.

The elopment of a daughter at the *Bhagoria* does not worry the father because the latter now knows that she has found out a mate. Terms of bride price are settled later on.

After passing 2-3 days, the young man goes home with his lady-love. Then it is the duty of his father or guardian to inform the parents of the girl that their daughter has come to his house. Sometimes, it is the other way round; the parents of the girl come to the house of the young man searching for their daughters. But in either case, there are bitter feelings and the girl or the boy is not scolded for what he or she has done. The elders sit in a meeting with the tribe's elders and decide about the bride-price to be paid by the boy's father or guardian. Once this is paid, the relationship of a couple is accepted and the boy and girl are granted approval to live as husband and wife.

It may also be that, after meeting her swain and roaming about freely with him in the *Bhagoria hat,* the girl takes leave of him and goes with her people to her house and the boy returning home discloses his choice to his parents, or the *Bhangadya* may do this for him. Knowing his son's mind, the boy's father goes to the girl's house and asks her father for her hand. The tribal elders meet and a bride-price is settled. Some amount, say 5 to 10 rupees, is offered as a token present.This is immediately spent on drinks. When the full bride-price has been paid the girl comes to the house of the boy.

The third course is a little tortuous though somewhat more chivalrous. In the *Bhogoria,* the boy casts his eyes on a girl and applies *gulal* on her face but she does not return the compliment. He does not lose hope, follows her and goes on applying *gulal,* but with no results. He then tries to forcibly take her away with the help of his friends. But the girl is not alone. There may be other suitors or there may be her relations. And then starts the 'fight for the mate'. Bloody quarrels ensue, murders may take place. But it may also happen that the chivalrous boy is successful in carrying away the girl by force. In that case, his parents go to the girl's father, decide about the bride-price and the girl becomes his wife. The amount of bride-price in such cases is, however, higher than in the other two situations.

It is not always that the unmarried boys and girls select their own mates in the *Bhagoria hats* sometimes a married woman also falls for some man in the market and elopes with him. In such cases, the exchange of 'gulal' does not usually take place, because so open an overture is fraught with every possibility of a breach of peace. If a married woman runs away with her lover, her former husband is entitled to a compensation from her new husband.

Bhagoria is a fair which falls when all the agricultural operations are over and they have only to reap the harvest. The success of the fair depends upon the crop condition.

Another fair, particularly popular with the Bhils, is held at Banshwara in Udaipur. This is a joint *mela* celebrated by the temple of Vishnu and Shiva, when a silver image of Mavji, a local saint is carried in procession. Barebreasted unmarried Bhil tribal girls jostle the married girls, whose legs and arms are covered with ivory bangles. And at night, Bhils lads gather round bonafies to sing their tribal epics with high pitched voices.[11]

Language and Literature

Bhils of Jhabua speak Bhili dialect which is a mixed form of speech. According to Varma, many characteristic features agree with Rajasthani or more especially with Nirmadi.[12]

The broad pronunciation of a short a or a is very marked. Thus, *ghor,* 'a horse', *moru* 'I am dying'. The palatals and s have the same sound as in western Hindi. Thus, *chal,* 'go'; *chhori,* 'daughter'. V and W become b as in Rajasthani where Gujarati and the western Bhili dialects have V and W; thus, *bis,* 'twenty'; *baras,* a year'.

With regards to the formation of words, we may note the frequent use of the suffix— lo; thus *waru* and *warlu,* 'good'; *ghodo* and *ghodlo,* 'horse'. The use of this suffix is of interest as it agrees with the use of the corresponding suffix— illa in Maharashtri, Prakrit.

Majumdar[13] opines that the Bhils dialects form a continuous chain between Rajasthani through Gujarati, Khandeshi and Marathi. The Marathi influence is only a superficial kind and the general character of the dialect reamains Gujarati. It forms a complete arch resting upon two distinct pillars one representing the aboriginese of India and the other Aryan. About 84 per cent of the Bhili words, compiled from Rajputana and Mahikantha, being derived from Sanskrit, corresponding to those used in Gujarati and 10 percent were of Persian origin. Moreover, there are some Bhili words for which there is no Gujarati equivalent, these may have been introduced into the Bhili dialects by contacts the Bhils have had with other tribal people.

According to Shah[14], the most remarkable is that the language spoken by the Bhils is based on a grammer which is more similar to the Gujarati language than any other. But the building of this superstructure on the foundation of Gujarati grammer points both to the closer cultural contact of the Bhils with the Gujarati speaking population and the geographical origin of the tribe. Out of the total population of about 22 lakhs Bhils, about 7 lakhs are returned from the Rajputana agency, about 6 lakhs from Central India agency, about 4 lakhs from Bombay Presidency proper, about 2 lakhs from Bombay states, and an equal number from Baroda state. It might not be possible at the outset to approach the Bhils in Rajputana and Central India agencies, but it is up to the custodians of Gujarati culture to see that the ancient Bhil population near Gujarat is reclaimed fully to the language and culture of the land to which they originally belonged.

On the basis of samples, Sir George Grierson opines that Bhili shows definite traces of a non-Aryan basis. The basis may have been Munda or it may have been Dravidian, perhaps more probably the former, but has been completely overlaid by an Aryan superstructure.[15]

It appears that Gujarati and Bhili are too closely related to admit of separate headlines. "The Bhili dialects, for example, are Gujarati as far as Jara (south of Udaipur), Dungarpur, Banswara, Alirajpur and Barwani to the east and they become slowly and more alien to the different neighbouring Rajasthani dialects as we go further to the east.

The Bhils have some fine oral literature. Their mythology can stand comparison today of its kind in the world. Their birth-songs refer the relationship between mother and child. It also expresses love and affection between the two. Their marriage songs have fine emotions; the daughter to be married is compared to a bird who will very soon fly away. The mother feels the absence of the daughter. Worship songs depict yearnings for supernatural help.

Notes and References

1. C. E. Luard, *op. cit.*, p. 19.
2. R. V. Russell and R. B. Hiralal, *op. cit.*, p. 291.
3. C. E. Luard, *op. cit.*, pp. 91-97.
4. *Ibid.*, p. 65.
5. C. S. Gupta (ed.), *Census of India 1961*, Rajasthan, A Village Survey Monograph : Kailashpuri, Vol. XIV, pt. VI-C, 1967, p. 9.
6. C. E. Luard, *op. cit.*, p. 37.
7. K. N. Srivastava,'Bhils of Maiwar', *The Indian Geographical Journal*, Madras, Vol. XXI, no. 2, 1946, p. 77.
8. Kalasinh F. Kishori, Ahwa, "The Ehils of Gujarat", *Vanyajati*, April 1962, pp. 67-68.
9. Sir James George Frazer,*op. cit.*, pp. 353-352.
10. C. E. Luard, *op. cit.*, p. 38.
11. Roloff Beny, *Rajasthan*, Frederick Muller Ltd., London, 1984, p. 73.
12. S. Varma, *Bhil Dialects and Khandeshi : A Linguistic Analysis*, Punjab University, 1978, p. 13.
13. D. N. Majumdar, op. cit., p. 22.
14. P.G. Shah, op. cit., p. 26.
15. Sir George Grierson, *Linguistic Survey of India*, Vol. 1,pp. 178-179.

5

The Bhil Religion

There are different opinion among scholars regarding religion of Bhils. Venkatachar[1] opines that though Bhils have a long contact with Hinduism and inspite of their preference of Hindu Gods and Godlings their appearance is animistic. Ahuja[2] has elaborately differentiated the term Animism and Hinduism. Animism means "a belief in individual spiritual being..." The concept of animism first arose as a result of difference between the dead and the living, and such phenomena as sleep, trance and dreams so that each person might be presumed to have a physical life as well as a phantom life.

Hinduism on the other hand is based on Vedanta Philosophy. It believes in 're-birth', *karma-yoga,* and *bhakti. Bhakti* is an extreme love for God; *karma-yoga* refers to unselfish good and hard work as the goal of life; rebirth to soul as eternal and immortal, perfect and infinite. Bhils believe in all those characteristic of Hinduism. Bhils also call themselves Hindu and assert that they are followers of Mahadeva and appropriated all the well known gods of the Hindu pantheon.

The religious practices and beliefs of the Bhils have changed under the influence of Hindu religion. They have made some necessary adjustment to fit in with the new cultural configuration, and the constant contact with new patterns of culture.

The area of our study exhibits different religious cults followed by the members of the Bhils. The Bhils of Bhurighati which typically represents the primitive pattern of living, is a representative village throwing much light on the primitive type of religious practices. But the Bhils of Kila Jobat do not exhibit the animistic ways of the practices as they have embraced Christianity. The Bhils of Thandla Block have been largely influenced by the Bhagat movement.

The Bhils do not build temple but install stone images smeared with red lead and oil. Their offerings, animals and liquor to gods and lighting a fire infront of the image, exhibit survival of the primitive idea of burnt sacrifice. The head of the tribe 'Tadvi' presides over social and religious functions of the village.

The Muslim Bhils of Khandesh, being disorganised in matter of religion have not yet been divorced from their primitive concept of gods. Idol worship is still prevalent. They pray to Muslims saints and to Khande Rao and in doing so they make a mud horse and offer it to the god who answers their petition.[3]

The Concept of Supreme Being

The Bhils consider Bhagwan as the supreme god and creator of the universe. They state that the Lord Bhagwan was the first to be born in a statue. Then Bhagwan thought within himself that in the world there was neither Earth nor man. Then the earth appeared to him in a dream and he went out in all directions to seek earth, and in so seeking he came to Gujarat. There he found two handfuls of earth and took them with him. Opening his hands on the way he saw the earth had been melted into water. Then Bhagwan went once more on the way. In a dream the Earth said to him : "Bhagwan thou shalt not take (or keep) two handfuls ! Take rather seven pinches." Then Bhagwan cut his little finger and applied blood to the seven pinches, and took them with him. Having come to an open place, he laid them down. From that spot the earth spread itself out in all four directions. Then Bhagwan made the five Pandawas, all the trees, water, day and night, moon and sun, animals and lastly man.[4]

The Bhils do not generally worship him much; they rather fear him, especially because of the judgement which according to their beliefs each has to undergo after death. Bhagwan performs this task himself and above all he asks whether it has given alms to beggers. When the soul answers this question in positive, all is well; but if he answers in negative the soul fares ill in the other world. They prefer to believe that it is Bhagwan who decides the fate of the soul after death.

The Bhils believe that the Bhagwan is Lord of life and death. On the occasion of death, they allow themselves to be carried away and to cry out against Bhagwan. "In their passionate grief and sorrow they go even so far as to accuse Bhagwan, the Supreme Being, of being merciless and cruel. They curse God, whom they hold responsible for the early death of their beloved relative."

With regard to God and gods, Kopper established the following hierarchy: Bhagwan, Rama and Laksman, Sita, Sun and Moon, Earth and then all the others.[5]

The Bhagwan and Rama are occasionally identified identical. This can be traced back to the influence of the Hindu, whose greeting : "Ram, Ram " is often used also by the Bhils.

Gods and Goddesses

The Bhils worship *Hanumanji* (God in the form of monkey). *Hanumanji* is held in great veneration; the emblem of the deity is only a few rude stones fixed in the ground, painted red with vermillion (*sindur*) and decorated with shining pieces of mica to represent the eyes, the mouth etc. The deity is worshipped very often and supposed to give them vigor, valour and courage. If anyone goes insane, they sacrifice goats and offer wine to the deity.

According to the Ramayana, Hanuman is the helper of Rama in his fight with Ravana. He is half monkey and half man, being represented with a long tail, and carrying a mountain in one hand and a staff in the other. He always looks southwards because he went this way to Lanka. However, this god is very popular in Jhabua. One of our informants of Kila Jobat said though he is a Christian, he reveres Hanumanji.

The Bhils believe that they are the followers of *Mahadeva*. *Mahadeva* i.e. 'the Great God', is usually identified with the Hindu god Shiva. But he is more like the Bara Deo of the Gonds. It is doubtful, therefore, if the Bhils really mean Shiva when they speak of Mahadeo. For them Mahadeo is more the agent and mouth-piece of the supreme being whom they now call by the Hindu name *Bhagwan* Mahadeva is second in rank to Bhagwan and has many functions with other tribe ascribe to *Bhagwan*.

If Mahadeva is really Shiva, it is strange that the Bhils do not worship *Lingam*, which is the symbol of Shiva, in fact they do not form any image of the god. Though they erect uncarved stones for every god of veneration for Mahadeva. It is likely that the Mahadeva of the Bhils was only later identified with Shiva, when Bhils came into closer contact with Hinduism. Originally he was simply their "Great God", either their original high-god, or a culture hero and agent of the high-god.

A large number of Shiva shrines in Central India suggests that Saivism was in the past quite strong in this area. When a cultural and religious fusion took place, the Bhils naturally identified their 'Great God' with Mahadeo-Shiva. But originally they must have been two different gods. It appears true, that the Bhagwan and the Mahadeva were sometimes inter-changeable gods among the Bhils. In some areas, Bhagwan performs a certain task while in other areas Mahadeva performs the identical benediction.

The Bhils also revere Ganesh (legendry son of the lord Siva) and is called as 'sonda deo' or the god of the trunk. When a Bhil begins to plough, he will often call on "Uncle Ganeh" which is the same meaning "Honourable Ganesh." When Bhils start any sort of magic incantation or any undertaking, first address Ganesh. But it is very much clear that they do not take this god seriously as other Hindus.[6]

The Bhils worship many other Hindu pantheons like Ramchandra, Bhairon, Indraj, Chandra (moon), Surya (sun), Prithvi (earth), Sharda (Goddess of learning), Kali devi, Jam or Yama and Chandi mata, representing by colour gards (Chindi). They believe that all the deities reside on tree, hillock or sky and each have their separate supernatural power. For example Indraj gives rain while 'Mesta Kuhaja' can make cows and buffaloes much milk.[7]

The God Bhairon is also worshipped by the Bhils. A Bhairon's image on a Bhil amulets has been found The image apparently appears like a female deity, but the Bhils worship it as a minor god. The image, encircles by a line of 101 tiny dots, has a corpulent belly, a large size chest, fatly thighs, short legs with large feet and two arms bifurcating into each at the elbow. Four hands hold different objects: (a) the upper right holds a *Trisul* (trident) alongwith a sickle, (b) the lower right holds a small drum (c) the upper left holds a sword alongwith a bunch of corn while (d) the lower holds a decapitated human head. The image has two eyes, but on its forehead a small circular eye is also present. The mouth part is erased through constant use of amulet. A tuft of hair, almost looking like hemispherical ornament, adorns its head. Only its lower portion from waist to knee, is clothed having ornaments for the waist besides bracelets and anklets.[8]

According to Crook[9], Bhairon, another favourite god, is often confounded with Bhumiya, who is one form of the consort of the Mother goddess. He has been partially adopted into Hinduism as Kala Bhairava, who is often depicted with eighteen arms, ornamented with a garland of skulls, with ear-rings and his armlets found form of snakes, a serpent coiled round his head, in his hands a sword and a bowl of blood. He is thus a fitting partner to the goddess Kali. Another school of thought, however. considers Bhairon as Bhairava, an epithet of Siva. Bhairon or Bhairava the terrible one, is a deity whose personality is a little difficult to graps. He is in the orthodox mythology the same as Siva: Bhairon or Bhairav one of the many names of the deity.

Another form of Goddess which Bhils worship is known as Mother Kali. A reference of Goddess Kali is made in the *Markandaya Purana* where the Goddess is supposed to have assumed ten incarnations, including Kali the terrible, (which form was assumed in order to destroy Raktavija Rakshasa). She is represented as a huge Goddess, desirous of animal sacrifices, particularly blood with which her image is bathed on sacrificial occasions. Her image is shown carrying a head in one hand and a dagger in the other. She wears the necklace of human skulls and presents an awful figure with her tongue coming out from the mouth. The Bhils do not observe feast or festivals associated with the worship of Kali-except the Navaratri days. During Navaratri Bhils go on fast for eight days and live only on milk.[10]

Village Dieties

The Bhils have appropriated all the well-known gods of the Hindu pantheon. Baba Deo is a generic term for the village tutelary deity. In *shrawan* (July), he is specially worshipped. All the villagers collect at the forest where he is making his abode and offer liquor, grains and fawl. Many other forest, woodland

and mountain deities are worshipped. Local gods vary with almost each village.[11]

The Rathia Bhils worship Bhilat Deo. The origin of the worship of Bhilat Deo is as follows: 'Bhilat Deo was the son of Ruparela Gaoli and his mother's name was Mehinda Ranj. He was a great simpleton when young and in consequence was always being chaffed and made fun of by everyone. Accordingly disgusted of life, he left his country and after wandering far and wide arrived in Gaur (Bengal) where he met a spirit *Karanda Jogan* by name who taught him magic. He studied the art of perfection and then returned to his native place to pass the remainder of his days. On one occasion while many people were collected together, he took his harp and began playing when a snake came out of a mole-hill. The snake was so large that the earth vibrated beneath the lashings of his tail. The *Bhilat Deo*, however, caught the snake and took it to Indar Raja (*Indra*) who was greatly pleased to see him marvellous strength and power and ordered the people to reverence him as a Deo (God) in future, thus, his worship started. The Indra Raja gave him *Bhera Deota* for a personal attendant, and also presented him with some cows as reward of his merit. The *Bhilat Deo* selected a spot under a tree on Mangalawri hill near Sondwa in Indore State, to settle. His cows increased daily in number, so much so, that he employed 900 cowherds to look after them, each man taking up his abode with his cows on a separate hill. Thus each of these spots represented the site of Bhilat Deo, gods being kept under a tree or under some rude cover or in a small temple.

The Bhils have great reverence also for hill tops difficult to ascend, as being the abode of spirits which must be propitiated during sickness calamity or to obtain offspring. In such cases, after the usual offerings the forest is often set alight.[12]

Many other minor gods are also worshipped, the most important Kampawara, his wife Kajal, son Balaraja and his brother Kudharana. Kajal Rani, as she is called, is supposed to have introduced Desarya, Diyari and Holi. Baba Deo is a generic term for the village tutelary deity. In *shrawan* (the month of August) he is specially worshipped. The whole village collects at the post marking his abode and offers liquor, grain and fawls. As a rule, each village has its own day in *shrawan* for the ceremony.[13]

The Bhils of village Khajoora (Rajasthan) worship a number

of gods and their own village deities. According to them, Siva is the supreme God and referred to as Bhagwan. The female deities commonly worshipped are Hovan, Mata, Lal Mata, Hithla Mata and Kalka Mata. Hovan Mata is, however, the village deity and worshipped by the entire village during Navaratra. Lal Mata is worshipped when the maize crop is harvested. Maize grain and Maize cobs are offered to Lal Mata. There is no particular day fixed for her worship. When the maize crop is ready the villagers fix week day which is generally Friday or Sunday for the worship of Lal Mata. Hithla Mata is worshipped during Navaratra and also when any member of the family suffers from small pox. In each *tapra* (house) a space, about twenty five centimeters is reserved on the left side of the wall while entering it. This space is purified by giving it a coating of cow dung. Three human beings, two in an erect position and the third below in between the two in an upside down position, are made on the wall. The *tadvi* of the village perform worship and offers grains, *dhoop* (incense), *deep* (ceremonial lighting) etc.

The *Dasa Mata* is worshipped by musical women on the festival of Dasa Mata-ka-varat, on the tenth day of the dark half of chaitra, for welfare of the family. It is, however, the god Kasumar who commands the general recognition. It is symbolised by a silver horse. A special priest is appointed to invoke the deity. The post of the priest is hereditary. Each year on Chaitra Purnima (Full moonday in April) he comes with a silver horse in a palanquin. The place dedicated to god Kasumer is worshipped. People pay homage to the god when their desires are fulfilled as a result of his supposed benediction. It is on this account that the worship offered is called *Jatar* which is currpt form of *Yatra* (pilgrimage). The local musical instruments are played.

The other god worshipped is *Vhotia Bavsi* whose place is in Bori Gaman. The Bhils also worship the Jain Rishabh Dev whom they call Kaliaji. There is no Bhils in the district of Jhabua who worship Rishabh Dev. It is prevalent among the Bhils of Rajasthan.[14]

Nature Worship

Besides worshipping various gods and deities, Bhils are also worshipping the nature. They worship the sun, moon, and other planets. Bhils of Katthiwara worship the moon on full moon days. They observe fast throughout the day and take their food at night after offering homage to the moon.

On the natural powers, Bhils worship fire and water in most of their religious rites. The worship of water in the form of river and springs is prevalent throughout our study area.

The Bhils consider the water of the Ganges to be sacred. They use the Ganges water for worship of deities and other sacred rituals. The Bhils of village Bansla (Rajasthan) worship river water too. Some auspicious day is fixed in consultation with Brahmin to pay homage to the water, to which village women too are invited. Some 15 to 20 earthen pots filled with ordinary water are given to women. Few drops of water from the Ganges are sprinkled into these water pots. Then, the women who have taken a bath and have put on clean white Sari, carry the water pots on their head in a procession. All villagers, irrespective of castes, join it. The village drums keep up their incessant with unfaltering throbbing, so that the Goddesses Ganges is invoked through some of the women. When the deity is invoked, the women keep hands of the village elders. They are offered coconut in abundance. When the procession reaches its destination the womenfolk come to normalcy.

The fire is considered to be sacred and therefore light is used in the worship of various Gods and Goddesses. At the time of invoking the deity at a village shrine, a flame is kept continuously kindled near the idol. Diyari and Holi festivals are also linked to the worship of light.

The fire is revered in another way who follow the Bhagat cult of Govind Giri. It is obligatory on their part to keep fire (Dhuni) continously burning in the parlour of the house. If the family members go out on a journey or attend a marriage, some one is left behind to see that the fire does not extinguish.

The fire is also worshipped at the time of marriage. It is offered grains oblations and the promise made before it, are considered to be sacred. The fire is considered as a sacred as well as goddess. But the Bhils of Jobat block take it as physical significance as majority of the people have adopted Christianity.

Worship of Animals, Trees and Stones

The Holiness is attached to some animals in Jhabua district.

The horse for example considered holy as gods like to ride on horses. The Bhils do not ride on the horse, as they consider it is meant for god only. When the vow is fulfilled, the devotee places the clay model of a horse (*ghoda*) at the foot of a stone representing the deity.

Now a days, cows are considered most sacred and are considered as Goddess. In old times, Bhils used to eat the flesh of cow. Due to impact of Bhagat movement, it has been completely stopped.

Some of the beliefs and ceremonial observations are mainly connected with the Bhil occupation of agriculture— the chief source of livelihood. The bull which is the main source of production, is venerated by all the Bhils of the district. It is supposed to be the favourite vehicle of the pre-historic father-God. The worship of the bull is performed twice a year— once in the beginning of the agricultural year and also at the harvest time. On the first day of the rising moon in the month of *Shrawan* (July) the bull is worshipped with a red mark on its forehead. On this day, it is not used for ploughing, pulling the cart or for any other work. On the day of Ekadashi or the eleventh day of the rising and wanning moon also, it is not used for ploughing. It is also worshipped when the harvest is ripe in the month of October.

The skin of lion and deer are considered sacred by the Bhagat Bhils. Some trees are also supposed to possess supernatural powers.

The Bhils worship various trees which are considered to be animated with spirits. Pipal, mango and banana trees are also held sacred by them. They use mango and banana leaves in the sacred rituals. The Bhils also worship *Tulsi* and its leaves. It is considered very sacred. The Bhils worship pipal tree on Saturday. Large and very old trees usually supposed to be haunted by evil spirits. Some trees are believed to transfer magical influence. If the 'Kheriya' tree (Acacia catechu, wild) is offered a piece of red cloth, a chronic cough is cured. Any tree having three roots of various trees over it also possesses magical power, for a feast enjoyed under its shade, cures intermittent fever (Akantra).

In Kotra Bhomat, every senior house holder's hut, there is a stone or a small image or a low consecrated mud plateform : these are the house protecting deities. Commonest is the Goddess

Melri, with her executive male spirit, Vir; but most dreaded is the male god known as *Kamriya Pat.* It is to his name that little empty plateform is constructed, and a house in which he is worshipped is obliged to devote many nights in the year to singing his epic songs, with music and dancing. To show that he is pleased, his spirit comes and possesses one or several of the dancers. Only the *devalo* (witch finder) knows the secret charms which can be used to enlist the help of these gods in striking down an enemy.[15]

Besides these household gods, there are shrines in many jungle glens and on hill-tops, some of which are regarded as particularly helpful when one is going on a robbing, others on a hunting expedition. Besides these, there are some of the Gods and Goddesses of the Hindu pantheon. In Kotra Bhomat these are reffered to as : "The Gods from Mewar"— that is, from the civilised, plains part of Udaipur. They are in fact manufactured of baked red clay, brightly painted, in the Udaipur village of Molera, and it costs the Bhils a six-day journey on foot to obtain new ones. These Gods are kept in a little shrine, usually roofless and unattended, so that they soon lose their paint and begin to crumble just twice a year there is an all-night session of worship, singing and dancing at this shrine. The priest of these gods known as the *bhopa,* becomes possessed with their spirit, and is then connsulted about the fate of the next harvest.

Worship of Tools

The plough and other agricultural tools are also associated with the Bhil beliefs and rituals. They are the means for exploiting the resources of production and the people therefore in all three village, attach great importance to the implements. Any mishandling of the tools leads to the destruction of the family. Even the Christian Bhils pay homage to, and worship, the agricultural implements. The worship of the tools begins on the Akha Teeja or the third day of the rising moon in the month of *Vaishakh* (April).

The Hindu festival of 'Raksha Bandhan' falling on the full moon day in the month of *Shrawan* has a special significance for the Bhils as its proper observance is intended to protect their tools. If the tools survive, no one can injure the tribe. On this day they tie sacred cotton thread (*Rakhi*), to the implements.

The Bhils also attach importance to manure. In all the villages including the Christian village, manure is taken as a form of deity.

Yet another channel of religious activities is followed by a number of men who have come under the influence of one of the wandering hymn-singing revivalist holymen. Such people are known as Bhagat and they hymns which are a muddled, limitative form of the ecstatic *bhajans* which are sung by low caste village all over northern India. Few Bhils *Bhagat* have a very clear understanding of what their hymns are about; but they regard themselves as being superior to their untutored fellows, and are given a grudging sort of respect.

Bhil Calander

Since the Bhils depend on the monsoon, many of the primitive customs and codes, rites and rituals fall during the period between July and November. The local new year's day accordingly commences on the first day of the rising moon of the month of *Shrawan* (July). The new year's day seems to have been fixed by the early settlers on the basis of the monsoon which assured them with food for the whole year.

Taking Oath Rites

There are some oaths and ceremonies which no Bhil will venture to break. One is swearing by the dog; the Bhil placing his hand on the head of the dogs, prays that if what he says be not true, the course of the dog may fall upon him. It appears that the dogs, the companion of the god Bhairon is specially looked up to.

Another oath is taking a small quantity of *Jowar* into the hand and holding it up praying that the grain he eats may bring curses and destruction on him, should he speak aught but truth. The third oath is laying the hand on a son's head and swearing ; taking up one of the village gods (image) in the hand. In case of boundary disputes, a goat is beheaded and then skinned and the skin placed on the man's head who with his face to the east, swears his cause is good, and then drags the skin along the line of the boundary. Certain oaths are inavoidable.[16]

Another forms of oath were taken by swallowing of live coals in the hand, piercing the palm of the hand with an arrow, eating poisonous herbs or fruits, etc. The simplest form consists in making the man take a solemn oath and then waiting for seven days. If (within this period) any mischance befalls him, or his family, or possessions, he is considered to have perjured himself, and the case goes against him.

We have an instance of taking a common form of oath. The man is brought before the *sarkari Gaddi*. This is simply a chair in the nearest tehsil office. A clean white cloth is thrown over it and it is placed in full view. This represents the ruler of the state and is in fact the emblem of authority. The man touches the chair with both hands and swears by Barabij. The Tadvi, who is administration the oath, turns to the east, and draws a circle on the ground with the point of a sword, commensing on the east and passing round by the north and west. Within this circle two lines are drawn joining north and south and east and west. The sword is then placed in the circle with its point to the east. The Tadvi then turns to the man and says : "If your cause is a good and true, raise *Bhavanimata* (name of the goddess) in your hand (i.e. the sword)." The man does so exclaiming "Barabij visit me with evil within seven days (or other period) if I swear untruely." He then lifts the swords, bows and replaces it. The Barabij are the twelve bij or second day of each month, on which the new moon is usually first visible, and is a day held in reverence.[17]

In many instances when these oaths are made use of, written agreements are given by which the person swearing, agrees that, should any serious or extraordinary injury happen to himself or his family within a certian time, he will consent to be guilty or to have stated a falsehood.

The Bhils are true to their words and never take false oath. They believe that he will certainly suffer if false oath is taken.

Notes and References

1. C. S. Venkatachar,op. cit., p. 243.
2. Ram Ahuja, 'Religion of the Bhils- A Sociological Analysis', *Sociological Bulletin*, Vol. XIV, No. 1, pp. 21-32.
3. G. Ahmed Khan,op. cit., p. 141.
4. W. Koppers, op. cit., p. 276.
5. *Ibid.*, p. 292.
6. *Ibid.*, p. 273.
7. 'Jhabua Ke Bhils', *Vanyajati*, Vol. XV, No. 1, 1967, p. 6.

8. K. Guha, 'Bhairon's Image on a Bhil Amulet', *Vanyajati*, Vol. VII, No. 1, January 1959, pp. 27-28.
9. James Hastings, *op. cit.*, p. 10.
10. S. L. Doshi,*op. cit.*, pp. 147-148.
11. C. S. Venkatachar, *op. cit.*, p. 243.
12. Ibid., pp. 243-244.
13. S. C. Varma, *op. cit.*, p. 40.
14. C.S. Gupta (ed.), *Census of India 1961*, A Village Survey (Monograph): Khajoora (Rajasthan), Vol. XIV, Pt. VI-A, 1964, pp. 32-33.
15. G. M. Carstairs, 'The Bhils of Kotra Bhomat', *The Eastern Anthropologist*, Vol. VII, No. 3 & 4, August 1954, p. 178.
16. *Census of India 1891*, pp. 219-220.
17. C. S. Venkatachar, *op. cit.*, pp. 244-245.

6

Birth Rites

The Bhils practise a variety of rites most of them revolving around fertility. The performance of these rites commences right from the marriage celebration. Several of the marriage rites are concerned with making the bride fertile. As soon as the day for marriage is fixed, the bride begins to wear red clothes. On the day of marriage, both the bridegroom and the bride invariably put on red clothes, with the exception of *dhoti* in the case of the bridegroom and the bodice in the case of the bride. Red coloured clothes, during the ceremonial period of marriage have a significance. Their being worn itself is a fertility rite. During the marriage celebration, when the bridegroom is taken in a procession, his mother throws rice over his body which is also believed to be auspicious from the point of view of the pair's fertility. When the marriage rites are over, the party is made to sit in the courtyard. A doll child made of rags is ceremoniously placed in the lap of the bride. The bride then places it in her husband's lap. The priest instructs them to be very careful with the child. The ritual performed on the occasion also suggests that they are for the purpose of bringing the blessings of fertility on the couple. When the marriage is over and the bride is taken to her new home by the bridegroom's party, the young girls of the village pay her a ritual visit carrying pots filled with rice and covered with pieces of red cloth. The rite is called *Ma Matula*. It also symbolises the boon of fertility which the higher powers are asked to bestow on the marrying parties. These rites of fertility are observed during marriage celebrations in the villages of Jhabua district.

Beginning of Fertility in a Woman

At an early age, the Bhil girl becomes aware of the facts of life. Not only does she see little boys and girls in their nakedness every day and notices the difference in sex, she also listens to the often uninhibited talk and gossip of the women in the house, courtyard, or at the water-place.

Thus she acquires sexual knowledge in a natural and gradual way and when her own maturity sets in and menstruation starts she is not at all surprised or startled. For long she has observed the separation of menstruating women in her own family, and knows well what has to do and how to behave when the monthly flow comes on her.

The Bhils know that the productive state in a woman's life starts with menstruation. Prior to that, she is like a field which grows nothing. Menstruation usually starts when a girl attains the age of 14 years. No particular ceremony is performed; not the girl required to spend the menstruation period away from the house in any specially built hut. She works normally in the house.

In the area of our study, during menstruation, women are considered ritually unclean for five days or as long as the menstruation lasts. Following the local custom, the Bhils consider her degradation to the status of a broom maker. This temporary degradation forces her to keep away from her house mates. She may not enter the main room of the house at all. During the days of her monthly period she may stay outside in the barnyard. During the monsoon she is allowed to stay in a corner of the verandah or, if there is shade for lumber in the backyard she may stay there. In the area of Nimar a menstruating woman stays in the stable.

She is not permitted to touch anybody or any object in the house. If she passes through a door, no one else may pass through the same door for five days. She is not permitted to prepare the meals for the family not to fetch water from the well. She herself receives her food from the house mates who place it on the ground so that any personal contact with her is avoided. The vessel is purified after use; if it is an earthen vessel it may be thrown away.

The Bhils believe that if a menstruating woman enter a house where a new-born child is kept, the child would certainly fall sick and get convulsions. A sick person too would suffer by her undesirable presence and get worse.

During menstruation her husband is forbidden sexual congress with her. A *Badwa* is prevented from performing his exorcisms during the monthly period of his wife. Nor can a person perform a sacrifice during the menstruation of his wife. But no menstruating woman is prevented from doing field-work or any other outside work.

When the days of menstruation have passed the woman takes a full bath, washing head and body either at the usual bathing place behind the house, or at the river, then she anoints herself with turmeric (*haldi*). This bath removes her impurity and from now on the woman can again associate with the members of her family and can assume her usual life.

It has been observed that among the low castes of the district only the first menstruation is observed with such strict rules of separation, while these rules are much relaxed for later menstruations. Because of urbanisation and impact of christianity, Bhils also do not observe such a strict rule. In some of the most interior areas, the Bhils women observe such a strict rules of menstruation.

Pregnancy

The Bhils are of a course well aware of the connection between sexual intercourse and reproduction. They believe, however, that repeated intercourse is necessary for a woman to become pregnant. Every Bhil wants to prove her fertility and to bear a child as soon as possible after her marriage. If pregnancy evades her, she is ready to undergo any penance and exorcisms. The usual procedure is to consult a *Badwa*. With his magic powers he is supposed to counteract the evil influences which had so far pervaded a pregnancy and to secure it by offerings and magic practices.

Cases of impotency do occur, but the Bhils of Central India attribute that sterility is due to a defect in the women, not in her husband. The Bhils consider that the sterlity is due to the evil influence of some witch. Therefore, a remedy is sought at the hands of the *Badwa*. Masturbation and homosexuality are not practiced in the Bhils community; the Bhils very vehemently refute the prevalence of these vices among them. The Wife of an impotent at times seeks a formal separation. Extramarital relation is not acceptable to the society; it often creates inter-personal problems and causes violence. A woman always tries her best to get rid of the stigma of sterility.

A Bhil is fully aware of the physiological origin of life. According to him, when the male semen, which is water, meets the female secretion, which is also water, a child is conceived in the womb. They believe that conception starts when menstruation stop; though the foetus is completely human in shape, life enters it only after three to five months. The foetus starts moving when it gets life. They are also aware that the foetus gets nourishment from the mother through the umbilical cord. That is why they are anxious that the expectant mothers should get nutritious food.

The Bhils believe that a woman gets child when a soul enters her womb. It is the soul of a Bhil who has died at least a generation earlier and meanwhile stayed in a place of bliss or of punishment. The respondents of village Ochaka, hold that a Bhil is always reborn in the same tribe at least a generation after his death. His former life has no influence on his next life, because during the interval between his present life and his former one he was either rewarded for the good deeds of his past life or punished for the evil he had committed. The Christian Bhils of Kila Jobat do not believe in rebirth and rewards of good or bad deeds.

Precaution or Taboos During Pregnancy

A pregnant observes certain restrictions and taboos. She leads a normal life but she takes care to avoid all sorts of dangers that may fall on her from the physical and spiritual world. During her pregnancy she has to observe certain restrictions in her movement and activities to save the child as well as herself from the evil spirits and other dangers. The following are the restrictions imposed upon the pregnant women:

(1) She is not allowed to visit a forest after sun-set, not to pass by places where evil-spirits are supposed to dwell, or which are otherwise inauspicious. The pregnant women are also not allowed to go to hill as they think that many evil spirits dwell there.

(2) They are also prohibited from going near giant trees, which are supposed to be the abode of *dakins* (ghosts), who may harm both women and their foetus. A pregnant woman should not pass under a mango tree because that would impair her fertility.

(3) She must abstain pork. In fact, this taboo applies to all Bhils women in the fertility age; only small girls and old women are not allowed to eat pork. However, Muslim Bhils do not take pork. She should not leave the house except in the company of a relative. She must keep away from menstruating women and from a woman who has recently given birth. She must not leave the house when an owl calls, not when dogs or jackals howl, and she must be careful that no snake crosses her path. If she wants a son, she should bathe in a full-moon night; if a daughter, in a new moon night.

(4) The Bhil women of village Surinala, Umarath and Kalyavav observe certain taboo at the time of solar and lunar eclipse. They believe that if they see sun or moon during eclipse, the baby in the womb may get physical deformity. During the period of lunar and solar eclipse, pregnant Bhil women are not allowed to see the sun or moon and also not to come outside. She is asked to lie on the bed dorsally in straight position.

(5) The women of village Kesharpura and Bhurighati avoid to see the lightening. By seeing dazzling light she may fall down or may faint. It may harm the developing child in the womb. During heavy rain she is not allowed to go out of the house. In case she is out, she should close the eyes immediately after a blaze of lightening.

(6) They also avoid to hear the noise of thunder. The loud noise may effect the ear of child, so the women close their ear at the time of thunder sound.

(7) The Bhil women have some restrictions in respect of eating certain vegetables. During pregnancy she should not eat jack fruit because if it is eaten, the child's foot will bear many cracks after birth. The informant could not cite any example of a birth of a child with a cracked foot or broken heel. He is simply told that it was their traditional belief.

(8) Old women remain very vigilant and cautious to see that a pregnant woman really follows these taboos and precautions. If any deformity in the body of a new born child is seen, they believe that some of the taboos might have been neglected.

(9) Practically there is no restriction imposed on food. Those who can afford give special food to their women during pregnancy. Most of them are below the poverty line, they can not afford to give rich diet. Those who afford give milk and some quantity of *ghee* (fat) to their pregnant women. The only restriction which is imposed on them, is not eat jack-fruit throughout the period of pregnancy. Sometimes they eat clay or powder of brick which is objectionable as it effect on the health of mother as well as child.

Speculation Concerning the Sex of an Unborn Baby

The Bhils speculate concerning the sex of an unborn baby. Like others the Bhils women are anxious to know the sex of an unborn child. Generally old women speculate about it on the basis of certain beliefs and signs visible during pregnancy viz., conditions, tempatations and movements of the expectant mother. One informant in the village Petlawad informed that the expectant mother does not vomit frequently in case of a boy; but in case of girl she does because food do not digest easily.

In the village Surinala, about tempatations it is informed that in case of girl pregnant lady likes to eat bitter and sower things, whereas in the case of a boy, she likes to eat sweet things.

Old women also speculate sex of an unborn child on the basis of the movements and condition of a pregnant lady. The Bhil women of village Sondawa visualise that if a woman feels heaviness on her right leg, it means she is carrying a male child, but on the other hand if she feels heaviness on her left leg, it is speculated for a female child. If there is heaviness in the right part of the belly, a boy is expected, but if it is on the left side, it is possibly a girl. If a woman drags her left leg while walking, she will give birth to a male child, on the contrary if she drags her right leg a female child is expected. In case of boy, a woman feels healthy and cheerful, but in case of a girl she feels dulness and laziness. But another old woman informed that a woman feels laziness in case of boy because the weight of the male child is more than that of a female child which seems to be more logical.

No one is quite sure about the expected date of birth. Generally they count nine months since the stoppage of menses. But most of them fail to ascertain this. It was informed that for such cases experts women are called to examin and diagnose the approaching time of delivery.

Such predictions are entirely based on speculations and they may not be fully correct. But in some cases their predictions become true. Their observations are based on long and continuous experience.

Safe Bearing and Delivery

For safe bearing delivery father too has to observe certain precautions. Form the fifth month of pregnancy onward, the parents start observing certain prenatal precautions for ensuring normal and easy delivery. To prevent miscarriage, after two or three months of pregnancy, a woman is advised not to lift heavy weight, for instance, a large pot of water or a heavy bundle of firewood. But otherwise she does not get any special care to which she should be normally entitled. She is supposed to do her household chores and even work in the field almost until the birth pains begin.

Cohabitation ceases after the sixth month and is not resumed before the child is three or four months old. The Bhils denounce the offenders in strong terms. Though both the parents are considered equally capable of influencing the child within the womb, a large number of precautions are to be observed by the father rather than the mother. A father is not permitted to cut anything growing, the mother should not eat anything which is jointed like a double banana or some double tuber. Neither of the parents should eat any animal which has died accidentally. None of them should tie a knot, drive a nail or stick a pole into the ground. A woman is not given liquor in order to avoid a miscarriage. Honey is also a taboo, for it is supposed to cause abortion. Meat and curd are not allowed as they are considered detrimental to safe delivery. Fried vegetables prepared with red pepper are also rarely given. The movements of the women are watched with vigilance and she is not permitted to carry a heavy load or move in the scorching heat. These are some of the taboos which the Bhil parents normally observe before a child is born. The Bhils consider it that if the health of the women is good, there are few chances of her miscarrying. Though the exact time of the birth of a child cannot be ascertained, they think that a girl is born exactly after nine months and a boy after nine months and nine days from the date of conception.

Since Bhils do not fortell the day when she will deliver the child, the Bhils women are generally carry out their duties in house, field and jungle even at the advance stage of pregnancy. It happens not seldom that they are surprised by labour pains when away from home. As they usually have some other person with them, this woman or girl may be obliged to assist them, in a case of emergency, or, if there is still time to go home and call the midwife.

Magical Means to Expedite a Birth

In the opinion of the Bhils of village Bhurighati, the cause of miscarriage are the disfavour of the gods or an evil eye. To avoid the evil eyes for safe delivery of the child certain rites are gone through. The expected mother is looked after with great care and concern. Charms and amulets are tied to the arms of the pregnant woman to protect the child in the womb against all evil influences.

In case of difficulty and protracted birth refuge is taken to magic and superstition. It is believed that for instance a birth can be effectively assisted by untwining a twisted thread before the eyes of the woman in labour. This obviously is imitative magic. Or she is given water to drink in which her husband's left leg, a gun-barrel, a pestle or a thunder bolt have been bathed. It is believed that each of these articles has the quality of direct and powerful expulsion; this quality will be transferred to the woman and will enable her to propel the child from her womb.

If these practices do not help, a magician is called in. He takes a brass vessel (*lota*) and pours into it water just fetched from the well and of which no one else has taken a sip. He takes the vessel into both hands, breathes three times on it and stirs it up with a finger. The vessel is then handed to a woman in labour and she drinks.

If even this water full of magic is of no avail the magician invokes his patron spirit till he falls into trance. He asks his spirit to indicate the cause of the difficult delivery and to reveal the necessary offerings. He prescribes some offerings and sometimes requests even the sacrifice of a goat. Then he ties a string over which he has recited some magic incantation around the woman's body. The sacrifice is, however, performed only a fortnight after the successful delivery. If the woman dies no sacrifice is made.

Pre-Birth Rites

The preparation for the arrival of the baby are made by the family itself. A room is reserved for the expectant mother. It must be far from the kitchen because a birth is ritually impure and would pollute the food. It must be far from the entrance because evil spirits, a woman with the evil eyes, or a person with evil intentions might enter through the door. Some indigenous medicines are collected before hand.

The Bhils women usually bear their children without great difficulty and pain. At the time of delivery, the expectant mother is made to lie on a cot. Generally, some expert old lady is called to act as the midwife and some women of the neighbourhood gather to help her. The midwife presses and massages the woman's body from the hips downwards.

In the village Kesharpura, a midwife is assigned for ten or twelve families. This midwife has never received any professional training and is helpless in cases of any complication. But she is a woman who has shown some ability for this calling and has a natural inclination to help women in labour. After she has attended several deliveries successfully she is generally accepted as an expert midwife and called for assistance whenever the necessary arises. Only if there are complications a second and even third midwife is called in.

Only in extreme cases is a man— usually the husband of the woman in labour— called in to belabour the belly of the woman with the feet. The man is blindfolded before he enters the delivery room.

There are cases when even such drastic methods of midwifery are unsuccessful. In such cases the woman in labour is left to die in great agony. No one can help her, as no trained doctors are at hand in the Bhils area to perform a caesarian operation. And even in places where a hospital is near, the Bhils are not usually in the habit of consulting a doctor when their women have a difficult delivery.

Fortunately most Bhils women have easy births. And in spite of the lack of cleanliness and hygines in delivery cases of puerperal fever are relatively rare, or at least not always deadly. When the time for the birth of the child approaches, all the male members leave the hut.

Cutting the Umbilical Cord

Cutting of the umbilical cord is an important rite from the cultural point of view among the Bhils. The custom of serving the umbilical cord with a piece of bamboo is widespread.[1] Some of the Bhils of village Kesharpura informed the process of making the bamboo knife for cutting the umbilical cord. They collect bamboos from the forest which have been cut in a single stroke in upward or downward direction. With the help of knife bamboo chips are prepared and the edge is sharpned.

As soon as the child is born, the umbilical cord is cut with the help of sharp bamboo chip and the part attached to the baby's body is tied up. The wound is smeared with a disinfectant orthodox medicine consisting of turmeric and oil.

In some of the cases the umbilical cord is detacted with the help of arrow head. They consider arrow head very auspicious.

Disposal of Placenta

As soon as the placenta is ejected it is taken in a bamboo basket outside the house and buried in a pit. In some areas, it is buried in the room where the delivery has taken place.

According to Doshi[2], the disposal of placenta is done by burning in the cattle shed. The naval cord together with a salt is buried in the left corner of the house. The belief regarding the disposal of the naval cord in the left corner of the house was not explained by the people. In contrast, the other castes in Bansla bury both the placenta and the naval cord in the backyard of their house.

The Bhils of Jaisamand Lake in Rajasthan bury the placenta outside the hut. The rite is performed by the younger brother of the husband.[3]

The Bhils of Jhabua dispose the placenta as soon as it is ejected. The midwife takes it and buries it at a secret place, usually in a corner of the verandah or in the house. It should always be under the protection of the roof. The hole is filled and then the floor given a coating of cow-dung paste. Great care is taken that no other person gets access to the buried placenta for this would endanger the life of mother as well as the child.

It is interesting to note that the remainder of placenta inside the house when considerable time has elapsed after the birth of a child, is supposed to poison the whole system and lead to the woman's death. The women in the house will therefore at once give her a shock by raising a cry of fire or by firing a gun. There are no proverbs connected with placenta among them.

Post-Birth Rites

Soon after the new-born baby is washed in lukewarm water, wrapped in a piece of clothes and put to the breast of the mother. The mother is also given a bath in hot water outside the house, where she goes with a sickle or an arrow or a knife as a security against evil powers. She sleeps on the cot and her clothes, bedding and utensils are not touched by anybody.

The birth of the baby is announced by beating of a drum *dhol* (of which there is generally one in every village). When this is not done, the *Guru* or some other persons carries the news to relations and neighbours who assemble at the hut of the parents and present gifts according to their means or wishes.

The father is prohibited from seeing his new-born child for the next two or three days. He may see his wife, however, the Bhils do not seem to observe any restrictions to the father's movements, which would suggest a king of couvade.

The Bhils of Gujarat and Rajasthan observe certain restrictions, not greeting a visitor, not plucking flowers or fruits and not bathing in a running stream. If a boy is born, the father must look at the son only after he has propitiated the deity with offering of a fawl and an earthen horse at the local shrine. Later, he is expected to go up the hill shrine with his wife and the child to make full offerings.[4]

If the father's services are not required in the house because he is sufficiently well off to keep the midwife a few days after the delivery, he is free to occupy himself with the usual pursuits.

He can do his work on the field or around the house and stable as before.

Among some clans, the *Badwa* or minstrel attends; he first places a small figure of a horse at the threshold of the door, and then, taking up his position just outside, chants a hymn to Sitla Mata, the goddess of small pox, who is considered much dreaded by all the tribes.

The room is set apart from the rest of the house by hanging up some sheets or blankets. This precaution is taken to protect mother and child against obnoxious draughts of air. But clearly they are also a protection against evil spirits and the evil eye. For some time nobody should have access to the mother except the midwife.

When the child is born, certain offerings of milk and liquor are made to the deities. Then some recongnisable marks attributable to any of the dead ancestors are searched for on the body of the newborn, because they believe in the rebirth of the ancestor in the family.

For five days the birth of the child, the mother is kept on a restricted diet and is not allowed to eat solid food. She is given instead of thin *kitki* (*Panicum psillipodium*) gruel, very thin on the first day, but progressively thicker on the following days. It is believed that *kutki* is a 'heating' dish and warm stimulates the exhausted organism of the mother. Cooking food is prohibited, thus she is not given any pumpkin or cucumber, or eggs, fish or sweet-potatoes.

The new born child is not sucked on the first or second day of its life. Usually it is given its first chance to drink only on the third day. In order to ensure an ample flow of milk the mother is often given some medicine which is brought ready made from the weekly market. It consists of a mixture of condiments, sugar, coconut pieces and other ingredients ground into a powder. In these first two days the lips of the new-born baby are often whetted with butter-milk.

Normally the mother rises from her bed on the second day after her delivery. Since the Bhils girl marry only when they are mature, they are physically well developed even at the time of their birth. Premature births and miscarriages, which seem to be comparatively frequent among Bhils women, seem to be rather dangerous and easily cause infection and fever.

The Bhils regard women who have given birth to a child as ritually impure. They are prohibited from touching anything in the house. They have to eat separately. Usually a woman who has given birth is fed first. The woman is not permitted to touch anything of common use or to do any household work.

Thereafter the plates and other vessels she has used are cleaned carefully and might only then be used by the other members of the family. The midwife too has to eat separately. For, by touching the woman in delivery and after; birth, she too becomes polluted. She, as also the mother, are dressed in old rags which can be thrown away afterwards. The midwife gets as her reward a rupee, two coconuts, some grain, pulse and salt.

Purificatory Rite for Mother

The mother takes a bath twice a day for the next few days. For the bath she has to stand on a bamboo mat so as not to touch the earth as she is impure. The baby is bathed by the midwife. As a rule, mother and child are ritually impure for about 25 days. But often, in the poor family, the mother has to take her purificatory bath earlier. Often the service of the midwife has to be dispensed with as early as the second day, and the mother has to assume her usual household work.

In the area of Alirajpur, Bhil women perform purificatory rites usually between the sixth and twelfth day after the delivery. In the areas other than Alirajpur the ceremony may be performed even earlier or later days. The mother and the midwife go to the river, or any other washing and bathing place usually on the bank of river and take their bath. Afterwards they dress in new clothes. If they cannot afford to throw away the clothes which they wore during the last days, they wash them as also the rags in which the new-born child had been wrapped. This ceremony usually concluded the period of pollution for the mother, and she is now free of any restrictions. A Bhil woman who has assisted a midwife in the time of delivery is not permitted to enter her own house before she had taken a bath and washed all her clothes.

The midwife is at the service of the new mother for labour three to five days after delivery. During these days she receives her food in the house where she serves. When her service is over she receives a small money present which is slightly higher when a boy was born. A wealthy Bhil may give her even a new garment.

Fifth Day Ceremony

On the fifth day (sometimes on the seventh day), the room and the house are cleaned with caw-dung. The woman takes her bath and gives an offering of *sindur* (vermillion) and coconut to the gods. Women from the neighbourhood are called a liquor party, but the men are excluded. From this day onward, the mother can do all the household work except cooking, which is taboo for a month. In the areas around Alirajpur, the period of taboo is only three days. Five children are invited on this party and given a feast of *Khichadi* or *Rabadi* along with a small quantity of liquor. This is known as the ceremony of fifth day.

The Bhils of Rajasthan observe the ceremony of the *Pansawu*[5] or the fifth day rite. The Sun God and the family deity are worshipped on this day. The mother is given a hot water bath after which she puts on new clothes. The nurse who attended the delivery officiates at this ceremony. The village drummer is also invited. The mother sits in the courtyard of the house facing the sun. She pays homage to the God with the child in her lap. She offers a small portions of wheat, bread and *ladoos* (sweet balls) to the deity. Then the totemic deity who is believed to reside in the southern wall of the house is worshipped. She is offered cooked grams, wheat bread, *ladoos* and coconut.

The village elders and women are also invited to grace the occasion. Sometimes when the delivery is difficult and the pains of labour are acute, vows to sacrifice a goat are made to the totemic deity. At this ceremony, such vows are fulfilled and the villagers participate in the feast which follows the sacrifice. The women dance and sing songs. The Bhils of Petlawad do not offer a goat or wine to the totemic deity as they have stopped taking meat and wine— they follow the *bhagat* way of life.

The worship of the totemic deity on this occasion has a special significance. She is supposed to be the Goddess of family progeny and is supposed to cause ample production of mother's milk. If she is annoyed, the milk in the breasts would dry up and the growth to the child would suffer.

The Bhils of Panch Mahals (Gujarat), on fifth day, perform a ceremony. After taking bath, the mother makes a circle of flour, piles little heaps of flour on all sides, and sits in the middle of the circle. The present relations who have been invited on that occasion give presents of money or clothes.[6]

On the fifth day ceremony, Bhils of Khandesh invite a party of women and both mother and child are bathed in warm water. Just outside the threshold of the hut, the mother cowdungs the ground and traces turmeric lines. In the middle of the drawing she places a lighted lamp, setting round it five stones corresponding to the number of days since the child was born. Round these pebbles she lays pieces of cocoa kernel, and over the whole sprinkles turmeric, millet, red powder and liquor. The guests drop a few grains of millet over the mother and child, and then re-enter the house. Next the guests are feasted with wheat and rice bread, mutton and liquor, and the whole night is spent in singing, smoking and drinking. The lamp is allowed to burn for twenty-four hours.[7]

Naming of the Child

There is not fixed day for the name giving ceremony to the child after the birth. Usually it is observed within a period of ten days. The Bhils of village Kailashpuri (Rajasthan) perform this ceremony soon after the birth. It is officiated by father's sister (*bhua*) or by some elderly person among the family who gives the child a suitable name.[8]

The name given to the child may be taken from the day of the week, on which the infant was born e.g. Dita or Ditya (Sunday), Homla or Homa (Monday), Mangala or Mangli (Tuesday) and so on, or from the season of the year, e.g. *Vasat* (the rain) or from some shurb, e.g., Thaura or Thauri, the beautiful red flowering shrub common in the hilly tracts. A child born may be called *Moti* (pearl) or *Rupa* (Silver) or, as a term of affection, *Kaura* or *Kauri* (Bitter).

In Alirajpur, on the occasion of the naming ceremony sometimes *Badwa* or a local renowned person is called in to perform certain rites. The rite performed in a brief way by offering some coconut and red powder to the village tutelary deity. The name of the child is given by some elderly lady. The name of the father and grandfather is not repeated, but the name of the paternal uncle can be adopted. The child can also be named after the day or the month in which he or she is born. If the childern of the parent do not survive some opprobrious name or pet animal's name is given to the child, so the gods may avoid visiting it with their ill-favour, such names are *Kidia,* "The wormy one," *Dhulia,* "dust of the earth," *Kachria,* "rubbishy," *Sadia,* "the putrid," and so on. The animals name like *Kuktru* (dog) or *Bilado* (cat) are usually given to the child. Some ugly name is also given to the child for instance, *Ukariya* (Dung Heap), *Kariya* (Blackish) etc. There is not much difference in the names of males and females except that the name of a male ends in 'aa' whereas female names end in 'ee' for example, *Vasta* and *Vasti, Bhura* and *Bhuri, Kodara* and *Kodari.*

The naming pattern of Thandla block would be more clear at a glance from the list of some names of both the sexes given in table-21.

Table-21

Naming Pattern of the Bhils

Name	Sex	Significance of Name
Guman	Male	Proud one
Rupji	Male	Beautiful
Sambhu	Male	Name of the god Siva
Galia	Male	Narrow street
Onkar	Male	Name of godess (wife of Siva)
Bhima	Male	Name of one of Pandavas
Somla	Male	Name of the day (Monday)
Mangla	Male	Name of the day (Tuesday)
Joti	Male	Flame
Rupa	Male	Name of the Metal (Silver)
Ukeri	Female	Dirty place
Sampli	Female	Name of the householdgoods
Bajli	Female	Name of ornament
Thauri	Female	Name of red flower

In the village Kesharpura, though, the naming pattern is the same, it is largely influenced by the practice of caste. On the day of the name giving ceremony the child is given the usual Bhil pattern name. But this is only a birth name and as soon as the child grows up and joins the neighbouring group or School, his name is styled according to some caste pattern. For example, the ritual name Vaga is changed to Vijaylal and Beriya to Bal Krishna.

The changing trends in the naming pattern of the Bhils of Kesharpura are illustrated in table-22.

Table-22

Urban Impact on the Pattern of Giving Name

Birth Name	Adopted Name	Sex
Rafel	Ashok Kumar	Male
Ramu	Ramchandra	Male
Toli	Hira Lal	Male
Bhura	Har Lal	Male
Tolia	Om Singh	Male
Kala	Dilip Singh	Male
Manji	Man Mohan	Male
Warju	Sarla	Female
Kunwari	Vimla	Female
Jhamku	Vanita	Female
Homli	Rukmini	Female

The naming ceremony of the Bhils of Jobat takes place in the church. The name is given in consultation with the church head, who adopts a Christian name. The names given are altogether different from those associate with the tribal traditions. Usually the names follow the English naming pattern, though recent names seem to be modelled on the Indian naming pattern. A few examples are given in table-23 showing the name on Christian patterns.

Table-23

Table Showing Christian Names

Name	Sex
Joseph	Male
James	Male
Samson	Male
Andrews	Male
Powel	Male

Tonsure Ceremony (*Balli Barna*)

Either in the first or in the third year after the birth of the child the tonsure ceremony takes place. Sometimes the rite is postponed till the child is of several years old. The ceremony starts with the worshipping the razor, proceeds to shave the child's head leaving one lock at the top which is never cut. While the barber performing the work, the women sing songs. As soon as the barber finishes his job, people attending the ceremony throw money which is picked up. The lock of the hair are placed in some cloth which are later on put into the flowing river water.

The child is bathed immediately after to purify him of the defiling touch of the barber. Then his toiled is performed.

Ear and Nose Piercing Ceremony

The ceremony relating to piercing the ears and nose is observed by the Bhils on any Basant Panchami day (which fall in the month of January or February) after the completion of one year of the child. Usually, this ceremony is performed after attaining the child at the age of five. The perforation is made by an experienced old woman of the community. She is offered some remuneration. It is obligatory in the case of a girl whose nose is so pierced on the right nostril as to allow wearing of *naths* afterwards. The holes in ears of the girls are made gradually larger so that they could wear big ornaments.

Rites— Growth of the Child

The period from birth to twelve years of age is marked by various rites and ceremonies. For the first two days the child is not allowed to suck the mother's breasts and some nurse feeds the child. Then, the milk sucking ceremony is performed. The neighbouring women are invited and the child is ceremoniously given to the mother for sucking by some elderly women. An offering of coconut is made to the totemic deity, that it may ever keep the breasts of the mother full of milk.

The next important ritual takes place only when the child attains the age of ten or twelve months. If, in infancy, up to the age of twelve months it weeps at night or indicates uneasiness, some evil spirits are believed to have harmed the child. To avert the evil influence, promises of offering are made to the totemic deity. Another way of driving out the influence is to put five red peppers, five salt crystals and lemon at the junction of four roads at the sunset.

Another important ceremony, performed among the Bhils Ghantali, is the branding of male children on the wrist and forearm. The ceremony takes place any time before the child reaches the age of twelve. Both the wrists of the arms are branded. A piece of cloth is dipped in sweet oil and burnt. The burning cloth, shaped in the size of a fifty paisa coin, is then placed on the wrist. The buring piece scalds the skin and to cool it, the boy is asked to run fast. The scalding is effected one to seven times on each wrist. The interpretation for the necessary of branding given by the Bhils is that on reaching heaven's gate a Bhil without it will be punished or refused admittance. They believe that if a Bhil has one mark (*dangla*) only he will be treated ordinarily but the greater the number of marks, the higher his status in heaven. Various proverbs with regard to the sacredness of *dangla* are prevalent.

The Bhils of villages Kawaria and Bansla (Rajasthan) do not practise this ceremony. The non-observance of this ritual seems to be due to the impinging forces of Hinduism and Christianity.[9]

Taking Solid Food

After about 10-12 months, the child starts taking some solid food. The Bhils of village Panara (Rajasthan) do perform special ceremony known as *Botan*. In this ceremony food is given to the child for the first time. *Halwa*, i.e. pudding made of jaggery and wheat flour, is put in the mouth of the child, and the women from the community sing appropriate songs.[10]

In Jhabua, generally Bhils do not perform this ceremony. But in few cases those who are economically well off perform this ceremony, a special solid food prepared by the elderly person is given to the child by aunt.

Socialisation

As soon as a child is born close kinsmen as well as other members of the family and of the society in addition to parents have the moral obligations to give him or her proper training so that it may become a full member of Bhils society. Family members play an important role in this regard.

Speech is a social heritage and transmitted by the members of the society. A little child cannot speak after birth. Generally a child smiles after three months. Then the older siblings, grandparents and parent try to make the child laugh by touching its chin or upper arm. After six months a child begins to produce some sound. The members of the family take much interest and care. They teach it to utter some simple words. They also say something or show something to which the child responds. From here a training starts to teach language and behaviour.

Learning to walk and talk go simultaneously, but walking is learnt earlier than talking. Parents and other members help in doing so. With one and half years most of the children walk and speak a number of words. Later on they learn the proper language under the strict supervision of the parents.

During the first year, children are bathed regularly in the morning, but as they grow and start moving outside the house, this becomes irregular, so much so that some grown-up children do not have a bath at all, unless forced to by their parents.

In the beginning toilet training is not given properly. Wherever they like, they defecate or urinate. But when they become older they go to the bush alongwith others for this purpose.

After attaining the age of a year or so, the child starts sharing the bed with its elder siblings or grandparents. Until the age of four for five, they usually do not wear clothes. When a Bhil child is among familiar people he plays and laughs, but he tries to avoid strangers. After the age of four or five, boys begin to put on a loin-cloth and the girls, a piece of cloth round their waist up to the knees.

Another phase of the socialisation process of the Bhil child begins from this age. He is taught to respect the elders, to behave appropriately with the different members of the family and to understand things using his own experience. In a nutshell, his education begins by perception, reward and punishment from this age.

As the child grows a little more, his professional education also begins. Boys are taught how to make ropes, how to give fodder and water to the bullocks and cows and how to tie or untie the bullock from their posts. While the girls stay with their mothers in the house and learn the essentials of cooking and other household works, the boys generally learn more of physical skills as to judge distance, straight throws, to estimate distances for jumping and diving, climb trees especially plam trees, and balance on narrow and precarious footholds and to shoot with arrows. The boys and girls learn a many good games and dances either by participating or imitating the elders.

The economy of a Bhil family, to some extent, depends on its children. From about the age of six to eight years, the children of Bhil families start assisting and accompanying their elders in all kinds of chores. Children, both male and female, go to the jungle to graze cattle and return at noon. When the children are not watching cattle, they do some household work such as preparing cattle feed, removing dung and cleaning the cattle sheds, and carrying firewood from the forest. Young girls fetch water from the streams and rivulets and help in the husking and pounding of grains. An idle child is always rebuked, whereas active children are praised and looked after well.

When a Bhil child is no longer a lad, he enters a world entirely different from that in which he had lived so far. They form groups of their own and prefer mostly to move among their group-mates. Generally, at the age of fourteen or fifteen, the Bhil boys become sex-conscious. They try to enhance their personal adornment, they dress their hair nicely, their clothes are cleaner, eyes brighten at the sight of a young girl and at times they get involved in some sexual intrigues also. Girls also become conscious of their physical developments and general appearance. This is the time when Bhil boys and girls get married. Their parent want it, they also want it, and therefore, preparations for marriage start in the family.

Affection for Children

The Bhils feel great affection for children. The more they have, the better they like it. This is given expression by a saying of theirs: "As long as God gives us children we shall take them on our lap."

If a marriage is not blessed with children, it usually does not last. It either leads to a divorce, or the husband takes a second wife, because invariably he blames the wife of sterlity. Bhils do not easily admit that the husband might be sterile.

The number of children in a Bhil family is rather high, not a few have ten to twelve. But infant mortality is also high. About a third of the children die of infant. Still, this is not a high percentage compared with the infant mortality in other tribes of Central India. In Alirajpur, more children survive because the climate is healthy and the Bhils are fairly well to do.

The fertility is high; it is often stated that a child is conceived by a Bhil woman while the last born is still in the suckling stage. "The one still drinks, while the other is being got ready." As Bhils women are generally rather strong and sturdy and marry comparatively late, the high frequency of births does not sap their strength to the extent it does among the other Hindu castes in which the girls are married very early.

The Bhils seem to be equally fond of boys and girls. A son remains in the family and support his parents in old age, while a girl brings money or bullocks into the house when she marries.

Sterile women often approach a diviner or medicine man for help in their difficulties. This is done especially in the *Chait* and *Desarya* festivals. The medicine man extracts a hair from his head and weaves it into a (black-yellow) woman's hair-string. The sterile woman wears this hair-string and hopes to be cured thereby from her barrenness.

Or she tries to obtain a hair from a woman who has already given birth to several children. The barren woman buries the hair under the stone on which she takes her bath. It is believed that the fertility of the hair's owner is transferred to her after repeated bathings.

According to the informant, *Tadwi* of Meghnagar, some years ago, sacrificed a goat to the local goddess to get a child by his second wife. The sacrifice was performed at night, at the confluence of rivulet Mahi. A medicine man (*Badwa*) from another village was called to perform the sacrifice. The goat could not be made to drink the water before the sacrifice. Unless the goat drink, it could not be sacrificed, as this is the sign that the victim is acceptable to the deity. The *Tadwi*'s brother, a magician himself, chanted some incantations. Then the goat was decapitated by the *Badwa* who in reward for it received the goat's head. The body was later cut into pieces and cooked the same night at the river side. There also the dinner was served. It took almost the whole night to perform this sacrifice. Soon his wife conceived and nine months later the *Tadwi* bore the child.

When the barren woman asks a medicine man for a charm, he gives it to her, but imposes certain restrictions on her; she may not eat coconuts or gram, or not drink sour milk etc. As few women brother to observe these conditions, the medicine man has a good excuse when his amulets fail to produce the desired effect.

Lulling of Children

A Bhil baby is practically always in closest physical contact with its mother. The latter carries the baby around with her wherever she goes, nurses it as often as it cries, cleans it, bathes it and lets it sleep on her lap when she sits and does her house or kitchen work, or chats with other women. When she sits on the ground, she places her legs in such a way that they form a soft cradle for the child, its head resting on one thigh, the legs on the other, while the body rests on the ground.

When the baby has grown somewhat, the mother carries it straddled on her hip while supporting its back with one arm. Also sisters and brothers even when quite small may in this manner carry babies on their hip without great difficulty. When a woman has work in the field or is cooking, she places her baby in a hammock lulling it into sleep by giving the hammock a few swings occasionally and nursing it when it wakes up and starts crying for the mother. The Bhil mothers nurse their babies as long as the milk flows; they do not nurse children not their own.

Rights and Duties of Bhil Parents and Children

The rights and duties with regard to parents and children are quite definite in Bhil's society. A father's first duty towards his wife and children is to feed and clothe them, and to give them the protection and affection which children need. In fact, affection must often substitute for any lack of food and clothing which the parent find hard to provide. During the first months of his life, a Bhil child might be fed adequately as long as the mother's milk flows abundantly. Then gradually the mother's breasts dry up and the child has to start eating other food. It is during this time the child often gets under fed through lack of suitable nourishment. It is more often ignorance about the choice of the right food for small children than inability to feed them at all which makes children suffer from malnutrition. One can often observe Bhil women feeding small children pieces of the heavy *joari* bread, indigestible for their tender stomach. Or they are given heavily spiced food which upsets their stomach. The absence of proper medical care for children is an additional hazard that Bhil children undergo. But those who survive the first years of life grow into strong and hardy men and women.

The parents are held responsible for the action of their children before the community. Though unmarried boys and girls are not punished severely for their offences against the tribal law and are never outcasted except when they get maggots in wounds, their parents and other inmates of the house might suffer indirectly for the misbehaviour of a child.

In general parents are held responsible for any damage their children might cause. On the other hand, they also get credit if their children turn out well. They gain in social prestige, something which is highly valued in Bhil society.

The Bhil parents have not only duties and responsibilities towards their children, they also have rights. They have first of all the right to discipline them. The mother or elder sister may occasionally give the child a slap if it is naughty. Most children are taught by tender and patiently repeated persuation to behave according to accepted standards. And children learn soon that certain things simply cannot be done, and that there is no argument about it. Public opinion is so strong in a Bhil village that children feel the weight of it from an early age and imperceptibly learn to accept it.

If the affection and the feeling of solidarity are not sufficiently strong motives for a Bhils to support his old parents and other dependents, public opinion forces him to do so. Throughout his life he has been used to obey tribal law more or less unquestionably, and he accepts this burden too as a matter of course. But he will not easily do what is beyong the strict demands of tribal law enforced by public opinion. There is still a wide margin left for individual generosity or stingness to show itself, and also among the Bhils certain men have the reputation of being misers while others are generous to a default.

Growing up in Bhil Society

During the first year of its life the Bhil child is mostly with the mother. It experiences the affectionate nearness of the mother who suckles land cleans it and keeps it warm and smug against her own body. It is given the breast whenever it cries, and is fondled and carries around or swung to sleep in the hammock. Occasionally, the father too fondles his child and carries it around, and so do the elder sisters and other women of the house. In fact, towards the end of the first year and later, the baby passes from one embrace to the other and is never left alone. Minding the baby is everybody's business, especially that of the elder sisters or of the grand-mother.

The baby gradually begins to increase its range of experience when it starts crawling on the floor. It now needs more supervision as it is ever pulling at things, or crawling into the fire and other dangerous spots. It is mostly in the company of the women of the family who stay at home, while the men and boys are often absent, or keep to the front of the house, when at home, doing some work or merely gossiping with neighbours and visitors. Even then a little child, up to four years of age, whether boy or girl, is never excluded from male company. It learns to speak; it may hear and see everything that goes on in a Bhil family. At night it sleeps either with the mother or the father, or with both. Its senses and intellect are stimulated by the environment which it explores and the persons whom it encounters, who treat it with affection but differently from the members of the family. During three or four years of age the child is happy and free in the security of its home; any discipline that is done is carried out by the mother or elder women. During this time the child usually does not wear any clothes.

By the age of five or six, the Bhil child begins to know about the sex. The boys begin to separate from the girls. They, as also the girls, begin to wear a small piece of cloth over their private parts. It is fixed to the waist-string which all wear. Before, boys and girls played together; from now onwards they refrain from it more and more. At this age the children still play much, but they also begin to imitate their elders. The little boys begin to accompany the father and the elder brothers to the field, and they help in grazing the bullock, while the girls go with their mother or the elderly women of the house to the well or river to fetch water. Proudly they carry a little brass vessel on their head, and carry it back home, filled with water. They help in sweeping the house, watching the smaller children and doing any odd they can do. At that time the boys begin to sleep with the male members of the family and refuse to sleep with women. They submit more to the authority of the father and expect orders from him, while the girls rely more on the mother and other women of the family.

The whole process of growing up is gradual; there is no sudden change, there are no age grades, no ceremonies which signify the reaching of a certain degree of maturity or age.

It is very often said that Bhil children change cosiderably when reaching puberty. This change is not only physical but also mental. While physically they now quickly grow into adults, mentally they slow down considerably. While their interest in the other sex grows, they lose their innocent gaiety and unbounded energy of childhood and turn into slow, clumsy and awkwardly shy youths. Puberty set in between the age of twelve and fourteen.

The boy are now integrated in male society and they rely completely on the father and the elder brothers. The girls draw ever closer to the mother and elder sisters or sister-in-law; they now share the initially frightening burden of menstruation with them. At the same time they are prepared in earnest for the married life to which every Bhil girl and at the same time is afraid of. They try to learn all the skills required for married life, in kitchen and house and in the fields, because they know fully well that if they do not acquire these skills now at home they will have to learn them the hard way under the supervision of a strict mother-in-law. The boy too try to acquire a good working knowledge of all the jobs waiting for them in the field as well as in the forest.

The teaching is done in the leisurely and patiently repetitious manner by the father, or the mother as the case may be, and elder relatives and inmates of the house. By the time, boys and girls reach the marriageable age, they have not only learned almost all they will ever need to know about field work or house work, but they have also acquired a general knowledge of tribal lore, and of the traditional beliefs and practices cherished by the Bhils.

Education

As soon as the Bhil children grow up somewhat, they are expected to take on tasks which of course differ according to age and sex. The boy joins the father and the elder brothers in work, imitating them, more in play than in earnest, the girls joining the mother and the elder sisters in their pursuits in the house, garden and field. The boys learn how to graze the cattle, how to do work in the field, even how to plough and to cut timber in the forest. The girls learn to weed, cut grass, collect fuel, fetch water from the well or river, cook and look after the younger children.

As in other castes and tribes, the Bhils children too observe a seasonal sequence in their games through the year. For instance, around Holi the boys begin to manufacture bows and arrows, and slings with great enthusiasm. At other times, but always connected with certain feasts, they begin to play games with stones or resort to kite flying. These are the games which Bhils children learned from the non-tribals or other classes and races of the society.

The girls separate early from the boys. They have no dolls. Their mother-instinct is satisfied with living children, their younger brothers and sisters, given into their care at an early age. Girls mostly remain at home; but when their mother or elder sisters go to work in the field, they may go along and play there at first, but soon they will be urged to do some work.

Informal education extends to other activities too. Sometimes an old Bhil takes it on himself to instruct the boys of the village in the songs and rites of the tribe. If he does it oftener and regularly, he might be called 'teacher' (*guru*) and receive a present occasionally from the parents for instance, a piece of cloth.

The Bhils children learn dances in the community or on the occasion of festivals and functions. In the specific cases they are taught by the village experts. On the occasion, children dance with villagers and the part of the mistakes are rectified by the elders.

Birth Songs

Among the Bhils, the song referred to the birth of a child are not numerous. There are some songs for the ritual of birth. These songs are fast disappearance from the tribal scene, as the Bhils are being more and more sanskritised.

Bhil birth-songs refer mainly to the relationship between mother and child in very simple terms. As in all classes of the Indian population, Bhil mothers, too, love their children dearly and take good care to them. However, great poverty often prevents them from nourishing their children properly and dressing them up as decently as they would wish to. Bhil society shares the general preference for male children; but they do not neglect their daughters on that account. Female infanticide, is not practised by the Bhils.

1. Fly, Sparrow, Fly !

Dear, sweep sparrow, deliver my message for me;
Tell my father that I have given birth to a son;
Tell my mother that I have got a son;
Ask my father to give me a new Saree;
Ask my mother for a blouse of many colours.
Tell my brother that I have a son,
Ask him to bring me some cloth for skirt.
Tell my Banvi that I have a son.
Ask him to give me a Saree, too.
Tell my uncle that I have given birth to a son;
ask him to bring me a blouse of many colours.

2. Blessed Events

My cow gave birth under a tree,
And my dear wife inside my house.
To her I shall give all the good food we have,
While I shall do with none.
She shall sleep on the cot, and I on the mat on the floor.
She shall sleep in the house, and I in the yard;
To her I shall give fine clothes, though I donot own a shirt;
She shall care for our baby, and I'll take care of the calf.

3. My Wagja Prince

In the courtyard of my Waja Prince
There is a perennial well.
Bring the infant prince to the well,
To wash his fingers and toes,
Wash also his umbilical cord,
And then his shoulders, too.
In the courtyard of my Wagja Prince
There is a perennial well.

4. Birth-Pang

Wait out of doors, O Sasro, do not enter the house, I pray;
The house echoes with the pangs of birth; please stay away!

Lo, the baby is born. O Father-in-law, come quickly!
A baby is born, O Mother-in-law, hasten to the house!
But, lo! the baby boy is born. O Brother-in-law, hastento the bouse!
There are birth-pangs in the house; O Sister-in-law, donot enter!
But lo! the baby boy is born, O Sister-in-law, hasten and enter!

5. Had I But Known Your Pain

Alas! dear wife, had I but known your pain,
I would have gone to Rajgarh, and brought a second wife,
To help you husk the rice, and make the sweet laddoos,
And disturb them among your friends;
For this, I'm sure, would give you immense joy,
And fill your stomach, too!

6. Bahu, Fetch The Water

My Sasro says: "Bahu, it is morning, go and fetch some water."
But my love says: "Sweetheart, do not strain yourself when
fetching it."
For my slim waist may not support me and I may fall into the
well.
My Sasro says: "Bahu, it is morning, go and fetch some water."
But my love says: "Sweetheart, do not strain yourself when
fetching it."
For my slim waist may not support me, and I may fall into
the well.
My Jeth says, "Bahu, it is morning, go and fetch some water."
But my love says, "Sweetheart, do not strain yourself in doing so."

For your slim waist may not support you, and you may fall
into the well."
My Bhabhi says: "Bahu, it is morning, go and fetch some
water."
But my love says, "Sweetheart, do not strain yourself in doing so."
For your slim waist may not support you, and you may fall
into the well."

7. My Baby's Needs

O husband! go to the plantation and bring for me some lime.
Bring a raw one, for little Nanad to play with.
I suffered the pangs of birth, while you were eating coconuts.
You never gave me any good food in your house.
My sister brought me a Saree, but you took it away.
You have never given me such a nice Saree.
Uncle, go and buy a golden swing for my baby.
Which has just been put up for sale.
Ah, which of my brothers will bring it for me?
My eldest brother will buy it for me.
It's nice to have these things in my house.

8. My Baby's Swing

I shall order a swing for my child from Piyor,
O my husband, too young to be one!
I shall have a pond dug before your eyes,
For my child to bathe in!
I shall fill the house with sumptuous beds,
And sleep peacefully on such beautiful beds.
I shall order a swing for my child from Piyor.

9. Let Me Fill My Pot

I want to join the dances near the well, naughty boy!
Let me fill my pot with water soon.

But when I fill my pot, he pours all the water out of
it!
Leave me, little boy; I want to fill my pot soon.
Give me back my hankerchief; for I want to wind it
into a
ring.
To support my pot on my head.
Leave me alone, to fill my pot.
I want to join the dances near the well, naughty boy!
Let me fill my pot with water soon.

Notes and References

1. B. J. Terwiel, *The Tai of Assam and Ancient Tai Ritual: Life Cycle Ceremonies,* Vol. 1, Gaya (Bihar), 1980, p. 31.
2. S.L.Doshi, *op. cit.,* p. 180.
3. S. C. Roy, op. cit., p. 10.
4. Kamaladevi Chattopadhyaya, op. cit., p. 61.
5. S. L. Doshi, *op. cit.,* p. 181.
6. R. E. Enthoven, *The Tribes and Castes of Bombay,* Vol. 1, p. 158.
7. *Ibid.,* p. 158.
8. C. S. Gupta (ed.),*Census of India 1961* (Rajasthan), A Village Survey Monongraph: Kailashpuri, Vol. XIV, Pt. VI-C, 1967, p. 11.
9. S. L. Doshi, *op. cit.,* pp. 184-185.
10. C. S. Gupta (ed.) *Census of India 1961* (Rajasthan), A Village Survey: Panarwa, Vol. XIV, pt. VI-B, 1965, p. 14.

7

Marriage

The Bhils do not make it easy for a man to enter matrimony. They take it as a serious matter and is not to be accomplished in a day. It needs considerable time on their hands. The leisure, whether voluntary or involuntary, they particularly like to fill with the many and varied ceremonies connected with betrothals and weddings. The bustle and activity with which the Bhils surround the marriage contract speak better than words of the fundamental importance which they attach to this institution.[1] This point is illustrated by one of their pithy proverbs :

"Zani Zoine hagun karwun, ane sanine pani piwun."

("Only after acquaintance and consideration does one form relationship (marry), as it is only after filtering water that one drinks.")

The Betrothal Ceremony

The betrothal of a Bhil boy usually takes place when he is about ten or twelve years of age, while a girl is betrothed from the age of five to seven years. Neither the boy nor the girl is informed of the intention of their parents to arrange their marriage nor have they any right of choosing their own partners. The betrothal of the children is entirely the affairs of the parents, and romance is not allowed to pay a part of it.

But there are exceptions and we find another proverb which clearly express disapproval of forcing an unwilling bride:

Gangarti unt nin palanwi

[Screaming camel not saddle (burden)]

["A screaming camel should not be further burdened" is often quoted by the Bhil when there is question of forcing a girl to marry against her will.]

Betrothal takes place in two phases : (a) *Chhoti mangani* (Preliminary betrothal) and (b) *Bari mangani* or *Sagai* (betrothal).

(a) Chhoti Mangani (Preliminary Betrothal)

When a boy attains marriageable age, his father, or the elder brother (in case of the father is not alive) is on the look-out for a suitable bride for him. Relatives and friends, or sometimes professional match-makers, help him to select the right girl. As a rule, the Bhils prefer daughter-in-law from a distant village, to avoid the interference of the young woman's relatives, later on, in case she does not find everything to her liking in her new home.

Occasionally, at a wedding or a funeral banquet, the fathers of a boy and a girl get acquainted, and each is informed of the other's character, family and economic status by mutual friends. If this first acquaintance turns out favourable to a future union, the boy's father expresses his desire to see the girl in question. Also the girl's father wants to know if the prospective husband of his daughter is sound in limb and mind and under some pretence pays an occasional visit to the boy's father.

If the enquiries made are satisfactory, the Brahman is consulted to cast the horoscope of the boy and the girl concerned. If the constellation of their stars appears favourable to a marriage, the betrothal is arranged soon. However, a bad forecast does not deter the Bhils from a betrothal, if it is otherwise satisfactory. The evil chances of a unlucky horoscope are made innocuous by giving alms (dan), consisting of a coconut, *supari* (betelnut), a small coin and grain, either to the Brahman or to a poor relative or begger.

The question of mutual relationship is discussed next. The Bhils of Nimar have concrete source for obtaining the information about their community who dwell distant villages. They have their own *bhat* (registrar), who keeps the family registers and yearly enters the names of new-born children in his book, and registers the marriages performed since the time of his last visit. The *bhat* is consulted, in case of doubt, whether a relationship in a forbidding degree does exist or not. But this form of enquiry is used rarely. Usually, Bhils know every one of their community very well to whom they are related and which degree.[2]

After these preliminary questions have been settled at a first or second meeting, the date for the official betrothal is fixed. It generally takes place in the month of *Srawan*(July-August), on a Sunday, sometimes also on a Monday or Saturday, but never on a Tuesday which is an auspicious day.The Bhils consider Sunday as the most auspicious day of the week and therefore like to settle all their major affairs on a Sunday. Even the main parts of their field-work, a ploughing, sowing, weeding and harvesting, are begun on a Sunday; no loans are given nor asked for on this day, and no Bhil will buy or sell anything on a Sunday before sunset, except at the bazar.

If both sides agree in principle, the next step is to carry out all the ceremonies and transactions which together form preliminary betrothal rites. This part of the business culminates in the paying of earnest-money to the girl's father and the drinking of *daru* (wine). With this purpose in view the young man's father, his agent and some friends and acquaintances set out to call on the corresponding representatives of the girl, but not without taking a many precautions. The most important is to make sure of good omens, or, as the Bhil express it to bring out good omens.

The Consulting of Omens

The Bhils take the omens seriously especially for ceremonial rites. Some of them recognize fixed and arbitrary omens. The fixed omen, being anchored in tradition and usage, do not change. It is for example universally held to be a bad omen if on the way to any serious undertaking one meets a woman carrying an empty pitcher on her head. The arbitrary omens are decided upon by those concerned, who can decide which are to be regarded as good and which as bad. Both kinds of omens may be made use of in connection with a preliminary betrothal; but the fixed ones, being easier to understand, deserve better attention. As long as the omens are not considered good the party will not set out. The Bad omens noticed en route may cause them to return back.

If some person in the house sneezes at the moment when the go-between is on the point of setting out he will prick up his ears and ask : "What kind of a sneeze is it?" If the sneezer or some member of the household answers : "A good sneeze", then the agent is satisfied and goes his way. But if they answer : "He (or she) is sneezing blood", the go-between will not start on his mission because such is an omen that presages quarrelling and mutual abuse. Notice is further taken whether a person sneezes once or several times. A single sneeze is regarded as a bad sign, a second one or ony even number of sneezes as a good omen.

If a running dog wags its ears, this taken as unpropitious; if it does the same while sitting all is well. If an ass brays on the right the prospects are bad and should this happen to the matrimonial agent he and his followers will turn back or else wait for some favourable omen. If a little black bird, known as *sari,* voice heard on the right soon afterwards, the expedition could safely be continued. Another small bird called *sibrun*is also considered of ill omen when singing on the left side, of good, when heard on the right.

A crow brings luck if it caws to the right while on the way. On the arrival at the destination when it (crow) caws to the left direction, Bhils take it as ill luck. The cry of a starling should on the other hand be heard to the left; but there exists another version according to which a starling to the left also spells misfortune as long as the marriage agent is en route and may be considered a good omen only when he has reached his destination. A crane to the left is a bad sign while on the right it brings good fortune.

The Giving of the Money

On that occasion the boy's father accompanied by village headman and some other worthies make a call on the girl's representative; then all go together to her house. If this is not the same village as that of the groom, then the headman and various "notables" of the girl's village will be invited there too. The young man's father then hands his go-between the sum which he wishes to have passed to the girl's father as a sort of earnest money. It is also known under the name of Omen Money (*Bakan na Rupya*). The amount varies from family to family as per their economic status but the number must in every case be uneven and end in a quarter, this fraction being, as the Bhil say, "good". The groom's agent immediately hands the money on to the bride's go-between from whom it passes through the village headman to the girl's father. The latter then hands out one rupee to his representative while the boy's father gives his one and a quarter. The two sums are put together and then two men, one from each party are sent to buy *daru* (wine) for the two and a quarter rupees. On their return they deposit the *daru* at the feet of the girl's village headman, who gives one of the men present the order to put it into a brass vessel that has been prepared for the purpose. The man half fills it, then stands motionless, waiting with the brass vessel in his hand, for the rupee which he is entitled to receive from the boy's father. The latter either gives it at once or else promises to give it at an appointed time. If he pays at once, the rupee is passed from one go-between to the other and then through the headman to the real recipient. This marks the end of the Omen-Money rite as part of the ceremonies connected with the preliminary engagement.

The Sprinkling of the Daru (*Dhar nakhwi*)

Before the village headman carries out the ceremony of sprinkling the *daru* the half-filled brass vessel must be painted with the so-called *tilak* (Bhili *wadawo*), a task allotted to the bride's sister or, if she has no sister, to her mother. She at the same time marks the bridegroom's brother with the same sign.

At this point the acting village headman takes in hand the sprinkling of the *daru*. As is usual for such ceremonies he stands with his face turned to the north, takes the brass vessel with the *daru* in his left hand and pours a little of the treasured liquid into his right palm. He then three times makes a circular movement over the earth with this hand, letting a few drops of *daru* drip between his fingers each time. Finally he opens his hand and throws what remains on the ground. The ceremony is a tribute to *Zami Mata* (Mother earth).

Then follows the so-called *daru* tasting by the village notables in which the headman is again the chief actor. If his colleague from the boy's village is present, then he passes him the first two trial drinks. The recipent lays the palms and fingers of his two hands together so as to form a *mussel* shaped hollow into which the officiating headman pours twice a certain quantity of *daru* with his right hand. The owner of the hands drinks this

without further ceremony. In the same manner the young man's go-between and his father and then the girl's go-between and her father are one after the other supplied with trial drinks.

The acting headman then passes the vessel with the *daru* to the girl's agent who hands it on to the boy's agent. The actor stands up and pours out two samples for each of the more important members of the girl's party. He then turns to the officiating village headman (who has so far been left out of the drinking) and pours him out four samples, two in the name of the girl's party and two in that of the boy's.

The Drinking of the Daru

Later on the officiating village headman gives the order for general distribution of *daru* so that all present can enjoy some of the precious drink. A man of the girl's party is charged by the headman to see to the pouring out. He first attends to the guests (the boy's party) in the order in which they have sat down, then to his own party. The *daru* is drunk out in a kind of cup or cup-shaped vessel. From time to time some older or more important person will remind the distributor of the headman and similar worthies so as to make sure that they get their full share, for special attention and consideration are due to such folk.

From the very beginning moment of the 'preliminary betrothal' both parties regard each other as kinsfolk. For the girl in particular this entails new duties as regards avoidence and veiling. She is now bound to avoid (and this is always connected with the duty of drawing a veil over her face) her future father-in-law, her bridegroom's elder brother, her sister's husband, the grown males of her bridegroom's clan etc. This avoiding and veiling does not apply to her bridegroom's younger brothers, the husband of her cousins, or the men of her own village unless one of them happens to be a member of the groom's clan.

(b) Bari Mangni or Sagai (The Betrothal)

On the day fixed for the betrothal, the boy's father, accompanied by a few friends or relatives, proceeds to the village where the father of the girl lives. Having arrived at their destination they sit down under a tree or in a neighbouring fieid. Not long after, the village headman and the girl's father appear upon the scene to welcome them with a hearty 'Come along!'

All the guests stand up, but sit down again immediately. In the meantime the go-between see to it that dry grass is fetched from the house of the bride's father and spread on the ground to serve later on as a shake-down for the night.

Gradually, amid lively conversation and tobacco smoking, the negotiations between the two parties are set going. The two groups, however, remain separated and the talking is done by the go-betweens. The main point to be settled is the bride-price and to her relatives. The former is called *dez,* the latter *dapan.* When all are agreed as to the exact amount, the young man's father gives a part of the sum to his agent, who passes it to the agent of the opposite party. From him it passes through the village headman to the bride's father.

After this the question of certain smaller payment has still to be regulated. A number of people are waiting for rewards recognized as their due and called *lag.* The women singers, for instance, the man who distributes the *daru,* the people make plate out of leaves, the women who prepare the meal, those who propound riddles and those who serve water for the guests to rinse their mouths - to all these a certain sum must be apportioned and paid by the bridegroom's father. If the man who distributed the *daru* on the occasion of the 'preliminary betrothal' was not then given the rupee promised to him, he expects to receive it now.

When accounts are being settled, the girl's father sometimes remits a small part of the *dahej* on the understanding that the boy's father will buy some additional silk-cloths or ornaments for the bride (*katni or katotri*). It is the bride's father who claims most of the rights on this occasion, the girl being in his gift. If the father is dead, then the girl's elder brother claims these rights, if she has neither father nor brother, then they pass to an uncle, the brother of her father or of her mother.

As soon as the financial question settles, the girl's father makes her a present of a goat and this opens up the prospect of the feast which is to be held in the course of the afternoon. Other preparations for this feast are made at the same time.

The bridegroom's father brought with him some clothes for the girl, *dhupti* (or *urni,* short veil), *ghagri* (petticoat), *choli* (bodice), sweetmeat and spices, a coconut and *kuku* (red powder). He puts on a brass plate (*parat*) the clothes for the girl, the other presents and two and a quarter rupees for the *panch.*

Before the girl's father accepts the plate with the presents, which the boy's father offers him, the headman of the *panch* gets up, dips his thumb in the red *kuku* powder on the plate and rubs his finger over the forehead of the boy's father, from the point between the eyebrows upwards. In the same manner he paints also the father of the girl and the other men present. The boy's father pays him few *paisa* for doing it.

Now the plate with the clothes, spices and other presents are handed on to the women of the house who have been waiting a little apart, singing among themselves. The money is taken by a villager who is told to purchase the required *gur* from the local shop. The women withdraw to the interior of the house, where the girl is dressed in the new clothes for the betrothal. After dressing the girl is brought by the singing women before the boy's father. A sheet is spread on the ground before his seat and the girl is told to sit down. The boy's father cracks a coconut, takes one half of the fruit, puts one rupee coin in its hole and lays it into the lap of the girl who is told to lift up the corners of her veil. A woman approaches, dips her fingers into the red *kuku* powder and rubs them across the forehead of the girl. Then she applies the ceremonial paint on the forehead of the other women. After that the girl is led away and the betrothal is over. The girl is allowed to eat the coconut presented to her and the sweets on the plate, while the one rupee coin go to the family purse.

Another part of ritual of the 'Final Engagement' consists in dabbing the hands with (bright red) Mehandi ink. The brother-in-law first paints the hands of the bride and bridegroom, then his own and those of all the guests who show any wish to have their hands decorated in this way.

The Feast for the Guests

While the betrothal is taking place, some men are busy with the preparation of the meal. The goat provided by the bride's father is slaughtered. The person to whom this task is entrusted, does his best to sever the head from the body with one sword stroke. If he fails to do so he is obliged to pay a fine of one rupee, which is of course added to the *daru* money. Among the other foods and relishes which have been provided for the feast or which are hastily procured at the last moment we find : rice, ghee, garlic, red pepper, salt, special kinds of shelled and split legumens and tobacco. The goat in particular should be cooked with salt, red pepper, legumens, oil and water.

Rice is usually provided, at least smaller quantities, so that the more important guests as also the girl's father, her village headman and her go-between can be served with it. When the rice and the roughly ground maize have been cooked, three, five or seven girls are told off to break up the big lamps into smaller portions. A number of the best brass or china plates are filled by the bride's mother or by the sister of her betrother's father. These are intended for the notables and when all are ready the mother or the aunt announces: "I have filled the plates." Then the bride's father, her village headman or her go-between bids some of the men of her party place the plates before the more important guests in the order in which he gives their names.

The majority of the guests must be satisfied with bowl-shaped receptacles made for the occasion by sewing together with bamboo splits the leaves of teak tree or palas tree. A special distributor passes round to each of the ordinary guests such a leaf plate for which he receives a coin of a rupee. Three things must be distributed: maize (or rice), ghee and meat.

After the meal, guests and villagers sit together to a friendly chat till it is time to go to bed. Early next morning the guests get up, take a light repast and return home.

The interval between betrothal and marriage may be anything from a few weeks to several years. During this time the father of the boy must send clothes for the girl twice a year: one at the time of *Holi* festival (celebrated in the month of March) and another at the time of *Rakhi* (celebrated during July-August). If he fails to send the clothes for any reason, the betrothal is not dissolved automatically, but the father of the girl enquires, why the clothes have not been sent.

Dissolution of Betrothal

The betrothal may be dissolved by both parties for any plausible reason. If a better match is in view for the boy or girl, or in consequence of a quarrel between relatives of the betrothed children, or in case of lasting of disfiguring sickness of one of the betrothed. As in the contrast of a betrothal, also in its breaking-up the betrothed children have no influence whatever. It seldom happens that they see each other at all till the wedding day.

Special Rites Practised During the Period Immediately Preceding the *Wane* Days

The so-called *Wane* days generally begin about a week before the wedding proper. The following ceremonies are carried out during the last days before the *Wane* period sets in. Both in the bridegroom's house and the bride's house a moderate quantity of rice is dipped in yellow turmeric solution. The order is given by the master of the house and by the village headman who also in every case appoints the messenger who is to convey the ceremonies invitations. He does so by strewing some of the yellow rice on the doorsteps of the house in question and saying : "The invitaion of name of the master of the house and of the bridegroom has come. The *Wane* days will begin at such a date, the *Notran-mameran* rite and the wedding will take place on such and such days."

One of the last days before the *wane* week begins, five or seven unmarried girls (*zanwanen*) "waiting-women" of the bride are sent out from the house of the bridegroom (it can also be from that of the bride) to look for ochre-coloured earth which they carry back in baskets on their heads. Together they go to a pit where such earth can be dug. The leader carries a brass vessel (*loti*) with *daru* in her hand and when they arrive at the pit she sprinkles a little *daru* on the ground. The rest of the *daru* they all drink together. One of the girls then with the help of an iron plough share digs out the earth and fills the baskets while the others sit round and sing. They all go home singing, with the full baskets on their heads.

On their return to the house of the marriage candidate they find one of the women of the family waiting for them holding in her hands a bowl of yellow turmeric (*haldi*) solution in which an oil light is floating. The basket carriers draw up in a semi-circle and the kinswomen of the marriage candidate swings the bowl with the burning light once from right to left in front of the baskets. Then she dips her thumb in the yellow turmeric paste and smear the tilak sign on the leader's basket. The earth which has been brought is then mixed with water to a thin yellow paste. Rags are dipped into this and the colour is applied both to the outer walls of the house as also to the *bharari* wall in the interior.

Halad Bhagwi

On the last market day before the beginning of the *Wane* week the bridegroom's father sends someone to fetch two-and-a-half to three pounds of turmeric. In the mean time, two, three or four girls are busy in applying the yellow earth paste there. When the turmeric of the same weight is brought from the market, the "women-in-waiting" first paint a *tilak* on the hard turmeric roots and then break them to pieces. The small pieces are left to dry in the sun for a couple of hours, then they are ground in the maize mill. This finely ground turmeric root mixed with water is used for painting the body and clothes and finds copious application in the course of the marriage celebration.

The turmeric root is destined to play another part as well in the course of the marriage ceremonies. Some members of the bridegroom's clan take care to prepare *haldi* knots for the morning of the day on which the *Wane* week is to begin. Five, seven or nine pieces of the hard yellow *haldi* root are tied with a woman's multicoloured hair-cord to a piece broken off an arrow-shaft. The bearer of this token must reach the bride's house before evening to announce to her officially the beginning of the *Wane* period and to inform her of the exact number of *Wane* days. The bride takes over the broken arrow-shaft with the *haldi* knots attached to it, lays it on her sleeping-place and, during certain ceremonies proper to the *Wane* days, carries it in her hand. Every day one of the knots is removed until on the last of the *Wane* days, the eve of the wedding there is not a single piece left.

The Wedding Ceremony

Marriages are celebrated generally in April-May. The reason behind it may be that with the coming of rains in July-August, the Bhils remain busy in their fields for four to five months, while in April-May they remain practically free. Secondly, because of the custom of bride-price, the Bhils have frequently to borrow money, and since borrowing and repayment of loans depend on harvest, getting loans in this period to much easier.

The Bhils marry for social as well as economic reasons. Marriage increases progeny and a wife adds to the number of workers in the family. For economic reasons sometimes Bhils indulge in polygyny and is very common among the Bhils. According to *Census of India 1961*, ('A Survey of Khajoora village of Rajasthan') two cases of polygyny have been found. One Bhil family got himself married second time because of economic reasons. He was finding it difficult to cope with his agricultural work with one wife and so he married another. The second case appears to have been due to the force of circumstances. The sister-in-law of one of the Bhils got widowed and she fell in love with the husband of her younger sister and consequently the man went through another married with the widow. Such cases have been found exceptional and marriage with elder sister-in-law is restricted.

Prohibition

The matters like marriage, succession, inhertance, adoption and maintenance, the Bhils have their own law based on customs and principles. Being an endogamous tribal groups, no Bhils member of a sept can marry another from the same sept. This prohibition is applied for three generations to any sept into which a man has already married. A man can also not marry into the sept from which his mother came for three generations, as the members of this sept are held to be the brothers and sisters of such man. The same rule is extended to the septs of grandmother, maternal and paternal. This prohibition does not allow with the children of a paternal or maternal uncle or an aunt's brother-in-law.

Amongst the Bhils of Rajasthan, it is also taboo to choose a mate from grandmother's clan but people generally tend to ignore it. Besides these restrictions, in the core of Bhil culture are where only one clan resides in the Pal (village) people cannot have a spouse from the same Pal, even if there are one or two families of other clans. Such families are considered as fictive kinsmen. But around Udaipur town which forms marginal area of this cultural unit, there is no restriction in selecting a girl from another clan from the same village. Thus there is no uniform pattern about the village exogamy.

An adopted son adhers to the same rules excluding his adoptive parent's septs. A man can marry two sisters, but the exchange of daughters between fathers is not usual.

Other Prohibitions

Social status is not a bar to marriage, at any rate in theory, though in practice apparently it does operate. Geographical position is no bar in itself nor are sectarian variations.

Certain occupations are now looked upon askance, due to contact with the non-tribe high castes influence, and certain families are inclined to reject marriage with a family which has taken up the profession of manufacturing of winnowing fans (*supda*), sieves (*chalni*), of a butcher (i.e. who kills an animal by cutting its throat as *kasais* do, but if he decapitates them he does not lose status), of a tanner, of a professional mendicant, of a Rawal or dancer and singer.

Age at Marriage

The Bhils have very little idea about the exactly age of a man or woman. They calculate the age on the basis of physical make up and the capacity to handle the household work and farm labour.

The boy is considered to be of marriageable age when he independently plough the field and work for the whole day in the field as an adult. The age of marriage for a girl depends on her physical capacity to fetch up a full big pot of water from the well, do the household work by herself and look after the fields. Besides, the efficiency in carrying out various tasks, she is also expected to possess bodily maturity. Maturation is no criteria for Bhils to fix the proper age of marriage for girls and no penalty attaches to the presence of an adult unmarried girl in her home. For the growth of her breasts determines the age of her marriage. When she has even just developed breasts she is supposed to have arrived at the thershold of womenhood and the members of the community remark: 'She has developed breasts, which require to be covered (*senke avi hei*)'.

It is general rule that girls marry at an earlier age than the boys. The earliest age of marriage of girls is 12 years, while most are married between 15-20. In the recent times the marriage of a boy is often delayed for want of money. The father is then obliged to wait for the marriage, till he can put his son to service with a landlord who employs him for a year and gives either half or the whole pay in advance, charging the usual interest of 25 to 50 per cent.

In several cases, for fair bride price and meet out economic hardship, parents of the girl settle their daughter's marriage in hurry. In such cases, the bridegroom may be too older or younger than the bride. Sometimes the parents like to have their daughter-in-law older than their son for she is considered as being capable of giving a better output of work. A rather young daughter-in-law is a liability to the family.

Among the Bhil there is never question of marrying or giving in marriage before puberty has been attained. They have refused to adopt the custom of child marrriage in spite of the persistent influence of upper castes of non-tribe. Nor do they recognize any law forbidding a widow to re-marry. There is, on the contrary, a proverb which says that "it is better for the widow, especially if she is young, to find a new protector".

Ram Ahuja's study on marriages based on 415 cases of Bhils marriage of Rajasthan in 1959 shows a change in attitude towards child marriage and a growing preference for post-puberty marriage. He found that 10.4 per cent of the Bhils interviewed were married before 15 years of age, 80.1 per cent after 24 years of age which shows that though pre-puberity marriages exist in Bhil society, they are not common. Majority of them prefers post-adolescent marriages.[3]

Early marriage also adds to the prestige of the bridegroom's father. The contact of marriage depends on the capacity to pay the bride-price and one who gets his sons married at the fairly early age enjoys a high status in the community.

Yet another reason for the performance of early marriage may be the motive of the families to be drawn together or to perpetuate their friendship. A man having only one son may cherish a desire to see grandchildren and contract a marriage. It is found that the marriages of the only sons are made at a very early age. The Bhils do not seem to arrange early marriages as a means of preserving the virginity of the girl. It is by no means a highly valued quality in a bride.

Among the Bhils, as a rule, the younger sons or daughters must not marry before the elder ones so long as there is a chance of the latter getting married. The villagers look at the marriage of younger child while the elder is still unmarried with suspicion.

Bride Price (*DAPA*)

Dapa for all practical purposes may be considered as a bride price. It is paid by the bridegroom's father a couple of week before the wedding actually takes place. The payment is delayed till a few days before the marriage, to avoid the money being wasted by the girl's father for other purposes.

The amount varies from area to area. In Dungarpur district the *Dapa* ranges between Rs. 350 to 1000. In Banswara district the bride price is Rs. 1000. In Jhabua district it varies from Rs. 100 to 1000 but now a days it has exceeded upto Rs. 5000. Thus *Dapa* is a costly affairs and it has become one of the major factors in increasing the rate of migration.

In addition, ornaments are also presented by the groom during marriage. It varies from family to family. The family of well economic status present even golden jewels. But the poor family presents only few silver ornaments. One of my informants of the Petlawad presented articles as a *dhapa* which are placed in table-24.

Table-24

Kind of Ornaments Presented as Dapa

Sl no.	Name of ornaments	Metal	Weight
1.	Hansi	(Silver)	20 tola.
2.	Pair of bangles	(Silver)	20 tola.
3.	A big chain	(Silver)	750 gms.
4.	Bajdi	(Silver)	10 tola.
5.	Nose top	(gold)	1 gm.

In Kota Tehsil of Udaipur the bride price ranges between Rs. 1000 to 2000. Out of this money the ornaments like *dayada* made of Silver, *kadora* made of silver and Nose top made of gold are purchased by the parents and presented to the girl. A set of clothes for the bride and its relations are also presented by the groom. This is called *palda.* Although there is variation in the quantum of bride price and number of clothes to be presented to the in-laws, there is uniformity in the pattern and system.

In case of Kalia Bhils the parents have to pay Rs. 16 as *dapa* out of which five Rupees is returned as the price of a blanket, being a return present to the bridegroom. Among the Kalia Bhils the bride price is as high as Rs. 65.[4]

In case of *natra,* the value of *dapa* comes down to less than half the normal rate and is paid to the women's parents and not to her husband's kinsmen.

If some betrothed girl becomes pregnant due to pre-marital relations, an amount equal to double the bride-price settled for her marriage is charged by the bride-groom's parents.

Payment of the Bride Price

For the payment of the bride-price, the bridegroom's father proceeds to the village, where the bride's father lives, accompanied by some relatives and members of his own village. On their arrival they are welcomed by bride's family. The Bride's father came with a *thali* (tray of brass) which contained *kanku* (vermilion), coconut and daubed vermilion on the fore-head of all the persons assembled. At the end of this ceremony the groom's father was given rupee one with a coconut. The settled amount of *dapa* was placed in a *thali* on which marks of *haldi* (turmeric) were already made. Grooms father daubed the fore-head of bride with turmeric and rice, and sum of settled amount was given to him as *dapa*. *Dhol* (Drums) were played by *dholi* (Drummer).

After the ceremony it is assumed that engagement is settled and will be binding on both the parties. The need of bride by bride's parents is explained in terms of compensation for the loss of a productive member of the family which is given in marriage. To secure the marriage all the requirements of bride's parents for starting the marriage is fulfilled by way of giving money. The boy's party spend first night at girls house and next morning the day of wedding was fixed.

It is not necessary to pay the whole amount in advance and after it the marriage takes place. Generally it is paid in instalments convenient to the groom's father. When the whole amount is paid then the date of marriage is fixed.

Fixing Marriage Day

After the payment of bride-price the date of marriage is settled. The members of both the parties go to neighbouring village to consult Brahmin for fixing the wedding day. The Brahmin fixes the date after some astrological calculations and gives the date of marriage.

In few cases the elders of the village proposes an auspicious date of marriage. In this connection no Brahmin is employed.

The day after this has been settled some rice dyed with turmeric is given to a Bhil or to several, as the case may require. The men take this round and leave it on the thresholds of all who are invited to the wedding. The recipients entertain the messager according to their means. This is the ceremony of *notra* or invitation.

Types of Marriage

There are different types of marriage prevalent among the Bhil society for acquiring a match. Some of them are popular and accepted by the society and some are objectionable and society does not recognize them, hence, occur rarely in the society. The following types of marriage are prevalent in the Bhil society:

1. *Lagan Mandwa* (Marriage by purchase) a form of religious marriage, 2. *Lugda-Ladi* (Economical or abbreviated form of marriage) 3. *Aa bharana or uchal jana* (Marriage by intrusion), 4. *Bhaga kar le jana* (Marriage by elopment), 5. *Ghis kar le jana* (Marriage by abduction) and 6. *Ghar jamai* (Matrilocal marriage).

1. Lagan Mandwa (Marriage by Purchase):

This type of marriage is very popular among Bhils and society gives them due respect. It is also known as orthodox type of marriage amongst anthropologists. The Bhils of the area of my study generally practise this form of marriage. The father accept the bride price, for he has taken pain in bringing up the daughter and incurred expenditure on her. The price for the bride called *dapa* is finalised when reliable persons of the two parties meet at the place of the girl's father. The amount of the bride price varies from area to area and little variation is due to the difference in the status of families.

The bride-price received by the father is not solely his own property. The rearing of the girl was in fact the responsibility of the whole family. The mother nursed her and the father provided her with food and shelter. The remuneration received by the father is, therefore, distributed among all the members of the family. The mother is rewarded, a share being given to her as the price 'of her milk'.

On the day of the marriage the bridegroom's party goes to the bride's place accompanied with friends and relatives. It is customary in Bhil marriages for the ladies of the household to join the party. Generally the boy is mounted. The party is led by a person or a group of persons beating drums in a singsong way. The bridegroom is dressed for the occasion in white *dhoti* and red *angrakha* and wears an imitation crown known as *maur*. The night is spent in an orgy of drinking and dancing to the accompaniment of wild and rousing music. After an exchange of presents, the upper-garments of the boy and the girl are joined and seven times the couple goes round the nuptial fire lighted in the middle of the *mandap*. Again there is feasting, singing and dancing. Next day the party returns with the bride.

The father of the girl loses his rights of ownership after giving her in marriage. But it is not exclusive disposal; for if she is unluckily widowed afterwards and consequently given in a re-marriage, he claims one half of the bride-price from her second husband. His ownership partly continues till the death of his daughter.

After marriage the husband gets the right over his wife. He has purchased her according to the customs and sanctions of the society. But it does not, however, confer on him the right to do with the wife whatever he may please. She is treated in the family and village in accordance with the sanctioned norms of the society. Despite the freedom accorded to her, she is by all means 'a possession' of her husband. If she runs away to her parents due to some maltreatment or for any other reason and decides to settle there, the husband may not permit her to do that. Either she is persuaded to return to her husband's house, or her father should pay back the amount of bride-price. Thus, if a woman decides to separate, the husband must be paid back the bride-price by the second man. Even if some other man cohibits with his wife, he demands the rent *bhada*.

During the minority of his son, the father may claim the *bhada* from the adulterer, but generally to prevent his adult daughter-in-law from failing a prey to an outsider with consequent economic loss to the family, he cohibits with her and this may continue even after his son has achieved adulthood. If the daughter-in-law objects to his sexual relations with her at any time, he can demand the bride-price from her father and release her. The son, however, cannot object to it as it cause no economic loss to the family.

The birth of a child as consequence of sexual relations with the father-in-law during the minority of her husband, ensures the daughter-in-laws remaining as a member of the family. The community, therefore, does not object to such relations even if the son, after attaining majority, raises his protests in the community council.

The function of bride-price among Bhil "serves as a compensation for the loss sustained in the giving up of the girl or a remuneration for the expenses incurred in her maintenance till the time of her marriage." It, however, does not give "a guarantee that the young wife will be well treated in her new house.

This is more or less the orthodox and Hinduised form of marriage, greater the degree of Hindu influence, the more would be the performance of the customary rituals and the greater would be the divergence from the truly tribal form. Hinduised tribal castes which regard themselves higher in the social scale insist upon the presence of a Brahmin priest to conduct their ceremonies. This type of marriage cost anywhere between Rs. 1000-5000 now a days. This, looking to the economic condition of the tribe, is an exhorbitant sum. The poorer and more humbler people take recourse to other forms of marriage.

2. Lugda Ladi (Economical and abbreviated form of marriage)

This is a more economical form of marriage as compared to *Lagan Mandwa.* The bride price is settled as in the orthodox form and on auspicious day the bride price is given to the bride's father. On a suitable day the boy's father takes the wedding party consisting of not more than five persons to the bride's place. The bride is presented with a new set of *lugra* (clothes) then the marriage is over. After a day or two the party return with the bride.

3. ***Aa bharana or Uchal Jana*** (Marriage by intrusion)

It is also called as *Uchal.* This type of marriage occurs when the girl takes a liking to a boy and enters the boy's house by the back door and silently started doing the household work. Generally this happens with the full consent and knowledge of the boy. After the girl has forced her entry, the boy's father informs the girl's father of the incident and invites him to talk over the terms of settlement of bride-price, etc. The bride's father accompanied by the *patel* and *panchs* of his village come to the boy's father for the talks. This is known as *Jhagra todna* or settling the dispute. The bride-price is settled and duly paid.

4. ***Bhaga kar le Jana*** (Marriage by elopment)

Elopement is one of the most publicized forms of acquiring a wife among the Bhils. There are number of opportunities which enable boys and girls of marriageable age to meet and share some of the pleasantry of life. It is common for Bhil boys and girls to rub their shoulders in fairs and weekly markets. The tribe is not wanting in fairs and festivals. These informal and off-meetings provide opportunities for love making. And Bhil girl is never annoyed when advancement made by the boy. There are chances when the boy runs away with the girl for the intention of marrying her. The usual time for the elopement of girl is on the *Bhagoria* festival, the day before the Holi pyre is burned.

In such cases the marriage takes place and the matter is reported to the *Bhanjgarhias* of the villages of the bride and the bridegroom. The *Bhanjgarhias* give recognition to this marriage and ask the groom's party to pay the amount of bride price. On payment of bride-price the dispute is settled and couple allow to lead normal life.

5. **Ghis kar le Jana** (Marriage by abduction)

Under this form of marriage the girl is forceably abducted by the young man with the assistance of friends for marriage. However, after this kind of marriage also the groom and his parents are obliged to pay the amount of bride-price determined by the *Bhanjgarhias.* In the Bhil marriages, the amount of bride-price assumes a central place for the recognition of any marriage. On the payment of bride-price the dispute is settled. Occasionally a simple marriage ceremony is performed.

6. **Ghar Jamai** (Matrilocal Marriage)

This is a very characteristic and economically significant form of marriage. When a boy is too poor to be able to pay the bride-price, he agrees to work for a stipulated number of years at the bride's place. The usual term is 7 to 9 years. It is commonest where the girl has no brother to assist the father at his work. Under this type of marriage, the man goes to stay in the in-law's house and during the course of apprenticeship they live like husband and wife and the children born during this period are considered legitimate. During the period, the boy works on the farm and does all other work which is required for him.

The term of his service and other relevant conditions are decided in the presence of village headman. The agreement is recorded on paper and preserved by both the parties. Usually when the man has worked sincerely as he passed a few years in the family, the girl is married to him. But still he has to continue the terms of services. Generally, after the expiry of the term the boy sets up his own independent household, not far from that of his father-in-law. Sometimes, if the girl's father has no son, the man lives there permanently and succeeds the family head in course of time. In few cases it is reported that the *Ghar Jamai* escapes with his wife after 2-3 years. In this case, the bride's father claims *dapa* to the groom's father.

Ordinarily, the two live amicably but after two years have no issue, the father-in-law has them anointed as if for a regular wedding and they are made to do seven 'Phera' as in ordinary marriages. The father-in-law provides the young couple with means to start their own home.

This form of acquiring a wife is a substitute for bride-price and such families are looked down by the tribe. The following witty proverb is given about a *Ghar Jamai*:

> "Son-in-law in a distance part, like flowers sweets, is deer to heart but should he come to stay in town, half his worth is at once down! And, god forbid! That his own spouse should lodge him in her father's house! A beast of burden, loaded at will: To this sad lot, he has condemned still!"

Remarriage of Widow

The remarriage of widows is permitted by the Bhil society and is solemnised without the usual pumps and show. There is, on the contrary, a proverb which says that it is better for the widow, especially if she is young, to find a new protector.

Zawan istri ne satar zoiye

(To the young women the safefuard should be)

A Bhil widow may marry after the completion of the mourning period. The marriage with the deceased's younger brother is permitted. It is called *Dewar Vatta*. As soon as the mourning period is finished, the family puts the proposal of the marriage of the deceased's wife with one of his brothers before the village elders. There is no question of the payment of any fresh bride-price as the woman has already been purchased by the family. She is only offered clothes consisting of a sari, petticoat and a bodice. She wears the dress and a red mark is put over her forehead by some old women of the village. A feast, in which liquor and meat are served, is offered to the village people.

In case the deceased husband has no brother the widow is married to someone else. As soon as the marriage consent of the lady is known the suiter alongwith four or five friends goes to her village with some clothes as presents. He pays some paise to the widow's elder brother's wife (*bhabhi*) or to her paternal aunt (*phuwa*), provided they have husbands living. A general drink is indulged in, in which the *Tadvi* of the widow's village takes part and the ceremony is complete.

The remarriage is always performed in the night as they believe that if the married widow enters her new house in the day, the famine will come. Any person who accompanied with man marrying a widow is bound to carry out this duty seven times.

The *dahej* (bride-price) payable by the man amounts to about Rs. 22 and other expenses coming to about Rs. 20 more. The widow's father has no expenses. This *dahej* is paid on the day when the ceremony takes place.

In case of widow married in another sept, a payment called *dewar bhatta* has to be made to the widow's late husband's relations. It amounts to about Rs. 5/-, a bullock being also given if means permit. The widow, and children by the remarriage have no interest in the property of the first husband after re-marriage.

In case when she marries her deceased husband's younger brother, should there be already a son by the first husband, children by the second have no right in the property of the first husband. If, on the other hand, there was no child by the first husband, children of the second inherit the property of the first husband.

According to Doshi, the Bhils of village Bansla, Banswara (Rajasthan) have actually launched a movement against the practice of *dewar bhatta*. They consider it the lowest form of marriage because of their conversion of Bhagatism. They consider elder's brother's wife as mother and she should be considered sacrosanct when after the death of her husband. The avoidence of *dewar bhatta* seems to be due to the impingement of the social forces current amongst the Hindu village. Even the lower castes abhor this practice.[5]

As per the present Bhil's social set up, widow remarriage seems to be absolute necessary for a woman in the home. The women, if young at the time of widowhood, would herself like to have a man for her sexual satisfaction. The usual form of marriage requires greater expenses and so the poorer families would like to have a wife brought in through widow marriage which means lesser expenses. A woman, if alone, would like to have a man to plough her field and so would marry another man, who would stay with her and help her in agriculture.

Divorce

There are few rites related to divorce which is known as *Chhuta Chheta* meaning dissolution of marriage. Among the Bhils the right of divorce lies both with the husband and wife. If the husband seeks divorce he can do it any time he likes, only with the loss of the bride-price he paid.

To effect a divorce the injured man calls together his village panchayat and in their presence tears off a piece from the end of his *pagri* which he hands to his wife, stating that finding that her conduct was bad he is divorcing her and that from this day forth she will stand to him in the relationship of a sister. A divorce takes the piece of cloth and hangs it carefully on a rafter of her father's house for a whole month or sometimes for a half month. It shows that her former husband has no further rights over her and she can re-marry. In case of remarriage no fees are payable to the former husbands but her father receives fees similar to those paid on a widow's remarriage.

But if the wife wants to part with, the husband has to be paid bride-price which he gave to her parents and marriage expenses. The negotiated part of the bride-price is determined by the village elders. This amount is paid by the second prospective husband, which is also known as *jhagda* money.

Pre-wedding Ceremony

The Wane Days

The general meaning of *wane baharwun* is to make a person sit down in festive attire in an appointed place. When speaking of the bridegroom the form used is *Wane baharwo*, of the bride *Wane baharwi*. The appointed place is with his or her face to the wall, the manner in which the village headman causes the bridegroom (or the bride) to be seated. From the first *Wane* day on the bride wears her hair hanging down.

As a rule the bridegroom begins the *Wane* period one day earlier than the bride because at the end, just before the wedding, he must occupy himself with other things such as the *notran parawan* rite and moving to the bride's house on the eve of the wedding. This evening of the last *Wane* is also known as *Wane* evening, *Mehandi-Wano*.

Kola Sitrwa

On the first of the *Wane* days the village headman begins to draw certain pre determined figures on the *Bharari* wall, that is the inside wall nearest to the sleeping quarters. Two colours are used: *haldi* yellow and rice-meal white. An exception is made for the human and animal figures, the *terhul* (trident) and the small circles used in two parts of the design; the latter are partly drawn in single outline, partly filled in colour. On the first day the headman begins by painting the upper *terhul* with its surrounding circles. These are drawn in outline and only one is filled in. On each succeeding day another filled-in circle is added, so that on the eve of the wedding as many filled-in circles are visible as there have been *Wane* days. From the second day on it is the bride-maid who see to it that the necessary circle is daily added. The bride-groom's brother or a certain uncle (the husband of the father's sister) fills in the rest of the design. The figures in the upper right and left hand corners represent peacocks. At the bottom of the drawing we see the bride and bridegroom, she with two water pitchers on her head, he proudly flourshing his sword. In the centre of the design we find a second *terhul* with representations of the sun and moon on either side.

The decoration of the outer walls of the house with *sarklan* (sparrows) is in the meanwhile carried out by the bride's own sister and by a sister of her father. The sparrows are regarded as lucky omens. They are produced by dipping a closed first in the yellow wash and hanging it against the wall like a hammer. The two artists receive a quarter of a rupee for their paints.

As soon as the village headman has painted the *terhul* (trident) on the wall he imprints a *tilak* on the bride or the bridegroom respectively. Then he says: "Lift white sesame seed over the bride (or the bridegroom respectively)!" Three or five girls and three or five boys holding some of the oily grains in the palms of their right hands then with one accord make a vibratory motion over the bride (or the bridegroom) sitting in their midst and as many upward movements are made as there are to be *wane* days.

Filling the Ghan

A certain quantity of some corn (usually rice), sufficient to fill up the pounding hole, has been set aside. The friends gathered round the bride (or bridegroom) then seize a ceremonial winnowing fan (*huprun*) specially coloured for the occasion and decorated with the leaves of the mango or peepal tree and begin to move in a circle round the sitting bride (or bridegroom). It is the duty of the master of house or his representative to keep filling the *huprun* with fresh rice which is scattered over the bridal candidate by those moving round. When the quantity set aside is exhausted, a few of the bystanders seize a rice-pounder and move round in a circle thumping the ground.

During the subsequent ceremonial washings with water as well as with *haldi* it is the bride's or bridegroom's sister who plays the role of bather, some of the maids-in waiting helping her. The bridegroom is washed and anointed three times daily.

After the washing two of the bride's maids stand opposite each other and lay their hands on each other's shoulders. The bride is then lifted on to the solid seat formed by their arms and carried in triumph through the house.

The final leading forth (*wane kadwun*) of the bride (or bridegroom respectively) from her (or his) house is effected in much the same way, the bride being carried on the shoulders of her sister's husband or of the husband of her father's sister. In the absence of these relatives a brother of the bride's or bridegroom's or even a brother of the gril's mother can act as carrier. Two men improvise a sort of canopy by fixing a cloth to four sticks and holding it over the bride (*asar tanwan*). During all these ceremonies the sister of the bride or of the bridegroom carries in her hand a little burning oil lamp.

It is especially during these processions that the bride carries in her hand the arrow with the *haldi* knots while the bridegroom bears the sword on his shoulder.

The last of the *Wane* days (*Sela wana no dan*) is called *mehandi* day because on the evening of this day, towards eight or nine o'clock the ceremony of *mehandi dewi,* the painting with *mehandi,* takes place.

Proper Wedding Ceremony

The last *Wane* days forms the transition to the wedding proper which include the subsequent ceremonies, comprises more than fifty separate rites. They take place partly at the bridegroom's house and partly at the bride's. Some are repeated, or may be repeated, in as much as the same rite is carried out in both places. Owing to these circumstances it is practically impossible to fix the time limit accurately. However, no time limit is fixed for performing any rite.

The invitation formula shows that the Bhil considers certain rites especially important and therefore of particular interest. Specific mention is made of the *Wane* days, the *Mameran* and *Notran* day and the wedding, in connection with which the *phera* or processional permutation round the ritual pole is regarded as the decisive rite.

1. *Mandwo Ropwo* (Putting up the Marriage mandap)

A special marriage booth is always set up close to the bridegroom's house and sometimes a second near that of the bride. Normally one booth is made in the bride's house and one in the bridegroom's. The brother-in-law, the uncle (the father's brother) and the musicians have to make all the necessary arrangements. The booths are built of the soft, easily fashioned wood of the *salar,* called *helero* in Bhili and also known as the incense tree. Its bark has a characteristically bluish tint when the trees are old. This wood is not used for building ordinary houses as it has no power of resistence and easily falls a prey to the ravages of the white ant.

Four stakes driven into the ground from the corners of the approximately square ground plan. The sides measured from ten to fourteen feet. While the height of the stakes is about six or seven feet. The ends of the stakes from a fork so that horizontal beams can conveniently be laid along the two opposite sides of the square. Five, seven or nine poles are then placed transversely over these beams, forming a support for the roof of green bamboos or other branches, which serves as protection against the sun.

Finally garlands of mango leaves are hung all round the edge of the flat roof.

2. *Bori Ropwi* (Setting up the Ritual Pole)

A necessary feature of every marriage booth is a wooden pole, about a foot and a half long and four to six inches in diameter. It is fixed in the ground on one side of the hut, halfway between the corner stakes and exactly under the edge of the roof, and is framed by four pieces of wood with their ends lying crosswise one over the other. It is possible that some symbolic representation of *lings* and *yoni* is intended. Even when no booth is erected at the bride's house, there will be a ritual pole.

3. *Sitran Rangwan* (Dyeing the Nuptial Garments)

When the marriage booths have been erected the village headman, the bridegroom's brother-in-law and his uncle (i.e. the husband of his father's sister) proceed to dye the garments of the young couple by dipping them in turmeric wash or by sprinkling them with this substance. The bridal veil is given a coloured border by dipping the finger in turmeric and then passing it along the four edges. The brest-cloth, from which the red trimming has first been removed, is dipped in the dye. The same is done to the two ends of the bridegroom's long turban scarf and his so called *uphanivun* cloth. The latter plays a role in all the ceremonies in which bride and bridegroom are bound together, one end being knotted with an end of the bride's veil.

4. *Gotriro Bharwo* (Taking another's place)

For a short time the bridegroom's brother takes his place in order to see to the drawing of the water and filling of the brass vessel which is to be placed upon a jar filled with *daru* (wine). When in this position the brass vessel is called *kaleh* and it marks the spot where the *mameran* ceremony is later to take place.

5. *Mameran Odwan* (Presents of Clothes and Jewellery)

This ceremony takes place at the bride's house on the day when the wedding procession is due to arrive in the evening; and at the bridegroom's on the day before. It takes its name from the word *mamo* which is primarily used to designate an uncle on the mother's side. But the same name also includes the brother-in-law (the sister's husband), the 'son-in-law' (the younger sister's husband), the father's sister's husband (i.e. an uncle on the father's side), as also all the friends and acquaintances who choose to take part in the rite, which is optional for them but obligatory for the above mentioned relatives.

The recipients of the presents are the parents, the uncle on the father's side, the bride's brothers (or the bridegroom's brothers) and their wives.

The donors are the blood relations of the wives of the above named persons, for instance the male relatives of the paternal uncles wives. For this reason the expression 'wives' kinsfolk (Bhili : *piyor,* Hindi : *piyar*) is also used in this connection to designate the fellow villagers and fellow clansmen of the women in question. It is therefore clear that the givers of the presents belong to various clans, while the receivers are all members of one and the same clan.

The fact that the mother of the bride (or bridegroom respectively) is not, or at least was not originally a member of the clan may perhaps explain why it is her brother who in this capacity of maternal uncle, is expected to furnish gifts and why it is from him, the *mamo,* that the whole ceremony could seem to have received its name of *mameran*. If the mother's father is still aliving, he is expected to give the most valuable contribution.

The bride and bridegroom receive nothing, their wedding day being regarded as a suitable occasion for presenting the gifts to their relatives.

The gifts consist of chiefly the articles of wearing apparel. Each of the men receives one article for himself, usually a turban, and one for his wife usually a veil.

In all these transactions, however, there is no question of giving in the strict sense of the word, for the "gifts" are all returned to the donors as soon as the circumstances are reversed and the latter have a wedding in their house. It is really only a matter of lending or depositing the articles; there is no genuine transfer of goods, and the whole business plays no role in the economic but only in the social and family life of the tribe.

The community could scarecely find a more impressive way of stressing the importance which it attaches to the foundation of a new family than by arranging for so many people actively to participate in the happy festive mood of the bride and bridegroom's families, and this not merely with fine words but also with genial actions. Although the goods have sooner or later to be returned there remains the valuable temporary material assistance and there is morever the constantly repeated act of giving which demands at least momentary sympathy and sacrifice on the one hand, while calling forth corresponding feelings of pleasure and gratitude on the other.

It is already mentioned that the *mameran* ceremony takes its name from *mamo,* the term used for a maternal uncle. In this connection it is pertinent to point out that at all the times it is considered the special duty of this relative to shower every sort of kindness on his *bhanez* i.e. his niece or nephew and on their families, if they happen to be already married. *Mamo* performs duties with all their means. He generally presents a cattle head to the *bhanez* during this ceremony. The Bhils have superstitious belief on it. They believe that the presentation of a cattle head to the *bhanez* during that period may lead him to the salvation.

It is interesting to note that the *mamo* has given his name to one of the fingers of the hand; the middle finger is known as *mami ni* or the *mamo's* finger. For it is one of the *mamo's* essential duties to give his nephew a silver ring for this finger. There should be a fine chain attached to the ring and this is passed down the outside or inside of the hand and fastened round the wrist, but a simpler ring without a chain will also be gratefully accepted. In general the young men have no ornament at all on their *mamo* finger; being poor like most Bhil, their good uncles, are simply unable to perform all that is expected of the ideal *mamo.*

6. *Notran Parawan* (Making the Guests' Money Fall)

We have already seen that the *gotriro bharwo* ceremony leads up to *mameran* and *notran parawan.* At *mameran* of clothes are returned and at *notran parawan* the same proceeding is applied to money. On this occasion the bridegroom's father recovers all the money which he has under similar circumstances temporarily made available for others. The sums vary; if he has given a man ten rupees, he will now get those ten rupees back. Actually this custom concerns only the bridegroom's father; it does not apply to the bride's father unless he has no unmarried son and consequently no other possibility of recovering the sums he has deposited, in which case he can make his daughter's marriage the occasion for doing so.

Considering the conditions under which the Bhil live, it is evident that *notran parawan* is often of great practical importance to them. It helps the bridegroom's father to defray the considerable expenses of his son's wedding. He has as it were deposited at the bank a part at least of the funds he requires for the occasion and can now lay hands on this sum just when he needs it.

7. *Khunt Mandwo* (Preparing the Place for the Daru)

The rite, *Khunt Mandwo,* is repeated several times in the course of the marraige festivities. This rite is performed same as the sprikling and drinking of the *daru* in betrothal rite. Here quantity is the most essential feature as regards *daru* (wine) at a wedding; the spirits are therefore copiously watered. The Bhil call this drink "married" *daru,* whereas the pure unmixed spirits are considered as "virginal". In some region of Central India, the rite which is continued for several decades has been completely stopped as a impact of Bhagat movement.

8. *Ukeri Dantwi* (Closing the Dung-heap)

The ceremony is carried out at both the bride's and bridegroom's house. It consists in burying in the manure heap of dry cow-dung a small open basket about three inches high and five to six inches in diameter. The bridegroom is assisted in this task by his father's sister's husband, his own elder sister's husband and occasionally the village headman. The corresponding relatives also help the bride. A bit of arrow shaft, about twenty inches long, is stuck through the basket and the part inside the basket is wrapped in a piece of white cloth containing a paisa and some raw sugar (gur). After the basket has been buried, the dung is smoothed down, the women actually dancing over it, so that the exact spot can scarcely be distinguished. This dunghill ceremony takes place some time before the *phera* shortly after which there is another ceremony in the course of which the basket is unearthed. This will be described in the chronological order in which it takes place.

9. *Khawun, Piwun* (Eating, Drinking)

The method of procedure is exactly the same as the sprinkling and drinking of *daru* in betrothal rite.

10. *Or Uglawo* (Getting the Bridegroom Ready)

Under this rite the bridegroom is prepared with the assistance of his friends for the procession to the bride's house and village. After washing and taking a bath, he puts on the wedding clothes and ornaments. Black circles are painted round his eyes with greasy soot (*Kazal harwi*).

11. *Mahat* (Sucking raw sugar from the Mother's Breast)

Dressing in full state the bridegroom leaves his parents' house and goes to the wicker gate where his mother is waiting for him and where for the last time she offers him her breast from which he sucks some little pieces of raw sugar (*gur*) previously affixed for this purpose. Then his mother kisses him on the cheek and goes away, taking care not to look at her again until he returns with his wife. If his mother is no longer alive, his elder brother's wife takes her place on this occasion. There is something of the maternal in this women's relation to her younger brother-in-law for, even were her husband to die, he can under no circumstances marry her.[6] Amongst the Kalia Bhils this rite is known as "Boba dena" or giving the breast. It is somewhat different to "Mahat." Just before the bridegroom starts for the bride's house for marriage, his mother has to give her breast to him, and the son sucks his mother's breast in the presence of all assembled relatives and tribes. In the absence of the mother, either the step-mother, if any, or the elder sister or the elder brother's wife or the uncle's wife enjoys the privilege. In the case of particularly of non-tribe castes, it is reported that it not unoften falls to the lot of a young girl to suckle a grey-haired bridegroom about to marry for the fourth or fifth time.

The Kalia Bhils believe that if this ceremony is omitted death or other calamity will overtake the bridegroom. The custom is ordinarily explained as the last suck indicating the termination of the dependence of the son upon his mother. It would perhaps appear more reasonable to regard it as intended to emphasize the inalienability of the natural tie between mother and son.[7]

12. *Kankar* (Village Boundary)

When the bridegroom and his followers reach the village boundary, the procession halts and *daru* (wine) is passed round. Then the crowd splits up, some returning home while others remain with the bridegroom.

13. (a) *Wizano dholwo* (Waving Fans)

On his way to the bride's village, the bridegroom must be fanned so that he does not suffer too much from the heat in the wedding clothes and so that no one can cast an evil upon him.

(b) *Kaleh Khakrawi* (Water-pitcher Noise-making)

In order to drive away all evil spirits those accompanying the bridegroom also shake a brass vessel with little stones in it so as to make a great deal of noise.

14. *Lada no Hantro* (The Bridegroom's Place of Encampment)

On arrival at the bride's village a halt is called in the neighbourhood of her father's house. The proceedings are the same as those described in connection with the final betrothal.

15. *Sukowani* (Paying out the Money)

A repetition of this rite takes place by agreement or as convenience may dictate. A further respite for payment of the remainder may still be granted.

16. *Hidun* (Food for a feast, including Goat's Meat)

The preparations for an appropriate meal (this time to be given in the vicinity of the bride's house) must be made in the usual way.

17. a) *Sitran Wadawan* (Applying the sign of the Tilak to Clothes and Ornaments for the Bride)

Some of the bridegroom's blood or clan brothers, walk up to the wicker gate of the bride's house carrying clothes and ornaments destined for her. They are met at the gate by the bride's sister. In her left hand she carries a brass plate with *haldi*(turmeric) paste. On a leaf placed on the plate there is also a little red *kanku* and a small earthenware vessel with oil in which a light burns. The girl dips the thumb of her right hand in the *haldi* paste and dabs some of it on each garment and ornament. Then she dips her thumb in the red *kanku* and marks the forehead of each bearer of presents with the sign of the *tilak*. When this is done she receives all the gifts and takes them into the bride's house.

b) *Sitran Perawan* (Putting on Clothes and Ornaments for the Bride)

The "maids in waiting" assist in putting the clothes and ornament brought for the bride.

18. *Zan Mandwe* (Wedding party goes to Marriage Booth)

If no wedding booth has been erected near the bride's house, this ceremony takes place at some other place in the vicinity. It consists in confronting the bride's and the bridegroom's parties, who now meet each other in full ceremonial attire and more or less challenge each other. There is much gesticulating and talking, both sides crying out : "Who will win?" "Who will lose?" Each party tries to outbid the other and their screaming drowns every effort at singing. Altogether a somewhat stormy meeting, in the course of which the latent and open antagonism between the two parties breaks through in very characteristic fashion.

19. *Or Ghoro* (The bridegroom on Horseback)

The bridegroom's sister's husband (Bhili: *benowi*) now takes the young man on his shoulders and carries him to within a short distance of the bride's house; he is then relieved by the husband of the bride's sister who carries the bridegroom to the marriage booth or in the absence of such a booth, to the wicker gate, which is decorated with garlands of mango leaves.

20. *Hala Katari* (The "Dagger" of the Bride's Younger Brother)

As soon as the youth gets down from his "horse" the bride's younger brother stands with both his feet on the bridegroom's feet, refusing to liberate him until he receives some amount of money due to him.

21. *Toran Sibwun* (Touching the Garland)

The bridegroom then touches the garland with his sword and the *Kotwal* is given half of the money received by the younger brother of the bride-groom during Hala Katari.

22. *Or Phunkwo* (Sprinkling the Bridegroom)

The bridegroom's mother-in-law now approaches holding in her left hand a brass plate on which there is a little oil-lamp burning and some *haldi* paste. In the fold of her dress she has a good handful of unhusked rice and she is wearing her special *uphaniyun* scarf round her neck.

Standing before the bridegroom she first waves the brass plate over his head; then she marks him with the *tilak* and hands the brass plate to one of the women standing near.

After this she puts her *uphaniyun* scarf round her son-in-law's neck; then seizing the two ends of the scarf and stepping back she pulls him forward three times. Taking some of the rice out of the folds of her dress, she proceeds to throw it at the bridegroom's head-dress, after which she pulls him forward once more. In all she repeats the pulling and throwing seven times. By then both are supposed to have reached the outer pillars of the house (*newan*).

23. *Kahar Khawarwi* (Ceremony at Bride's Sleeping Place)

Two or three men, together with the bride's waiting women now lead the bridegroom into the house and up to the bride's sleeping-place, where she is waiting him. He must sit down beside her, whereupon a large shawl is thrown over both of them by the husband of the bride's sister or the husband of her father's sister. While muffled in this cloth the bride and groom are given some *gur* (raw sugar) mixed with wheaten meal to eat. This sweet food is intended to symbolize the delights and joys of married intercourse.

24. *Sera Seri Gathalwa* (Tieing together "Man servant" and "Maid")

One end of the bride's veil is now knotted together with the bridegrooms *uphaniyun* cloth. As long as the young couple are tied together no one must come between them and especially no woman; for she might cut off a piece of the veil, take it away with her and swallow it, a proceeding by which the bride could be bewitched and deprived of progeny.

25. *Phera Parwa* (Making the Rounds)

Tied together, the bride and groom, accompanied by all the wedding party, march to the marriage booth, or, if there is no booth, to the place where the ritual log or pole has been set up. It is here that the decisive ceremony of marching round the pole is performed. The bride weeps aloud, being obliged to show how hard she finds the parting. The duty of supporting the weeping bride on her way to the ceremonial pole and during the perambulation round it, falls to the husband of her elder sister, who receives ten paisas for this charitable action. The young couple walk round the pole seven times (in the opposite direction to the hands of a clock); for the first four rounds the bridegroom leads, for the last three the bride.

26. *Ukeri Kholwi* (Opening the Dung-heap)

The young couple, accompanied by those who helped to bury the basket, now betake themselves to the dung-heap, where both bride and groom try to locate the basket, the one who first finds it being supposed to play the chief role in their married life. The girl is allowed to use both hands, the youth only one. The assistants are entitled to a certain amount of *daru* (wine) and to a ball of cooked rice each. The same rite is repeated at the bridegroom's house the day after.

27. *Lado no datun Kaglo* (The Bridegroom's Mouth-rinsing and Tooth-cleaning)

The husband of the bride's and bridegroom's sisters now offer their new brother and sister-in-law little sticks with which to clean their teeth and water with which to rinse their mouths and free their hands from *mehandi* ink.

The ceremony is followed by *daru* (wine) drinking. The husband of the bride's sister in particular, is supposed to offer a bottle to the husband of the bridegroom's sister. The village headman, the more important people present and the bringer of the bottle, however, also join in the drinking.

28. *Sak Walwi* (Turning the 'Potter's Wheel')

This rite may be carried out now or earlier, when the money

is paid out. There are two ways in which the *daru* can be drunk (to serve this ceremonial purpose). The first consists in one of the two drinkers holding his hands over those of the other, and this is the way that the bride's brother (by blood by clan adoption) drinks with the groom's brother (by blood or by clan adoption). The two sit opposite each other and each puts his hands together so as to form a shell shaped hollow, the bride's brother holding his underneath. The village headman then pours *daru* into the hollow made by the hands of the bridegroom's brother, who lets the spirit trickle through his fingers into the hands of the person sitting opposite, who immediately proceeds to drink it. This gesture is repeated three times, then the roles are exchanged and seven times in succession the bridegroom's brother holds his hands underneath and drinks the *daru* as it trickles into them. After this it is again his opposite's turn to drink four times. When it comes to the seventh potation, the bridegroom's brother lets a rupee glide into his partner's hands together with the *daru*. Then only are both free to open their hands; had one of them done so earlier he would have been liable to a fine of a rupee and a quarter.

The second method of *daru* drinking allows of each partner tasting the *daru* for himself. The same order is, however, adhered to and the last potation must under all circumstances be drunk out of the hollow of the hand in the manner described above.

The ceremony has been called 'turning the potter's wheel' because of the circular sweep of the arm over the earth accompanying the libation which introduces each draft of *daru*.

29. *Bol Sirwa* (Looping off a Speech, Cutting Short Speech)

There follows a short harangue from the bride's go-between. It is addressed to the bridegroom in particular, upon whom it impresses the following points:

"From today on this human being belongs to you. Good! Give her (the bride) to drink of the water on this side or on the other side of the mountains. But do not beat her, neither with a green nor with a dry stick. And if she should die from the blows you give her , the sum of money (the bride-price paid by you or rather by your father for the girl) will be maintained but together with our enemity. But if on the other hand she dies of disease or snake-bite, we shall all come together to burn her."

30 *Ladi no Zaniwaho* (Wedding Party Goes to the Camping Ground)

The ceremonies we have been describing take place in the vicinity of the dung-heap. After their completion the young couple, still tied together, and accompanied by the youth's party and some of the girl's people, betake themselves to the camping ground, where they sit down on the grass.

31. *Ladi no Kholo Bharawo* (Filling the Bride's Lap)

The bridegroom's sister (sometimes his mother or even his father's sister) throws four coins, a bit of coconut and some uncoloured rice into the young wife's lap. The Bhil themselves recognize this as a fertility rite, intended to symbolize the wish that she may be blessed with many children and also that she may not enter her husband's house empty handed but bring her 'portion' with her.

32. *Ladi no Kholo Kadarwo* (Taking out of the Bride's Lap)

The bridegroom's younger brother has the special privilege of picking the bits of coconut out of his new sister-in-law's lap.

33. *Ladi no Pasi Walawi* (Bringing back the Bride)

After the knots binding together the young couple have been untied, her sister's husband takes the bride on his shoulders and carries her back to her parents' house.

34. *Matha Soti Karwi* (Making Hairplaits on the Head)

The bride's hair, which she has been wearing open ever since the first *Wane* day, is now replaited. The bride's sister helps with this.

35. *Thalien Zhelarwi* (Causing Dish to be Taken)

The bride's sister goes to the bridegroom, holding a plate with *haldi* (turmeric) paste and a burning lamp in one hand and a brass vessel filled with water in the other. When she is close to him she puts down the *haldi* (turmeric) plate and proceeds to wash his face, hands and feet, afterwards, covering these parts of the body with yellow *haldi* (turmeric) wash.

The bride's mother, assisted by other members of her party, now brings seven or eight dishes of specially good food and places them beside the young man, who then passes his father-in-law and the village headman two drinks of *daru* each. The headman, as usual, pours out a libation before drinking. Then he and the father-in-law hand the bridegroom two "tastes." The food is emptied into a basket and some money laid on the dishes in its place, usually four coins on the mother-in-law's dish, and one or two coins one each of the other.

36. *Khawun, Piwun* (Eating, Drinking)

The youth's sister now brings a dish of food for her hungry brother. It consists of heavy balls made of wheat meal, *ghee* and *gur,* which have been prepared at his own home the day before and brought to the bride's house. The youth may eat of these only and is not offered any of the other good things. The reason for this is to be found in the fact that he will return again in eight or ten days in order to fetch his young wife home and will then enjoy a feast specially prepared for him.

While eating his sweet dumpings, the young man is covered with a cloth, which his brother-in-law has thrown over him. He must not, or does not wish to be observed at his meal. We are told that on the one hand he is ashamed before all the lookers-on (for he must eat first, all by himself, sitting among his wife's waiting-women, who might feel inclined to mock him) and on the other hand fears the effect of the evil eye.

When the bridegroom has finished, all the others begin to eat and drink.

37. *Ladi no Dharmeno* (Loving Gifts for the Bride)

After the feast, before the young couple with their train of followers start off for the youth's home and village, the bride's go-between speaks the following words : "If anyone among you wishes to present the bride with a gift, let him name the gift." One of the more usual presents is a head of live-stock.

38. *Ladi Walawi* (Bringing Home the Bride to her husband's House)

The wedding party now sets out for the youth's home village. The young couple are again tied to each other. The girl's parents retire to their house, not wishing directly to witness the painful farewell, but the rest of the party all accompany the bridal pair to the outskirts of the village. There is singing as well as lamentation. When they reach the boundary, the bride and groom take off their head ornaments and the knot that joins them is untied. The bride's followers now turn back, with the exception of five or six men, near relatives, who join the party returning to the young husband's home.

39. *Baenun Rokwun* (Refusing the House Door)

When the bridal party reaches the boundary of the young man's village, the couple are again tied together and have their head ornaments put on. At the door of the bridegroom's house his sister awaits the couple, forbidding them to enter. The marriage agent calls the attention of the groom's father to this, saying : Your daughter will not allow the couple to enter, give her a present so that she may let them pass. The father then gives or promises her a present (usually a newly born or expected head of cattle or some smaller animal). When the couple have entered the house, the husband of the youth's sister or of his father's sister takes off their ceremonial head ornaments and unties the knot binding them together. The young man's father then offers a goat to those who have taken part in the bridal procession so that a good meal can be prepared and enjoyed.

40. *Wahedun Kadarwun* (Clearing out Manure)

On the morning after the wedding day it is the young wife's duty to clear the manure out of the stable with the help of some of her 'maids in waiting'. The dung is filled into baskets and carries out to the dungheap. Five to seven journeys are usually needed before the stable is clean.

41. *Ukeri Kholwi* (Opening the Dung-heap)

The procedure is the same as at the bride's house on the proceeding day. The bride and groom must have their ceremonial head ornaments put on and are once more tied together. Those who put on and take off the head ornaments for them are each time entitled to a brass cup full of *daru*. Should this be denied them, they would be in no hurry to help to take off the uncomfortable ornaments and would leave the young couple to feel hot and ridiculous.

On coming back from the dung-heap the young husband and wife are led to the sleeping place where they are relieved of their heavy head ornaments. The bridegroom is then supposed to wait on his guests himself, handing round common clay pipes as well as big water pipes and seeing that they function properly. The bride in the meantime cleans the stable unless she has seen to this earlier in the day, as is usually the case.

42. *Pani Bharwun* (Filling or Fetching Water)

The young wife goes with five, seven or nine of her 'maids-in-waiting' to the water source. She carries a new red pitcher on her head on top of which a second, brass vessel is placed. When the girls come back with their pitchers full, the helpers place theirs on the wooden shelves outside the house, designed for this purpose, while the bride, who has not yet been formally received into her husband's clan, puts hers down close to her own people, that is close to the guests. As a pad under the pitcher she uses her husband's folded *uphaniyun* cloth which has, as we have seen, repeatedly served to tie the young couple together.

43. *Kaleh arwu* (Bringing Water Vessel)

Before the bride puts down the brass vessel filled with water, her father-in-law (sometimes even the bridegroom himself) drops a rupee into it and this money is then the girl's personal property.

44. *Pani Waparwun* (Pouring out Water)

The youth takes from his bride the brass vessel full of water and gives two "tastes" to each of the people assembled; first to the village headman, then to his father and lastly to the guests. When the vessel is empty he takes out the rupee and places it on the plate which his sister holds before the bride. The latter then hands round water to all the women present. Sometimes, the bridegroom looks after the women as well as the men. The following two ceremonies are frequently inserted at this point or sometimes earlier or later. First or seven or nine children are given a good meal, as happens on other occasions also. This is called 'Feeding the Sparrows'. After the meal, some water is sprinkled over the children. This might possibly be connected with a fertility rite, for the Bhil are conversant with the prolific habits of sparrows, who breed four times a year.

The second rite consists in some prominent person taking a piece of cloth and forming it into the semblance of a human figure, the head, legs and arms being more or less recognizable. This 'child' is laid in the bride's lap and she passes it on to her husband. It often happens that some joker comes along and sprinkles the doll with yellow *haldi* (turmeric) paste. This evokes much mirth : the baby has soiled its clothes.

45. *Pogen Parawni (Malwun)* (Bowing down and embracing)

Sometimes bride and groom are tied together while the foregoing rite is performed, but this is not always the case. The following description is based on the assumption that they are not tied together. Both are, however, in full bridal attire.

A. The bridegroom first embraces the village headman and pays him his respects. This is done by bending forward and almost touching the ground with folded hands, then raising the body and placing the folded hands against the forehead of the slightly bent head. After saluting the headman he goes to his father and the other men. Then he turns to his mother and his nearer female relatives on both sides. The other women he embraces without bowing before them.

B. The bride must pay her respects to the same people. But her manner of greeting them is somewhat different. She remains standing in a respectful attitude at a certain distance from each one of them, bows deeply and scatters some husked, uncoloured rice over them. Then she sits down, takes one end of her veil in both hands and raises it three times, accompanying each lifting with a bow of the head. She does not stand up until the person to whom she has paid her respects has given or promised to give her some present. She is always accompanied by the bridegroom's sister who holds out the *haldi* (turmeric) plate, where among other things lies the rupee belonging to the bride to which other similar gifts can be added.

Gifts are expected also from the women present, beginning with the mother-in-law, who may, however, get out of the difficulty by offering a second time what has already given or promised by her husband. If the bridegroom is only son it is customary for the father-in-law to say : Look, here is the house with all that belongs to it. One day you are sure to inherit it all. Most of the other women lay an ornament, a bracelet or ring on the *haldi* plate.

46. *Khunt Mandwo* (Preparing the Place for the Daru)

This ceremony is repeated as discussed in step no. 7.

47. *Dhuniyen Melawiyen* (Bringing presents)

The brother of the bridegroom's father and the husbands of both his parents' sisters contribute money for *daru*. The brothers give fifty to seventyfive paise each and the sisters' husbands one rupee each. This *daru* is first distributed in 'samples', of which two each are given to the bridegroom's father, to the young man himself and to the village headman.

The village elders sometimes receive what are known as 'witness samples' of *daru*. Having taken these, they are regarded as official witnesses of 'the great event'. If this 'witness' distribution takes place, the *daru* used is not provided by the men. It is bought by a group who give it, 'in deposit' as it were, expecting that the corresponding amount be provided by the other side as soon as an occasion arises. The village elders are also regarded as witness of this arrangement.

48. *Hara ni Harti* (Distribution of *Daru*)

The distribution of the available quantity of *daru* is carried out in the usual order or precedence: first to the notables and then to the general relatives and friends.

49. *Ukeri na Ladwa (Bakala) ni Harta* (Distribution of 'dung-heap' Rice balls)

The rice that was strewn over the bridegroom during the *Wane* days is now cooked and part of it formed into balls, of which one is given to each 'maid-in-waiting', to the headman, to venerable elders, to some of the bride's followers, to the *dholi* (drummer) and the *rawal* (master of ceremonies). If any are left over they are distributed among the remaining guests. A general feasts follows.

Among those who have a claim to the rice balls are the persons who helped the bride and bridegroom to bury the basket. Their connection with this ceremony is evident from the name given to the balls.

50. *Ladi Ramarwi* (Making the Bride Dance)

50. *Ladi Ramarwi* (Making the Bride Dance)

When all have eaten and drunk, the women call upon the young wife to join in the dance. The manner in which she acquits herself depends on the extent to which she has by now got over her shyness. After the dance the young couple are brought back to the sleeping place inside the house.

51. *Ani or Olawa* (Sending back Companions with Bride)

The bride's dancing marks the end of the ceremonies at the brdegroom's house. Escorted by those of her own people who joined in the procession to the youth's house, the bride now returns to her own home where she is to spend some days before her husband comes to take her away finally. His mother gives the party provisions for the road (five to ten pounds of rice) which it is the duty of the bride's brother to carry. His father adds one rupee so that the party may not suffer thirst on the way.

52. *Mandwo Ohalwo* (Pulling down the Marriage Mandap)

About four to eight days after the wedding the young man comes to the bride's village to fetch her back. He greets his parents-in-law in the usual manner. Sometimes his mother-in-law, seize with respectful administration, forestalls him and falls at his feet. In this case he will return the compliment holding the end of his turban in both hands. The father, however, will never bow down before the son-in-law. Nor will the youth be asked to sit on the *palang*; he must sit lower than his elders, that is to say on the floor, as it customary. Sometimes he is offered a low stool.

53. *Mandwo Warhawo* (Showering of sweets on the Marriage Mandap)

The new son-in-law brings sweets for the children and a breast cloth for his wife's sister. He either gives the sweets to his father-in-law to distribute or else, taking with him his go-between and the children, he goes to the ritual where he throws the sweets into the air, and the children then catch them with cries of joy. It also happens that he simply deposits the sweets near the family sleeping place, as every knows for whom they are intended.

54. *Sori Ukherwi* (Pulling out the Tree-stump)

Importance is attached to this rite. The bridegroom must take hold of the pole with one or other hand and try to pull it up. If he fails to do so, he must pay a forfeit of one and a quarter rupees.

55. *Khawun, Piwun* (Eating, Drinking)

This meal is taken inside the house if there is sufficient space, the idea being that the guests should eat their fill in peace and comfort and also form a good opinion of the cleanliness and easy circumstances of their hosts. There is yet another reason; when the meal is over the women of the bride's party administer a sound thrashing to their male guests and the better to accomplish their purpose, they lock the door before beginning the attack. The bridegroom is spared and the bride and her mother take no active part in the performance. The thrashing is done with the fists but spoons and sticks can be used as well. The beating is primarily intended for the men who come with the young husband to fetch the bride and finally take her away. At the present day the proceeding has, of course, merely ceremonial significance, but it is highly probable that it was originally the expression of a real conflict between matriarchal and patriarchal principles of social structure. According to the matriarchal system the young couple would remain in the girl's home; the patriarchal system put an end to this; but the women continued to make at least a ceremonial protest, and a pretty violent one, as we have seen.

56. *Dharmenun Hinswun* (Designating Loving Gifts)

In the course of the meal mentioned in the *Khawun, Piwun* (sl. no. 55) the father-in-law repeats his offering or promise of a gift to his son-in-law.

57. *Salu* (Mouth-Rinsing)

The bridegroom is offered the largest and tastiest portions of food. As he would be ashamed to eat so much, he passes some of the tit-bits on to his neighbours. At the end of the meal his father-in-law brings him water in the usual manner. The young man lays a rupee on his plate before returning it. This money is intended for his mother-in-law. Finally the water for rinsing his mouth is also offered to him by his father-in-law.

58. *Ladi nun Anun Mokalwun* (Seeing off those who Take the Bride Home)

When they are standing before the house ready to set out, the guests say to the people of the bride's party : "Sit down!" and these answer: "We are sitting." Then the bride and bridegroom, together with the people who are to accompany them home, depart, the bride first embracing her mother and the other women. Very often these go her part of the way. In this case the farewell take place where her people halt and turn back. One of the women who accompany her carries the bride's bundle, in which her mother has packed her dowry. When the women turn back, the bridegroom takes this bundle and carries it for the rest of the way. Later the young wife will of course have to carry similar bundles and burdens herself.

59. *Lada no Mandwo Ohalawo* (Pulling down the Bridegroom's Marriage Booth)

This ceremony and that of pulling up the ritual pole are rarely carried out at the bride's house but always take place at the bridegroom's home some days after the return of the young couple, when a number of men of the girl's household come to fetch her back to her parents' house again for a couple of days. The bridegroom is allowed to use both hands for pulling down the booth, but here, as at the bride's house, the pole may be pulled out with one hand only. If the young man does not succeed in doing so he must pay the usual fine. The ceremony is followed by a good meal in the bridegroom's house. This time it is the bride's escort that gets thrashed by the women of her husband's house.

Wedding Songs

In the Bhil society, wedding is the most important event and it is performed with the involvement and assistance of village headman (*Tadvi*), villagers and relatives. Thus wedding songs are not only addressed to the bride and bridegroom but it is also related to *Tadvi* and all close relatives.

In the wedding songs the bridegroom is praised and made happy throughout the wedding celebration, but on the other hand, the bride is made to cry everywhere. Her maid reminds her of all the problems she will have to face in the house of her father-in-law. Her departure is the saddest event of her life; and the songs accompanying this event are most touching. Most of the wedding songs especially the one attended to taunt the opposite clan playfully, are very obscene, employing a language which has a very bad impact on the inflamble imagination of the growing children. There are too much repetition of this undesirable theme and the tunes of the marriage songs. The songs are sung by a choir of women.

The Bhil songs are available, more or less, for all steps of the wedding ceremonies. Due to sanskritization most of the traditional wedding songs have been disappeared from the tribal scene. The selected twenty nine songs are most popular and are sung in the various Bhils region of Central India which have been represented in the translated form.

1. Tadvi

"Tadvi, start the marriage festivities;
All the guests are waiting for you."
We have invited the Tadvi of the village.
Has he come or not ?
We have also invited the younger brother of the Tadvi.
Why, then, this delay in starting ?

2. Memories of the Relatives

On this side of the river, Revan, and on the other, Devan.
Between the two, the bride sits and reads a letter.
"Bride, your Mamas live in a far-off land.
Do you feel their absence ?"
"My Mamas live in a far-off land, their absence fills me with pain.
I shall write a letter and invite them immediately."
"Your sisters live in a far-off land; do you feel their absence ?"

"Bhabhi, I shall invite them, immediately, and they shall all come to my wedding."

"Bride, your Kakas live in a far-off land. Do you feel their absence ?

"Brother, my Kakas shall be invited immediately; they will all hasten to my wedding."

3. Gotriro Bharwo

O brother Newo, we came to your well to draw water.

We came bringing gold and silver vessels to fill.

The water splashed out while we filled and filled.

So we came again to draw water.

O brother Newo, we came to your well to fill our vessels
with water.

4. Mameran Ceremony

Our crazy kinsman came to the mameran ceremony.

He brought with him a mameran garment chewed to pieces by
a horse.

He sold a broom and brought mameran garment.

Away with, your rascal, or we shall kick you; kick you and
make you howl.

Had you brought silk you might have eaten goat's meat.

You have brought a beautiful veil with a design of red flowers.

Away with you, you rascal, or we shall give you a kick.

5. Notran Parawan

I set out to invite the garden bumble-bee.

O bumble-bee come quickly to take the invitations.

The garden humble-bee has invited the guests

(The messenger bumble-bee speaks) I set out and invited your (paternal) aunt's husband. O bridegroom give your uncle *mehandi* ink and come back quickly.

(The messenger bumble-bee) I went and called hither your sister's husband. (The bridegroom) O my brother-in-law, if you are ready to pick up (to cleanse) leaf plates, then come quickly.

(The messenger bumble-bee) I went and called hither your own sister. (The bridegroom) O my sister if you would like to smear on *haldi* then come quickly.

(The messenger humble-bee) I went and called hither the village headman. (The bridegroom) O headman, if you wish to have the ritual pole set up, come quickly.

6. Invitation

My house has long and short staircases and decorated doors.
Come, my brothers, and sit down; for I have spread silken
sheets for you.
Come, Mamas, and sit down; I have spread silken sheets for
you.
Or shall I prepare cots for you to sit on ?
Come, Mamis, I have spread silken sheets for you.
Come, Kakas, I have prepared cots for you,
And brought the hookah for you to smoke,
Come, all my Kakis, I have spread silken sheets for you.
I have cooked the finest rice;
I shall clean the plates.
Come, my Kakas, I shall offer you liquor,
And then serve the rice.

7. Bring me the Turmeric

The bridegroom is very happy, for today he is anointed with
turmeric.
Your father has bought the turmeric for your feet.
Apply the turmeric and let's be gay.
Your sister is applying the turmeric all over you.
The night of your jewellery fills you with joy.
Your father has bought for you the best ornaments- be happy!
Also, a silver girdle for your waist.
The ornament for your head is gift from your aunts.

8. The Wedding Courtyard

"Near the wedding seat, who is thumping the ground ?"
"I think the childless ones are dancing like peacocks."
"No, not the peacock, but my brother is dancing."
"Oh no, it is the girls, raped by my brother, who are dancing."
"No, not those awful girls, but it's my brother who are dancing."

9. Beware The Cawing of the Crows

As we go to the Bana's father-in-law's house,
The crows are cawing; and that is a bad omen.
Do not go thither.
If you must go, take some food along with you.
Take a band of strong cousins;
For in some way or other, they will harm you.
Do not eat food there, for fear of poison.
Take the swords and guns with you.
Do not sit on their cots, if they ask you to.
Do not drink their liquor;

For it will be poisoned.
Beware ! The first cup of liquor will be the bait,
The second will have the poison.
So, drink only the first;
And the second you slip into your sleeves at the elbows
Your father-in-law is a dangerous man.
Beware, beware of him !

10. Mahat

The parrot (i.e. bridegroom) is walking in the garden of sandalwood-trees,
Drink your mother's milk,
Take, o take the breast, handsome parrot.
Drink your aunt's (wife of Father's elder brother) milk,
Take, o take the breast, handsome parrot.
Drink your aunt's (wife of Father's younger brother) milk,
Take, o take the breast, handsome parrot.
Drink your sister-in-law's (wife of elder brother) milk,
Take, o take the breast, handsome parrot.
Drink your sister's (elder) milk,
Take, o take the breast, handsome parrot.

11. The Golden Crown

Bridegroom ! on your head rests
A golden crown;
You speak only in a subdued voice.
Your father is calling you.
You reply in a very low voice.
Your mother is calling you,
Your answer is so silent.

12. Hasten, Bridegroom !

Bridegroom, harness the horses, Why do you delay so ?
We are going to fetch the bride for you.
Bring your sisters to sing and dance there.
Bridegroom, call your uncles
And also your aunts.
We are going to fetch the bride for you;
Do not tarry any longer.

13. Tilak song

The queenly merchant's wife applies the tilak.
While he with the thick lips stands there,
While he with the round, fat belly and the thick lips stands there.
The queenly merchant's wife applies the tilak,
While he with the heavy paunch stands there,
The queenly merchant's wife applies the tilak."

14. The Bride Awaits

O bridegroom ! decked in all your finery
Why do you sit here all alone ?
Your bride, she awaits you there.
With silver belts you do sit here;
With wedding crown you do sit here;
With wedding gown you do sit here !

15. A Bottle of Liquor

Bridegroom, why did you not bring a bottle of liquor from
Baria town ?
All your sisters are displeased with you;
All your aunts are displeased with you.

Show me, Vevan, where is the pain ?
I shall brand it away.
Do not feel shy, show me.
Or shall I give you an injection ?
For an expensive injection helps a fast recovery.

16. Consolation

O bride ! let us celebrate the wedding !
How sad ! no one comes to your house.
Yes, your brother shall come
And make you sit on his shoulders.
Your Bhabhis shall come and sit by your side.
Your Banvis shall come
And make you sit on their shoulders.
Your aunties shall come and sit by your side.
Your Mamas shall come and make you sit on their shoulders,
and dance.
Your Mamis shall come and sit by your side.

17. Oh, for a wife

I have travelled from Delhi to Bhopal,
In search of a wife for me.
I have been as far as Limdi-Jhalod to the West,
Searching, searching in vain.
Many were the places I searched,
With gifts of handkerchiefs and rings,
To attract many a girl;
But my searching is all in vain.

18. The Widower Veval

When the widower comes for the wedding,
I shall place burning cow-dung cakes before him;
And behind him, an itching cactus fruit.
If he gives a handsome present of a hundred rupees,
He will be pronounced a great man;
And if he brings the money, we shall welcome him at the
front entrance.
If not, he shall enter at the rear,
Sit there, and be made to break open nuts and collect the
berries

19. The Eloping Bride

Why did you marry a girl who will elope ?
She is so young, that she is too impulsive.
Ah ! But it is better for her to marry so young,
For she earns for marriage even at her age.
"Father, I could stop a flooded river
In the twinkle of an eye;
But I cannot subdue the surging passion of my youth."

20. Wedding Ornaments

Bana your father has brought the ornaments for you;
Place them under the light of the earthen lamp.
Your father has brought a love-letter for you;
Read it by the light of the earthen lamp.
Your brother has brought a bangle for you;
Put it on by the light of the earthen lamp.
Your father has bought a silver belt for you;
Wear it by the light of the earthen lamp.
The wedding crown has arrived in the mango grove;
Crown your head by the light of the earthen lamp.

21. Think before you marry

It is easy to get married, O Bride.
But think a while about it;
Think before you invite the elders to your wedding.
It is easy to invite the matrons of the village;
But think of all the consequences of their coming.
Why did you invite the whole village for your wedding?
You will have a trying time to host such a crowd.
You have even consented to be married thinking about it.
You will be delivered to a stranger,
Who will fill you with sorrows,
And sadden your days.
It is easy to get married;
But sad days will be your lot !

22. The Bride's Lament- I

I cannot bear the conflicts and bickerings in my husband's house.
I can never forget my father's house.
I have no strength to bear the naggings of the Sasro,
I can never forget my mother's love.
I can never tolerate the burdens of my mother-in-law.
Dewar speaks so bitterly to me;
How can I bear that ?
My Jethani ever scoffs at me.
I have never suffered such indignities.
My brother's love and care is ever in my mind.
Father, I cannot bear the conflicts and bickerings in my husband's house.

23. The Bride's Lament- II

I cannot grind so much maize, o father !
There are too many people to feed in this house;
And too many cattle in the stable
For me to carry so much cowdung away.
My husband has sisters.
Who never lend a helping hand with the work.
There are so many children in this house,
I can't make chappatis for all of them.
I can't carry water for all the people,
Nor can I milk all the buffaloes, alone.
The ache in my fingers and hands is too great.
There are Jethanis in this house;
But they never lend a helping hand !

24. Bride's farewell song

My father, I am leaving you for a father-in-law.
My love for you has given way to something stronger.
My mother, I am leaving you for a father-in-law.
My love for you has given to something stronger.
My brother, I am leaving you for a father-in-law. You will find the corn that is to be ground lying on the grinding stone.

O sister-in-law, I am leaving you for a father-in-law. You will find on the hearth the earthen forms for baking the bread.

Bring your neck hoops, o sister-in-law. Help to free your missy from her prison-house.

Bring your silver bracelets, o my uncle (elder, on the father's side), and help to free your daughter from her prison-house.

O my uncle (younger, on the father's side) I am going to my father-in-law. There is manure lying on the ground in the stable.

O my uncle (on the mother's side) bring your ploughing oxen. Help to free your niece from her prison-house.

O my uncle (on the mother's side) bring your silver hip chain. Help to free your niece from her prison-house.

25. Bride's arrival at her future home

The daughter-in-law has come,

I have brought her with me.

The daughter-in-law has come.

She has brought water buffaloes with her.

O bride, send back your people who have come with you. I am ashamed to death.

No matter where I look, I see a one-eyed father-in-law.

If I look at the feet I see a crippled father-in-law.

If I look at the figure, I see a pot-bellied father-in-law.

26. Gifts to bride at her in-law's house

You may be sure, o bride, that your father-in-law will give you something,

He will give you a water buffalo cow, o bride.

You may be sure, o bride, that your mother-in-law will give you something,

She will give you a fine zebu cow.

Your brother-in-law (husband of your sister-in-law) will be sure to give you something,

He will give you a rupee, o bride.

Your sister-in-law (the wife of your husband's younger brother) will be sure to give you something,

She will give you a rupee, o bride.

27. New Life with in-Laws

O bride, you must leave the affection of your brother;
You must forsake the love of your sisters, too.
And accept the taunts of Jeth,
And the scoffings of your Nanands.
No more for you the soft love of your mother,
And the dear nearness of your father.
Your mother-in-law will dominate you.
In exchange for the fond love ot your Bhabhis,
You now have the stings of the Jethanis.
Poor bride, gone is your family forever!

28. Who will fetch me

(Return of the bride to her parents' house)

There came a marriage offer from Kushalgarh.
Who then am I, o bridegroom ?
I am the daughter of a herdsman.
Oh do not accept the proposal.
My father is a withered leaf.
My mother is a withered leaf.
My brother is a small child.
Who will come to fetch me back ?
My uncle will come and fetch me back.
The marriage offer came from afar.
I shall be on the lookout from the hilltop.
Memories of my father fill my heart as I climb the hill.
And memories of my mother keep crowding in.

29. When the Bridegroom was Young

When the bridegroom was young,
He used to play with heaps of dust.
When the bridegroom was young,

He used to go to graze the cattle.
Now then he is grown up,
He uses bow and arrows.
He has now interest in girls,
At times he makes love with the Vevans.

Notes and References

1. W. Koppers and L. Jungblut, "Betrothal Rites among the Bhil of North-Western Central India", *Artibus Asiae,* Volume IX, nos. 1-4, 1946, p. 6.
2. Stephen Fuchs,"The Marriage Rites of the Bhils in the Nimar District, C. P.",*Man in India,* Volume XXII, nos. 2 & 3, 1942, p. 109.
3. Ram Ahuja, "Marriage among the Bhils", *Man in India,* Volume 46, no. 3, Sept. 1966, pp. 233-234.
4. S. C. Roy, op. cit., p. 11.
5. S. L. Doshi, *op. cit.,* p. 133.
6. W. Koppers and L. Jungblut, "Wedding Rites among the Bhil of North-Western Central India," *Anthropos,* Volume 46, 1951, pp. 113-120.
7. S. C. Roy, op. cit., pp. 11-12.

8

Death Rites

For Bhils, sickness is a frequent occurence and a heavy burden. Often they are helpless when a disease strikes them. As the government health service rarely reaches their remote areas, they frequently suffer from diseases for which no proper treatment and no adequate medicines are available. Nor do the Bhils always seek for such, as they usually attribute the incidence of disease to the influence of offended deities or evil spirits. They believe, therefore, that the best way of curing a disease is the propitation of gods or spirits causing the illness.

However, the Bhils do not completely deny a natural cause for illness. That old people get sick and die is generally accepted as the natural course of human life and no evil spirits are blamed in such cases. And even in other cases of illness the Bhils first apply curative herbs and minerals as traditional remedies. Some Bhils are particularly successful in the treatment of sick domestic animals, though in their eyes even such animals are subject to the evil influences of spirits and godlings. If a human or animal patient does not respond quickly to such natural treatment, a supernatural cause is assumed for the illness and treatment by the expert diviner or Badwas.

The Bhils do not have specialists for the treatment of medicinal herbs. Every man and woman seem to know some medicines, though certain persons naturally are supposed to have a better knowkedge if natural remedies. Usually such knowledge is inherited from father to son, and from mother to daughter. But in general these two tribes soon resort to treatment by their diviners and Badwas or magicians. And there is no doubt that this type of treatment often achieves remarkable healing results.

Many medicinal herbs, roots and leaves are obtained from the forest. In every village certain persons can be found who have a good knowledge of such herbs. *Sarpagandha* (*Rauwolfia serpentina*), for instance, is a cure for high-blood pressure, *dhaval* (*Lobalia nicotinae folia*) is used in treating asthma and bronchitis. *Dhudi* bark and leaves (*Holarrhena antidysenterica*) cure dysentery. *Pangli* (*Pogostemon parvificrus*), its leaves and stems, and the root of *Jamrasi* (*Elaeodendron rotburghii*) are used in snake bite cases.

Rather drastic remedies take the form of burning the temples with red-hot iron for headaches or the stomach area when pain is felt in the stomach. This pain curing treatment is not useful among them as it overcome the pain by the pain of buring part and after subsiding the pain again it relapses. It is only a psychological treatment. It does not cure the patient.

The Bhils rarely take advantage of the medical facilities provided by government. They usually do not think of going to a hospital and rather die before they undergo an operation. They seem to have less reluctance to go to mission dispensaries and to visit doctors. Mobile dispensaries have made them familiar with modern medicines and proper adequate medical treatment.

The diseases most common among the Bhils are respiratory ailments, influenza, stomach complaints, fevers and epidemics such as small-pox, cholera etc.

In former time malaria has always been endemic in the Bhil tracts. Due to heavy rains in the hills and the many stagnant pools in the jungle malaria-infected mosquitoes were up to the recent times breeding everywhere in the adjoining forests. National Malaria Control Scheme has to a great extent control this disease but it has not been completely eradicated. Still malaria is prevalent in the inaccessiable areas.

Every year in the monsoon cases of 'gastroenteritis' show an abnormal increase. This also coincides with the increase of flies. Flies have frequently been shown to spread the dreaded disease. Since Bhils are ignorant of the role of flies as disease carriers they do not take any precautions against them.

In the *Sushrut Samhita,* it has been mentioned that cholera was present in India since very early times. As everywhere, cholera is an almost invariable concomitant of distress arising from want of food. Since 1817, epidemics of cholera have been recorded systematically by the British administration of India. The records also mentions that it has never been entirely absent for more than two or three years, at a time. The worst recorded year is 1891.

The disease is a frequent occurrence among the Bhils. Most probably it is spread by flies which carry the germs from one house to the other, or they are carried into the house from the garden where the Bhils defecate. The disease persists throughout the year, but cases increased in the hot and humid months of June and July.

The disease last only four or five days. If the patient does not die of it, through dehydration and uraemia, he soon recovers and becomes normal again though he may have become very weak. Cholera is very frequent in times of famine, when the tribals are forced to eat anything and frequently also contaminated food. The Bhils are reluctant to get inoculated against the disease. Even at the time of epidemic they hid in their houses or ran away into the jungle to escape inoculation.

The small-pox is another scourge that takes a heavy toll of human life. Though the National Small-pox Eradication Programme is sending vaccinators and sanitary inspectors around the country, the Bhils often try to escape from vaccination. They claim that the children often get sick of the dreaded disease after vaccination. Sometimes they bribe the vaccinator not to vaccinate their children.

The Bhils, of course, frequently suffer from various other infections which cause diarrhoea and dysentery and often lead to death.

The fever is said to be the most frequent cause of death among the Bhils. But fever might be caused by many different disease, not only by malaria, also by cold, pneumonia, tuberclosis and typhoid, etc. Respiratory disease and dysentery and diarrohea are also frequent causes of illness and death among the tribals.

The leprosy is rare among the Bhils. It prevails among them due to their dirtyness. If there is a case of leprosy, the patient is allowed to stay at home until the disease has advanced far and the bad odour of his wounds compels his family to expel him from their midst. The patient is usually allowed to stay near in a hut erected for him in the garden or just outside the village. He has his separate plate and he is fed and given water by his relatives until his death. But nobody will enter his hut, or touch anything used and touched by him.

The custom of abandoning an incurable patient is found among the Bhils not only in the case of leprosy. According to one respondent, once a Bhil had a wound on his foot that became septic. As neither medicines not the exorcisms of the Badwa were of any avail, the relatives gave up hope of his recovery. They removed him from the house and brought him to the threshing ground outside the village where they built a small hut for him. The dying man was removed from the house for fear of evil spirits. If he would die in the house, his spirit would find its way back to the house and it would make other sick. To prevent this danger, the dying patient was removed from the house and sent to the threshing ground to die there.

Sometimes the Bhils try another remedy, when their illness does not go. They leave the place and go to settle with relatives in another village. Sometimes the house is altogether abandoned and a new house is built, either in the same or in another village. In Jhabua district, we found many instances of abandoning houses, phalias or villages. Out of 1760 villages, we have record of more than 50 uninhabitated villages. This happens due to spread of epidemics or cause of evil spirits.

The illness caused by supernatural agencies may be of various nature. Some diseases are caused, in the opinion of the Bhils, by dead ancestors or relatives for whom the funeral rites have not been performed properly or who did not receive the necessary offerings. The omission of the funeral feast may also cause disease in the family. Also certain deities may send down a disease on a member of the household if, for instance, a vow has not been fulfilled or offerings due to them on certain feasts have been neglected.

An illness may also be caused by a breach of certain taboos, especially of the incest taboos. Thus the appearance of worms in wounds are usually attributed to the sin of incest, either in this life or in a past life. This belief is so strong that persons in whose wound worms appear are excommunicated from the tribal community.

The sickness may also be caused by black magic and witchcraft. It is the task of the diviner or *Badwa* to find out the supernatural cause in each case of sickness and to advise the proper forms of appeasement of offended deities or spirits.

Rituals Concerning Death

The Death is supposed to be physical and the soul is believed to survive in the form of a spirit which is disembodied on the extinction of physical activities. A man is not allowed to die on a cot, for it is believed to be the inauspicious. As soon as death approaches a man he is placed on the floor.[1]

The Bhil becomes an old man in his fiftieth or sixtieth year, and is then treated by his people with consideration.[2]

Except among the muslims, cremation is practised for the disposal of the dead bodies. Persons dying of smallpox and dead bodies of children upto the age of 5 years are buried. All these are buried in sleeping position. An ascetic is buried in the sitting position.[3] In case of pregnant woman after fourth month of pregnancy the foetus is taken out from the womb by the husband and cremated alongwith the dead body of the mother. If the husband of the woman is not present this is done by some close relative.[4]

The Bhil believes that when death is about to enter a house, a cracking sound is heard for it is *Joring Padhsha* coming to take away some one from the house. Sometimes, a bird is seen on the top of the house. After the death, relations and friends gather around, and each pours a little liquor into the dead man's mouth saying, 'Drink my share'.[5]

On the occurrence of death all members weap loudly and notice is given by firing off guns before the deceased's house while the villagers are informed by monotonous beating of a drum (Dhol). The relations and neighbours, who come to attend the ceremony bring some quantity of grains in their hands. The Jogi, also called Kamaria, is invited to officiate at the funeral ceremony. "He sits outside the door of the house and an image of a horse, and an earthen jar full of water are placed near him. Each visitor who has come to attend the ceremony gives him grain and sprinkle a little water over the image of the horse in the name of the deceased.[6] Some quantity of flour, ghee and sugar is placed by the side of the dead body, with the belief that it will be used by the departing soul journeying to the next world on horseback.[7]

In case of the death of the husband, his wife is to lie with the dead body for some time, and when it is wife, the husband is to do the same.[8]

Amongst the Bhils of Gujarat and Rajasthan, an elderly woman, called Harwani, a widow acting as one of the performers of the death rites, puts on the fire a clay cooking-vessel filled with water into which all those gathered together are put with a handful of grains (rice) saying, "If any of our dead ancestors come, give them something of this." A fawl and finally some fish is also cooked, then is tied in the piece of cloth to go into a basket placed on a new winnowing fan, and laid on the lap of the deceased man's wife or daughter. It is called *Petio.* The Harwani then puts it outside on three stones. Nearby is also placed an empty blackened pot inside a net, and covered by a basket containing a little rice and some coins.

A near female relative goes to the stream with a new earthen pot and a sickle to which is tied a black string to bring water to bathe the deceased. On this errand, she is followed by a man carrying an axe on his shoulder. Before filling up, the woman makes on the water two intersecting cuts.[9] Then the beard, hair, etc. are shaved off the corpse in the case of a man; in the case of a female the hair is dressed as in life.

In the meantime, a small wooden plank is placed under the dead man's feet, and the hair is rubbed with curd to prepare for the bath. Then the corpse is bathed in the water which has been brought in a new earthen vessel. The corpse is then dressed; in the case of a male in *dhoti,* and *chaddar* of new cloth, in the case of a female in a new petticoat (*ghagra*), *lugra,* and *kachli,* where the corpse is that of an unmarried adult some turmeric is thrown on the dress.

A little bread is made of flour freshly ground, care being taken that the hand in grinding always moves from left to right. This is then mixed with *ghi,* and *gur* and made into a ball. The ball is called *hamla.*[10]

A *tarkhati,* of the shape of a ladder, is made by tying seven small pieces of bamboo, each about half a meter in length, to two bamboo which are about two and a half metres long. Some leaves of *dhak* or of some other tree are spread over the ladder and the dead body is placed on it. Each person present then put a coin or a small piece of silver into the deceased person's mouth. A shroud made of four and a half metres cloth is spread over it. After covering the corpse women throw rice, asking the dead to give it to their own relatives. The corpse is then tied to the ladder with a string. The prepared ball (*hamla*) is then tied up near right shoulder of the clothe's garment. Afterwards a strange scene is appeared. The partner of the dead, the husband or the wife has to lie down beside the deceased for a little while or, at least, sit beside it. In the case of male white cloth is used for shroud while in that of female it is red.[11]

The eldest son or a near relative, if there is no son, takes an ignited cake of cowdung in his hand and the corpse is carried to the cremation ground, the man with the ignited cake leading the way.

The corpse is always carried so as to lie north and south, the feet pointing to the south. Guns are fired off as the procession proceeds and sometimes music and drums are played softly, accompanies the bier. The women are also allowed to accompany the procession. The deceased's house is meanwhile laped with fresh cowdung, and then sprinkled with maize, a small lamp being placed upon the spot where the man died, covered over with a bamboo basket. This lamp is called *diwania*.

On coming to a *ber* tree (Zizyphus jujuba) the corpse is set down, while all the persons present proceed to take up stones with which a heap is made. A piece of cloth is then torn off from the dead man's garment and thrown over the tree. The corpse is then picked up again those formerly at the head going to the feet.

The tradition of taking rest under the *ber* tree has some reasons behind it. A story relating to this tradition is prevalent among them. Once the son of an aged dame died. The old woman carried his corpse as far as a *ber* tree but could go no further. She then decided to appeal to the gods by fasting, for the restoration of her son's life, and sat for three days fasting beneath the tree. This was not the fruit season, but seeing her piety the gods gave the tree fruit, and also caused hunger to attack her. She could bear her pain no longer and rose to seize the fruit, suddenly the tree grew and raised the fruit beyond her reach. At length she propped the corpse against the tree and standing upon it reached the fruit. She had broken her vow, and the village people approaching took and cremated the corpse. To avert any such evil each corpse is now halted under a *ber* tree, and a piece of the garment is offered to the gods. The earthen vessel containing water to wash the corpse is taken and broken under this tree on the heap of stones.[12]

The man's widow is taken to the tree where her ornaments are taken off.

The burning *ghats* are situated anywhere near a stream or tank. The corpse is put down near a stream or tank while the pyre (*hela* or *chita*) is being made. The fire carrier meanwhile bathes and then approaching sprinkles water on the corpse.

The body is then placed on the pyre with its head to the north, and burnt together with man's bow, club, etc., and in the case of a women some favourite ornament. The face is uncovered before the fire is applied. A piece of cloth torn off the face is used to wrap up a piece of silver money, some of the balls mentioned and some *darbha* grass. Every person present puts a piece of sandal-wood on the chest of the corpse. The pyre is ignited by the fire carrier, who approaches it backwards so as not to see the pyre, holding his hands behind him. When alight all retire and sit down to watch.

When all is over, the company bathe and then go back the deceased's house. Here liquor is produced for all. Only the men may drink it. Food is then given to all, to the men by male and the women by female relatives.[13]

In case of the Bhils of Gujarat and Rajasthan, the bier is carried by four mourners while a man with a sword goes in front, the tur or musical pipe playing all through. Then a gun is fired. When the funeral has gone 500 yards, the cot is put down, the Harwani takes away the plank from under the corpse's feet, and break on it two white pumpkins and a black pot. After this, the man alone go to the burning ghat, and the women go to the river or stream carrying with them the sickle, the black pot, grains, pulse, vegetables etc. At the waterside, a small rectangular plot is marked to be divided into five parts, into which are poured the grains and the vegetables. The pot is broken, the water sprinkled and some offered to the dead by the Harwani who says, "Drink this."

At the cremation ground, the body is placed with its head to the north. The mourners sit on the cot fanning the body or holding an umbrella over it. The Harwan, male version of the Harwani, brings with him a burning cowdung cake in a black pot along with the *petio* and the empty pot in the net. The pyre is arranged with three fire-logs kept at a distance of about two feet from each other, and on these, the other pieces are placed to raise its height. The cot is taken five times round the pyre, then placed on it with the head again to the north. While the ceremony is going on, cows, bulls, buffaloes or wherever the person owned in life are tied near at hand, and taken away when the rites are over. It is said that when a prince was being consumed in the flames, an elephant was tied nearby.

The Harwan brings water, passes the crushed end of a tooth-stick used for cleaning the teeth over the deadman's mouth, splits it into two, waves it round his head, and throws the pieces away. He then washes the dead man's face, after which he washes his own hands. The food from the petio is taken out in two clay-lamps, and thrown away towards the feet of the corpse. The mourners then place food one by one into the Harwan's crossed hands, touch him and say, "This relative of yours feeds you. He does everything for you, and for you, he opts into indebtedness. Give him plenty, do him no harm, do not harass his cattle." The Harwan throws all food towards the corpse's feet. This is feeding the dead. A small piece is torn off from the cloth covering the deceased, and tied to a tree. Then some money is tied to the dead person's waist, everything the mourners have brought is thrown around the pyre, a pumpkin is placed near the head, some leafcups with rice are put at the foot with the injunction, "Eat this from us. Take some of it to our relatives who are also there." Silver coins are dropped into the mouth, and the body is covered with ornaments and even some agricultural implements. The Harwan with the fire moves from west to south, from south to east and from east to north, after which the pyre is lit from the side of its head.

As the body burns away, the mourners move towards the stream with the Harwan giving the lead. Each picks up a handful of grass, which is all deposited in the stream. The Harwan places a maize-head with a coin and tobacco in it. After which the Harwan and the others pour water on the grass requesting the dead to drink it. Then they embrace each other. The Harwan takes away the coin put there, crushes maize, but lets the tobacco leaf lie. The day after, the Harwan takes two slices of bread and an egg to the cremation place. The Harwan places the bread, egg and some tobacco in three shares. If any valuable pieces of ornaments remain unburnt, they are collected by the Harwan, and put beside the stream on a head of maize.[14]

In Khandesh, when a Bhil is on the point of death, his relations distribute money among the poor in his name. When he dies, the body is laid on a blanket or on a piece of cloth spread over a blanket. An earthen pot full of cold water is placed near the door of the house and the body is brought out, held in a sitting position outside the door, and water poured over it. The old clothes are taken off, and tying a new piece of cloth round the loins, the body is laid on the bier and covered with a new white sheet, leaving the face bare, and the head covered with a turban. Red powder, *gulala,* is sprinkled over the face, and some red and cooked rice are tied together in a piece of cloth and placed on the bier. The body is then tied with a string to the bier and carried to the burying ground of the shoulders of four near male relations. In front of them go the sons of the deceased, the chief mourner carrying fire in an earthen jar, and one of the others carrying an earthen jug full of water. Half-way to the grave, the bier is lowered, and some of the cooked food is laid near a bush. The bearer change places, and without further halt the body is carried to the burning ground. Here the bier is lowered and the mourners help in digging a grave, long enough for the body, and to prevent it opened by wild animals, about five or six feet deep. In this the body is laid, the head to the south and the arms stretched along either side. Cooked rice and bread are placed in the mouth, and the body is sprinkled with water. Before leaving the grave, the man who is last arranging the body tears a small hole in the winding sheet. Then the whole party sit round the grave, so far off that they cannot see the body, and the chief mourner throws a handful of earth on the corpse, and, all joining, cover the corpse with earth. When the body is covered they rise and fill the grave, cutting a small trench round it. In this trench, beginning from the north, they pour water out of an earthen jug, and when the circuit of the grave is complete, drop the jug and break it to pieces. Then the bier is turned upside down and burned, and the funeral party, going to the nearest water, bathe and accompany the chief mourner to his house. In front of his house a fire is lit, and into it some women's hair is dropped, and each of the funeral party, taking some *nim* (Melia azadirachta) leaves, throws them on the fire, and passing his open palms through the smoke, rubs them over his face. The mourners are now pure, and after taking a draught of liquor, go to their homes.[15]

Among the Gujarat Bhils, when life is gone the relations bathe the body, spread a waist cloth *dhotar* over it, and carry it on a rough bamboo bier to the burning ground. At the burning ground the chief mourners sit near the body while the rest of the party gather wood for the pyre. The son or other next-of kin sets the pyre alight. When the body is half burnt the mourners bathe. On the way back to the deceased's house the party rest half-way between the deceased's house and the burning ground, place five stones near each other, and to the branch of a neighbouring tree tie a small piece of the deceased's winding sheet. On returning to the deceased's house the party smoke tobacco for a short time and after saluting each other go home.[16]

On the occurrence of the death of Kalia Bhil of Jaisamand Lake in Rajputana, the dead body is carried out of the house with head forward on a bamboo bier. Female relatives accompany the funeral procession, weeping and lamenting in chorus. Female relatives from the settlement who may have received the information join the procession and the ceremonial wailing. Fire in an earthen pot, and one big *laddu* or roundish cake made of flour and molasses and ghee, are carried to the cremation ground by the chief mourner- either a son or next-of-kin. Arrived at the cremation ground or *masan*, the *laddu* is broken into pieces which are scattered all over the *masan* and then the bier, with the corpse on it, is placed on the ground. The chief mourner once circumambulates the bier and then places a lighted faggot underneath the corpse.[17]

On the second day the old man and two other Bhils go to the cremation ground. If the body is not properly burnt they put some fire-wood there and set fire to it.[18]

Third Day Rites:

The *tiya* or third day rites are arranged in accordance with the means of the family. The man who ignited the pyre then remove the basket from over the lamp, see if is burning well and then replace the cover. Some *darbha* grass is scattered round it.

The unconsumed bones are carefully collected from the pyre, and separated from the ashes. The bones are placed in an earthen vessel and buried near the house until the *nukta* (12th day ceremonies) can be performed. When this takes place they are dug up. If there is no chance of their being carried out the bones are thrown into the nearest river. The bones must be thrown into a river before *nukta* is carried out.

The ashes are thrown into water on the 3rd day. After this the new master examines the flour round the lamp and the shape of the marks determines what animal the spirit of the dead will next inhabit. If it like a human footprint a man is his next abode, if like a hoof a horned animal, if like a bird's foot a bird, if like a scorpion or snake one of these animals. If the spirit assumes the form of an awful animal, it is painful to all. If per chance the spirit comes in human form the member of the family speak very high of the deceased and his achievement. The form assumed by the spirit after the return to the world is so important that the next day it is topic of conversation in the village. A good form assumed by the spirit bestows a higher status on the family. The lamp and basket are now thrown away and spot liped.

The deceased is provided with food and drink on the third day, the provisions being placed under the *ber* tree, where the corpse is rested. The stones heaped up there are scattered. Those performing this ceremony are then feasted at the deceased's house. It is not considered ill for a mourner to touch any person or thing, but no religious observations other than those of mourning may be performed.[19]

Amongst the Bhils of Khandesh, on the third day, one of the mourning household rubs the right shoulders of the pallbearers with oil, milk and cowdung, and washes them with *nim*, twigs steeped in cow's urine. Then the four men bathe and are treated to a dinner. In the house the only sign of mourning is that every morning for five days the women wail for about a quarter of an hour.[20]

On that day a ceremony is performed at the side of the river and the Bhils of the village and relatives gather together. The moustaches and beards of deceased's relatives are shaved.[21]

The third day ceremony is little bit different amongst the Bhils of Gujarat and Rajasthan. On that day, the Bhils of the village gather together. This is known as the *Kol Padsha mandal.* There the moustache and beard of close relatives are shaved. The *kotwal* invited for this special ceremony arrives with a new basket, and cooks a complete meal. This is put on leaf plates, and kept in the basket along with two bamboo tubes, one with milk, the other cow's urine, an accepted disinfected used in purification ceremonies. The basket is then tied with a cloth, with grass over it. The *kotwal* carries the basket and four pieces of dried bark of teak, and the mourners follow him to the cremation ground. The four bark pieces are put on the four sides of the pyre, and with them, the ashes are gathered. A near relative of the dead touches the *kotwal* and says, "If anything remains to be done, tell us. We will do that, but don't trouble us." Some of the cooked food is strewn there, water poured on the ash heap and basket torn on it.

The *kotwal* then erects a small booth a foot high with a few sticks, and spreads grass on it as a thatch. Under this, he divides food into three parts, and pours milk and cow's urine in each of them. It is called building the house. The *kotwal* is paid for his services that day.[22]

Fifth Day Ceremony

Amongst the Bhils of Gujarat a fifth day ceremony is performed. On the fifth day after death, ten to twenty friends and relations of the deceased come to the place where the small stones were laid, and without drinking any liquor eat boiled maize *ghugari.* After the meal they throw away the stones and the pieces of the winding sheet, and return to their homes. On the fifth day as well as on the day of the *kaita* (12th day ceremonies) or death-dinner the Jhalod Bhils have the special practice of shaving their moustaches only.[23]

Eleventh Day

This ceremony is performed amongst the Bhils of Khandesh. On that day the chief mourner goes to a river, and there has his head, beard and face shaved and bathes. Next he makes a dough cow, sprinkles it with red powder, and setting it on a leaf plate, bows to it, and throws it into the water. He then bathes and goes home.[24]

Twelfth Day

In Jhalod (Gujarat), where they are well-to do, Bhils give a death dinner or *kaita* on the twelfth day like other non-tribal families of upper castes. Among the poorer Bhils family of five or six deceased persons subscribe and give one combined death-dinner, in some cases two or three years after the death.

For this death-dinner much liquor is distilled and a dish called *ghugari* made of Indian corn, gram and wheat boiled together is prepared. When the guests, who often number two or three thousand, come together, a Raval pours a quart of milk into a metal salver and in the milk sets a brass horse. Two of the deceased's near relations squat down holding the dish at arm's length above their heads. Then while the Raval plays a one-stringed *guitar* or *tamburo* with a hand drum accompaniment, the mourners for an hour or two keep throwing into the dish money, rice and corn. At last the salver shakes and the image of the horse falls on its side in the milk. The mourners weep and wail. Liquor is handed round, and, in a leaf, each guest is given a small dole of boiled corn, gram and wheat. When the meal is over, all but relations leave, the Raval taking his perquisites, the brass horse and the salver full of grain. The relations usually bring a goat or young buffalo or a few yards of country cloth as a present for the son of the deceased. If they bring cloth it is given when the villagers leave; if they bring a goat or young buffalo it is at once beheaded and the head thrown on the roof of the deceased's house. The body is taken to a distance, cut up, cooked and eaten, the relations bringing liquor to drink with it.[25]

Then there is drinking and merry-making, beating on tom-toms, shooting arrows into the trees and singing and dancing. For a year from then, the dead person is offered food and water twice a day out of the daily food that is cooked, as also on all festive occasions.[26]

Amongst the Bhils of Khandesh, either on twelfth or the forty-fifth day, a potter, Kumbhar, is called and a seven-step hemp ladder, *chodhvan,* is set against the wall of the house that the soul of the dead may climb by it to heaven. The priest sits at the foot of the ladder and chants a verse from the *Purans,* the string by which the ladder is fastened to the ground is burnt, and the ladder pulled down and thrown away. The spot where the ladder was tied is then covered with flour, and a small plate with a piece of bread and cooked rice is laid over it. In the plate is set a small water pot, and alongside of the water pot is a lighted lamp covered by an empty bamboo basket with a cloth drawn over it. This day a grand dinner is prepared, and before it is eaten, five mouthfuls are burnt near the basket.[27]

Conception of the Departed Soul

In the creation myth of the Bhils conviction is expressed that *bhagwan* had to infuse a soul into the human bodies which he had shaped in order to give them life. But not only one soul, in fact, several souls exist in man and are active in him.

One soul is called *jiv*, the life spirit. It is conceived as the efficient cause of all functions in the human body. As such it is present in all parts of the body and acts in it and enlivens it even when man is asleep or unconscious. The *jiv* makes the body breathe and the pulse beat. In severe sickness it may leave the body for a short while, but not for long or else the body would die.

The Bhils religious beliefs and practices have their roots in the concept of the life of the dead. It is their belief in the world of the dead which forms the basis of their religion. To them death is not ghastly; as they wander completely unafraid of a wild animal, or an enemy killing and dying for them do not inspire excessive horror.

The Bhils are of the believe that the life spirit survives at man's death and goes after death to *bhagwan*. There the spirit is rewarded or punished according to good or bad deeds in the past life. If his bad deeds predominate, the *jiv* may even go to a place of punishment, called *narak khundo* (hell). But most souls go to *bhagwan's*.

According to the beliefs of the Bhils of Bansla, however, the soul may take the form of an evil spirit and return to the earth to fulfil its unsatisfied desire. The Bhil of Kawaria who are Christians, however, believe in the immortality of the soul which dwells in the heaven or hell.[28]

It is believed that as soon as the fire is lighted, the soul leaves the place for it has thereafter no physical body to live in. But the soul hovers in search of its body. The spirit is assumed to possess the power to think as well as all the human desires and sentiments it possessed in life. When it does not find the body in which it lived a worldly life, it hovers around the place of its earthly residence— the last place where the body when living, resided— for it cannot altogether forget previous attachments and contacts. It is also supposed to hover under the cot where it lay at the time of death. Sometimes, the soul does nuisance. In order to avoid it, the Bhils erect a heap of stones known as *pariya* on the way to the cremation ground under a ber tree. *Pariya* is considered as a residential abode where the spirit lives for twelve days. During these days, family of the deceased offer, twice daily in the morning and evening, milk and rice at the *pariya* as food to the spirit. After twelve days, the spirit goes to the land of the deed.

The Bhils have some definite ideas about the future of the departed soul. They consider that after the death most souls go to *bhagwan's* abode. However they are not sure whether the souls remain permanently with *bhagwan* or not.

The World of the Dead

There are not many rites among the Bhils that might give us the idea of the world of the dead. The general belief is that spirits enjoy themselves or live a miserable life according to their good or bad actions respectively during their lives. The journey by the spirits to the land of the dead is full of hardships and difficulties. There is no food to fill the stomach, and no water to drink.

It is believed that *Yama* comes from the south and carries the soul of the dead man to the north. On the way the soul passes over a thorn-strewn plain. Hence shoes are given as gift on the day of the funeral feast or else his spirit suffers greatly. He then passes between two heated pillars; the spirit then encounters a *bhatyari* (keeper of cook shop) who offers him cooked food. Their relatives realising this difficulty tie a few copper coins and *laddus* to the corpse. They also pour a few drops of water over the dead body. The spirit may get over the difficulties of ration, but there is yet another hardship, which can hardly be surmounted. On the way to the land of the dead a turbulent river flows. It can be crossed only by clinging to the tail of the mother-goddess the cow. Therefore, a Bhil should during his life time, and more particularly when death approaches give a cow as a gift to a Brahmin or to his daughter after washing its tail three times so that he may safely land in the world of the dead. On reaching the end of the journey *Yama* determines which of the three hells (lit, kunds or tanks) he is to enter, one being full of nectar, the other of varying degrees of foulness (worms, blood etc.) until he is born again.

Life of the Dead

The rites of giving food and water to the dead show that the spirits partially lead a life which is similar to their lives led in the world. They eat, drink and wear clothes. If, per chance, they are dissatisfied with the living conditions of the world of the dead, they visit to the womenfolk specially and they see them mostly in a needy state, wandering without food or dress. On the morning following such a dream, the women invite a virgin or a Brahmin to a dinner. Another kind of dream, usually associated with the dead is the dream wherein the spirit of the dead is seen in miserable plight for the non-performance of rites by living relatives; a similar plight befalls a spirit for having troubled or injured a person during his lifetime. Relatives of the deceased, therefore, perform the necessary rites to liberate it and keep it happy in its world.

Evil Spirits

The spirits who have evil designs do not confine their stay to the world of the dead. Their association and attachment to the human world are so deep-rooted that they are happy only if they are once again in the vicinity of mortals. Sometimes the evil spirits are forced to leave the world of the dead to take revenge on an enemy who was a threat to them throughout their lifetimes. Spirits which come to live in the world of mortals are called evil spirits.

When spirits return to the world of the living they make their permanent abodes in certain ruined places the usual places of their residence on earth being graveyards, or crematories where their bodies have perished, or yet lie buried inside. In the village of Bhurighati there is a thick grove of Mahua trees. The villagers believe that a host of evil spirits have been living in this grove. Were a man to pass by the trees at night, the evil spirits attack him and he becomes horror-sticken. According to one of the informants, a Bhil of Bhurighati was going to Petlawad late in the evening when he was attacked by a host of evil spirits who came in the guise of thieves. The man cried at the top of his voice, 'Thieves, Thieves'. The villagers heard the call and rushed to the spot. There was no one on the spot and the man became a laughing stock among the people. But a little later the significance of the thieves was fully realised by the abnormal behaviour of the person victimised and this was confirmed by the village elders.

The spirit of a woman died in child-birth or in pregnancy is believed to become a *Churuel,* and those who die a violent death like killed with a sword, gun or arrow is believed to become a *bhut;* others become *hatris,* who however cannot harm human beings but only animals, and others *deos* who are beneficent spirits. A sinner is also believed to the transformed into an insect.

These *bhuts* are buried at the spots where they have been killed, and stone heaps are placed over their graves. Curiously enough these stone heaps are known by the name of Palias. When any Bhil passes by the side a *palia,* he is required to place a pebble over it.[29]

The evil spirits who have their abode in the cremation ground also somehow make their existence known to the people. In the village Bhuraghati, the cremation ground lies on the river bed, close to the village. Once is so happened that an evil spirit in the guise of a woman began weeping. It was late in the evening, when darkness had enveloped all the area around. The weeping of the spirit and its cries were so pitiable that almost all the village gathered at the house of a villager near the river bank. The voice of the spirit resembled the shrieks of a woman whose spirit it was supposed to be.

Other places haunted by evil spirits are old ruined houses or old trees which usually have an atmosphere of awe and mystery. Places where some accident has occured may also be considered to be a haunted spot. The spirits are classified according to clans and villages. The spirits of a particular village may stay in that very village and not to haunt places in other villages, for this is considered to be breach of their convention. Similarly, the spirits of a certain Bhil clan affect the members of their own clans only. In no case would the spirits of Bhil haunt the Hindus. The spirits seem to have their own territorial and tribal limitations. The taboos and modes of behaviour which controlled the spirit when it was in the human world, are also adhered to in the spirit world. The customs relating to sex are also observed in the world of the dead. A male and female spirit would never live together in a single spot. How could a woman lie down in presence of man ! And therefore the spirits live in the company of members of their own sex. The spirits are also marked by their character constitution. Of a spirit belongs to a Ninama or Maira clan, it will behave very desperately, and all the high handedness which is the characteristic of the clan would be markedly observable in the behaviour of these spirits. It is believed that a spirit is very powerful and therefore there is no charm or remedy against its revengeful actions. It is capable of bringing, and does bring, immense trouble to the people, and can be driven out— its resistance is great— by the Badwa or the magic-man by special and difficult means. While the individual possessed by an evil spirit is being dispossessed, it takes revenge even upon the Badwa. The spirit in fact are supposed to possess their own social structure even to the extent of . leadership and following.

In Rajasthan the evil spirits living in this world supposedly all the human drives and impulses. They eat and drink like man, perform excretary functions, possess all human appetites and often dress themselves in fine clothes. The appetites of the women spirits seem to be so powerful that in Bansla when the women are confined to bed in the post-delivery period and take delicious food, spirits possess them and satisfy their appetites. The spirits are quite fond of meat and when a Bhil Bhagat dies and assumes the form of a spirit, his spirit takes meat in large quantities— a thing that it had been denied all his life by way of compensation. They also relish liquor and tea. It is believed that they do not feed upon corpses. Householders, whose abodes are haunted by spirits, often complain about the theft of their bread. The spirits indulge in sex and even possess ethnical standards. The women spirits would never possess the body of a man, for a woman should not have male friends. Similarly, if a woman is possessed by a spirit when he is in sexual congress with her husband, the spirit would leave the body, for how can it have adultery with another man? There is also sexual jealousy among evil spirits. Evil spirits are conceived as small children with long hair and four fingers on each hand. They resemble air and can appear or disappear at any time.[30]

The Bhils are greatly superstitious and have faith in the supernatural beings and evil spirits whom they consider responsible for all ills and evils and, therefore, wear amulets to ward off their evil effects and also offer special sacrifices to them. The Bhils of village Kailashpuri (Rajasthan) are careful in propitiating the spirits of the dead in whose memory, stone memorials known as *chheero,* are raised and invoked on all occasions for blessings and protection. In appeasement worship and sacrifices they are helped by the Bhopa who minister to their needs by prescribing various rituals. To get rid of a ghost a pitcher full of water is kept at the cremation ground where some magical recitations are given by the Bhopa. Rice, coconut; kajal (soot), henna and vermilion are offered to evil spirits (*dakans*).[31]

Way to Fulfill the Desires

The spirits have their own desires to be fulfilled. There are various methods of satisfying these desires. They sit in their abodes with open eyes and whenever a person of their choice is seen they satisfy their desires through him. Persons usually possessed by them are pregnant women, young girls and men of fickle mind. Scent and flowers are greatly liked by the spirits. They may also obtain dresses, ornaments, and other things which can be provisionally acquired by force of magic, as the power of magic is considered to last for not more than one-fourth *ghari* or about half an hour. The method of taking revenge upon anybody is generally harassment, infliction of some mysterious disease often resulting in death, or possession— a method often adopted for the satisfaction of sexual appetite. Often they harass human beings if the latter insult the spirit by passing urine or stools on their abode or disturb them in the dark night when they are free to play or if a woman during the period of taboo, the monthly course, passes near them. They allow torment a man when he cuts the branches of a tree which is the abode of spirits or violates any rites to which they are otherwise entitled.

The Bhils of village Bhurighati know the haunted places. But they are not unduly afraid of the evil spirits. They understand that the evil spirits are the dead once and in no case are they stronger than human beings who are alive. A little patience and courage can overcome the harsh created by the spirits. The villagers relate that a few years back a young man of the community was entrapped in a valley by a host of evil spirits.

But he did not lose heart, with the result that he lived with the spirits for about a week and learnt many a magical formulae from them. He came back to the village and narrated the story of the living conditions of the spirits. He excelled in the art of benevolent magic and cured many a patient. His death considered by each villagers as loss of a potent powers.

The inhabitants of the village Sondwa are easily terrified at the appearance of the evil spirit. If a member is posssed by a spirit, his face turns blank and immediately a magic man or Badwa is called. In the village of Kila Jobat the Christian Bhils do not believe in the spirits and therefore they little care about their activities.

Attachment of the Spirits

The most important phenomenon associated with the activities of the spirits is that of attachment. They attach with a man, who is capable of satisfying their desires. Such a man is easily influenced by the spirits, for he is fickle minded and weak at heart. The spirits, it is believed, cannot possess people with strong minds and saints who have a strong will and can therefore control and direct the spirits.

Among the Bhils the male spirits attach with a man in order to gratify their sexual desires. The man is often attached at night when he is supposed to be having sexual congress with his wife. It satisfies the sexual desires of male spirits. On the other hand female spirits do not attach a woman for sexual satisfaction. But if a spirit lived a life of adultery during its lifetime on earth, then it attaches some women to satisfy its sexual desire. In no case would a female spirit attach a man or a male spirit attach a woman. But it is feasible that a female spirit may follow a man who has annoyed it and may pass urine or stool and then later may attach her wife mother or daughter.

The spirit may attach a bride when she moves outside the house during the marriage celebrations. It may also attach a pregnant woman while passing a haunted place. The most dreaded days are the days of the darker nights, falling in the month of Kartik, when the spirits pass through the sky to roam about and attach human beings. In the whole district this month is believed to be associated with the frequent visits of spirits. No one is permitted by the family to move during night time. The cremation grounds are believed to be the abode of various spirits and therefore if a man passes through them in the hot mid-day or in the night, the spirit immediately attaches him. The spirits are active after midnight, as all the spirits of the neighbouring haunted places assemble at the cremation ground and indulge in dances. They play hide and seek. If their 'Night Club' is interrupted by human beings, they get enraged and attach the man out of sheer vindictness. There is no hard and fast rule as to the age of the attached person. Normally an adult is attached though teenagers are not exempted.

The man attached by a spirit can easily be recognized. If the attachment is ordinary and not motivated by revenge, the spirit is reflected in the eyes which become red of the person. The man gets a serious headache and feels acute pain in the stomach. He talks irrelevantly and at random. He may also cry in fear of some dreaded image which he remembers. In serious condition, when the spirit attaches him to take revenge, he becomes pale and weak. He suffers from diseases which cannot be cured by a herb or medicine. Such diseases are vomiting, continuous weeping without cause, insanity or other kinds of physical or psychical disorder. When a patient is not cured with medicines, it is believed that he is attached by a spirit.

The spirit can often be driven out by charms prepared by the *Badwa*. But if the charm fails, the Badwa may take the assistance of a stronger spirit. The Badwa is skilled in the practice of driving out the spirit. He acquires the power to disposses the spirits by constant practice and *sadhana* (penance) observed on special days of the year. He goes to the cremation ground with a hen, powder of red oxide, lemon, and flowers, preferably on the darker nights of the month. All the spirits hover round him. The *Badwa* worships the deity which is powerful enough to control and direct the minor spirits. The deities worshipped by the Badwa are Hanuman and, Bhairawa Kali. It is through the power acquired by the *sadhana* that the Badwa derives out spirits from the attached man.

When the charm prepared by the Badwa fails to drive out the spirit, the rite of Mandor is observed by the Badwa. It is usually on the 11th or the 14th night of the waning moon. In the morning of the day when the rite to disposses the spirit is to be performed, the Badwa takes a bath in a stream and invites (*Notru*) the deities whom he has propitiated to attend the ceremony. All the articles required for Mandor such as a hen, a goat, liquor, sindor (red oxide) and lemon are kept on hand. At night, the Badwa comes with his associates who play on metal plates to excite the subject. The family members sit round the attached spirit man and observe the progress. The subject is made to sit in front of the Badwa and his associates. Music is played and the Badwa drinks large quantities of liquor. Sometimes a drink is also administered to the subject (to bring him into a state of trance) under the belief that evil spirits desire liquor, without which they cannot be hypnotised.

If the subject is a man, his turban is taken off, while in the case of a woman her hair is untied. Now the Badwa swings his head forward and backward and this induces the spirit to possess the subject and swing his or head. Thus, the subject is induced by the hypnotic suggestions of the Badwa to come into the desired abnormal condition and answers the questions put to him. If the deity propitated by the Badwa is powerful enough, the spirit is subjected to great pressure. The replies are given by the spirit who attaches the medium ,or, in echnical language, it is the secondary personality that dominates the consciousness of the subject that replies to the Badwa. The normal personality is completely submerged when it is suppressed by the secondary personality. In case the controlled power of the Badwa turns out to be the weaker of the two the subject is not induced hypnotically, and the Badwa himself replies to questions relating to the subject.

However, after some time has passed, the Badwa gets stronger and tries to overpower the subject. He compels the spirit to answer all his questions without any loss of time. If required, the spirit is appeased by the sacrifice of a goat or hen. The Badwa keeps a large iron chin and hot iron spears by his side. Incase his questions go unanswered, the spirit is beaten with these. He may also burn the subject with a hot iron. The spirit reveals its desires through the medium and promises are made by the Badwa that the desires will be fulfilled. The whole night passes and with the break of the dawn, the spirit says that it has dispossessed the subject. When the spirit leaves the person, it indicates this by demanding a glass of water or by crying loudly or weeping bitterly. When the person is dispossessed, he is found to be utterly exhausted and to be completely mentally dull. He is forced to rest.

In some villages *Badwa* acts as a priest of the community as well as magic-man to drive out evil spirits. The Badwa in some of the extraordinary case when he fails to dispossess a spirit, the subject is brought to the great *Badwa*. The great Badwa commands the supernatural power as a result of great 'Sadhana'. On the sacred days i.e. saturday or sunday the subject is brought to the great Badwa for relief from the influence of spirits. He invokes the goddess. At the very sight of the Badwa, the spirit promises never to adhere the man again. The magical driving out of the spirit by the great Badwa is so effective that the spirit never possesses the man again.

Belief in Re-birth

The villages of our study indicate that the people do have a belief in the theory of re-birth. When a person steals anything, the remark made in reaction is : "He would pay for it in the next birth." The general tenor of the belief is that when the spirit leaves the world and goes to the land of dead, in course of time it is re-born in the form of an animal, a tree or a person. If it is an evil spirit and wanders alone in the world, it will continue to live in the world till it has satisfied its desires. When its evil desires are fulfilled, it returns to the land of the dead and is re-born in this world. Some people believe that the souls of the dead even pass directly into wombs and are born later as infants. The Bhils do not cremate infants but bury them in the belief that the spirit, after going to the land of the dead, will return to the family. Similarly, a woman dying during the labour pains, is also buried under the belief that the soul might return to the family. If, however, the funeral rites are not properly performed, the soul may wander in disappointment for ever.

Ancestor Worship

The Bhils believe in ancestor worship though they do not practise the *shradha* ceremony like the non-tribal castes. The worship of ancestors consists in the ceremony observed during the Navaratri celebrations. The ceremony called 'Purvaj Ramana' or the recreation of ancestors. On this day, the ancestors are appeased by offerings of liquor and meat. If the annual worship to ancestors is not observed, the lapse, it is held, may bring some calamity to the family. On no other occasions, are the ancestors appeased or worshipped by the villagers. The Bhils of Jobat who are Christians do not worship their ancestors.

Magical Operations

Magic plays a very important part in everyday life, and it is two main types, harmful or protective. In case of sickness, the *Badwa* is called for, and he practices divination with the aid of a handful of grains of maize. He is able to announce where the sickness is due to the action of a witch, or a demon, or one of the village gods, or whether it is none of these things, but just plain sickness : and he will suggest the appropriate remdey for each case. There are many potentially harmful magical influences, but of all these the commonest is witchcraft.

Witchcrafts

Witchcraft is very common amongst the Bhils of Rajasthan. The Bhils of village Ghantali have a belief that there can be no village on the face of the earth without a witch. Witchcraft is so rampant that it is difficult to distinghuish a woman from a witch, because for them, women who are matured enough to put a bodice to cover the breast are supposed to be witches.[32] This is so prevalent in Jhabua district that Bhils believe that every young girl, once she is married, is initiated into its arts by her older friends. Most of them are thought to be if not well-disposed, at least harmless : but others are very malignant and will not stop short of killing their victims unless they can be bought off.

Certain physical characteristics are said to be peculiar to a witch. Her eyes are dark, red and specially so at morning, noon and evening. They are supposed to be red because of her predilection for eating human hearts and drinking blood. Her eyes have evil effects even for her own family members. And, therefore, she is invariably found covering her face with her Sari lest her own children might be injured. The villagers know her to be a witch and nobody dares to pick up a quarrel with her. In all public places such as wells and pastures she gets a primary position.

The power of witchcraft can be acquired by both the sexes—though men practise it rarely. The woman who has acquired this magical power is called a 'dakan' and the man a 'dakana'. By means of divination, the Badwa ascertains the woman is witch. There are some other sorts of ordeal through which the witch can be identified. The most common is ordeal by water. The woman is placed in one side of a bullock's pack-sack and three dry cakes of cow-dung in the other; the sack is then thrown into the water, and if the woman sink, she is no witch, while if she swim, she is.

There is an another ordeal known as water test performed in such a way. A bamboo is stuck up in the middle of any piece of water. The accused is taken to it, lays hold of it, and by it descends to the bottom. In the meantime one of the villagers shoots an arrow from his bow, and another runs to pick it up and bring it back to the place whence it was shot. If the woman is able to remain under water until this is done, she is declared innocent; but if she comes up to breathe before the arrow is returned into the bowman's hand, she is a true witch and must be swung as such. The other way of trial is by sewing the suspected one in a sack which is let down into water three feet deep. If the person inside the sack can get her head above water, she is a witch.

By means of magic power *Badwa* find out what offerings the witch requires: and then it is his business to have them conveyed to the supposed witch in secret because if it is done openly, the witch will be furious. If the sickness still persists, he may then ask: "Do you wish to be swung ?", and if the reply is 'Yes' then the men of the village lay hold of the witch at the Badwa's instructions, and take her out into the jungle by night. There, they bind red pepper over her eyes, and then suspend her by the heels from a high tree, and swing her side to side by means of ropes. From time to time they shout to ask her if she has had enough, if she will leave off devouring the victim now, and the unfortunate woman's ordeal is not over until she has tacitly admitted to having been a witch. Sometimes they are very stubborn, and refuse to capitulate for as long as two or three days and nights on end. Most 'witches' will settle for a goat-sacrifice, or a quantity of cloth, but if they are so malignant that they will not be bought off, you simply have to exterminate them.

The practice of 'witch-swinging' is a very old one. It is described in an account of the Mewar Bhils, written by the then Surgeon to the Bhil Crops, in 1875. Should any of their relatives die without appearance cause, they consult the Badwa, who, generally a shrewd, clever fellow, manages to find out before hand what ugly, disagreeable old woman may live in the enquirer's village, and he proceeds, apparently oracularly, to describe this old witch. Witches with the Bhils are tried much in the same way that they were in civilized England two centuries ago.[33]

The magic power of witchcraft can be acquired by a woman of any age. But ordinarily, unmarried girls learn the secret formulae and practices from some old woman who excels at witchcraft. A tendency prevails amongst witches to take the initiative and persuade girls to become their disciples so that their followings is enlarged. Some unmarried girl is invited by the old witch to her house under the pretext of helping her in daily routine. She offers her bread or liquor which she has laid a spell on. Quite unconscious of the existence of the charm the girl takes the bread and eats it. That night, the girl dreams about tanks and lands submerged by water and human hearts being eaten with relish. The following morning, she has an intuitional desire to become a witch. The effect of the magic becomes obvious. The girls goes to the house of the old lady and express her desires to become her disciple and learn the magical formulae. The old witch really agrees to her proposal. She awaits some suitable day. Meanwhile the girl is induced to inveigle some other girls of the village for a batch of girls could easily be taught this knowledge. Usually five or six girls of the village join in a group to learn witchcraft. The auspicious days for learning the magical formulae are the darker nights of Navaratri and Diwali and especially the fourteenth day of the waning moon in the month of Ashwin (Roop Chaudash). The witch fixes the day and asks her would-be disciples to assemble under a tree at night. The *dakan* takes a coconut, lemon and liquor along with the meat of a hen and a goat to appease her favourite deity, who may be either Hanuman, Bhairawa or Kali. She therefore applies red marks on her forehead and recites certain incantations over her husband so that he becomes unconcious until she returns. She leaves the house and joins the group of girls who await her under the tree. As soon as she comes to the first junction of the four roads of the village, she draws a big circle around a cross and puts four pieces of lemon inside it, after reciting some incantations. Anyone who crosses the circle the next morning gets a serious deformity in one of his limbs.

After reaching the village cremation ground, the party sits along a circle drawn by the old lady. She prepares a mixture made up of the juice of lemon, liquor, red oxide (vermillion) and meat while reciting her magical formulae and administers it to the girls one after the other. Now they are under the spell of her magic. She then gives some secret formulae which are central to witchcraft to learn. The formulae possess a variety of powers which injure the victim against whom they are used in different ways. The power so acquired is called 'Veer'. A 'Galat Veer' is the power of melting the human body in gradual stages. The 'Rakata Veer' causes skin diseases to the victim, while the 'Hujania Veer' gives swelling all over the body and the 'Balunia Veer' creates a sort of burning in the body.

It is believed that when the girls have learnt the formulae, the old lady takes them for a play. Again on some dark night the old witch goes to a river bank along with the girls and through her magic, calls a crocodile which comes to her. She has gained command over the animal; she puts a copper ring in the nose of the crocodile. The thread of her skirt is tied to the nose-ring of the crocodile and this serves as reins to the riders. Then the whole party rides on the crocodile and moves about in the tank. The witch conjures up a few human hearts for the party's feast. The party enjoys the feast while riding on the animal. They sing and play in the waters of the river and slowly the night passes. The party of girls has by now gathered courage to resort to such magical adventures. They reach their houses before the dawn breaks.

The witches possess a multitude of magical powers. The people of Petlawad believe that they can order the leaves of a tree to fall to the earth and again order them to cling to the branches. A witch does not necessarily harm a man for any sound reason. A trifle may provoke her to harm a person by throwing of charmed grains of *urad*. She may put a stone in the corner of a man's stomach, or she may add a bone to any human limb.

A witch not only harms human beings, but also kills cattle. If she looks with an evil eye at a milk-giving cow or buffalo, the result is a gradual decay of the animal.

If an enemy of the witch is living at a distant place which is separated by a river, the witch floats the charm on a small boat (*tapa*) putting lemon, *sindur* (red-oxide) and grains of *urad* in it, as the charm cannot cross a river or a water tank. When the charm reaches the house of the victim and if the latter is resting in a room with closed doors, the doors crack into parts and the charm harms the victim. Sometimes, the witch even harms a tree. Good mango trees are often supposed to be affected by the power of the witch. The Bhils of Petlawad assert that there seem to be nothing in the world that the witch cannot affect or injure. There is a peculiarity attached to the potency of witchcraft— once a witch inflicts a particular disease on a man it cannot be cured by her. The disease is inflicted forever.

The witch is most dreadful during the Navaratri and Diwali celebrations. She cannot restrain herself from injuring a man who happens to cross her during these days. During these nights she is believed to ride on the back of wild animals and roam about in the wood creating a sensation in the woods.

She is also harmful at the early morning, during the day, at noon and during the evening. People avoid contacts with her during the period when she is particularly capable of causing harmful effects. She is very fond of human blood and hearts. It is believed that when she causes injuries to a person, she acquires small pieces of his or her heart and eats it regularly, and with the last piece she calls for the patient's death. Her fondness for human heart is so strong that she would not even spare her own kinsmen.

The Bhils of Kattiwara believe that a witch possesses a man without any difficulty. She causes a specific disease in a man. The Badwa can diagnose the ailment and say whether it is an ordinary disease or an abnormal one inflicted by a witch. If the disease is caused by a witch, the process of curing the victim by the Badwa is adopted. A suitable period for curing the effects of witchcraft is Sunday night which is supposed to strengthen the magical power of the Badwa. A coconut, a red cloth, liquor, a hen, a goat, lemon and cotton threads are the goods used for this rite. The Badwa drinks liquor and recites his incantations while his associates sing in order to invoke the deity propitiated by the Badwa. The subject who sits near the Badwa is influenced and after a few hours a *dakan* possesses his body. It is believed that whenever a *dakan* possesses someone, she has to leave her physical body in a closed room. The wicked soul leaves her body and possesses the victim. She is supposed to be able to do this miraculously for she possesses magical power to travel through the air without her physical form. When she possesses her victim, she is persuaded to reveal her name. For sometime, she refuses to reveal her name as that would affect her prestige in the village; but a little later she starts misleading the *Badwa* by giving wrong names. Only if the Badwa is stonger would the witch would reveal her correct name. The Badwa knows that it is very difficult to eradicate the evils brought by the witch and therefore he usually adopts the procedure of appeasing the witch. She is offered liquor and chicken-meat. If she expresses her fondness for mutton, it is offered readily. The offerings to a witch are not made in the ordinary way. A rectangular earthen pot is made from earth removed from a junction of four roads. Six marks of powder of red oxide are drawn on its outer layer. Some quantity of the powder is also poured inside. Then, it is filled up with the blood of a hen. Six wicks are lighted and put around the pot. The lighted pot is waived round the head of the victim and put up on the roof of the house. It is supposed to appease a witch. In the morning the earthen pot is submerged in a stream. When the witch is appeased, she makes a promise to make the patient recover and if he subsequently does not recover, he is taken to some greater and more powerful magic-man.

The *Kajali* is a famous term used in connection with the driving off of a witch's spell. There is a shrine in the Jhabua district where the *Badwa* is powerful enough to drive away any witch. In extraordianry circumstances, the people of Ranapur Block or Rama Block visit the shrine. The Badwa fills a brass plate with water wherein the image of the witch becomes visible. This is called *kajali* or the screening of the witch. Ordinarily, every witch is supposed to be frightened when people resort to the process of *kajali*, for it will expose her to the whole village community. A witch would ordinarily, it is believed, leave her victim for fear of the performance of this rite.

The Memorial Feast for the Dead

After one year, or after several years, as soon as the money is available to cover the expenses for a grand feast, the spirit of the dead is finally set to rest. It is known as Memorial feast. It is celebrated for every deceased Bhils, man, woman, or child; but since the surviving relatives generally cannot afford the high expenses of the feast so often it is performed for all those who have died since the last feast performed in a certain area, or by a particular family. It is natural that men, rarely women, of some importance due to their personality or wealth, especially when they die in advance age, are the main recipients of such a celebration. However, all the other deceased members of a family or relationship (*kuthumb*) are also included and commemorated in the memorial feast.

The feast is arranged by a family-group or a *kuthumb*. All kinsmen and relatives by affinity are invited to attend it. The chief performer is, of course, the man who bears the main expenses of the feast. He is usually the eldest son of a deceased Bhils for whose credit the feast is primarily celebrated. For the dancing and other more public ceremonies not only the fellow villagers, but also the Bhils of the neighbouring villages are invited. These guests are, however, not entertained by the celebrating family; only kinsmen take part in the festive dinner which the host is obliged to provide.

The purpose of the feast is to set the spirit of the dead at rest, through the final disposal of his remains, or their remains, in a symbolic act at the river side and by the erection of memorial post, the so-called *munda* or *mando*.

The *munda* is a square post of teak wood (*Tectonagrandis*) or *salai* (*Boswellia serrata*) wood, about three feet over the ground, two feet in the ground when erected. The top end is either pointed or squared in roof form. The figures of the sun in form of a disc, and of the moon in the form of an erect crescent, are carved upon one side of the *munda*. Beneath these figures appear the figures of a man sitting on a horse. More elaborately carved *mundas* bear instead of a relief image the full figure of a rider, carved more or less artistically out of the lower portion of the *munda*, between four or six pillars at the corners of the post. These pillars and miniature keep the upper and the lower parts of the *munda* together and at the same time provide protection to the figure of the rider in its centre. The care must be taken lest the total number of figures representing the dead exceeds that of the members of the family who have died during the period for which the feast is performed, for in that case another member of the family is likely to die for the extra figure.

The carver of the *munda* is always a sacred person. He is paid according to the work he does and the skill which he displays. In the Nimar District where the *mundas* are rather primitive and simple, the carver gets just a few rupees, a bottle of liquor, a loincloth, and some other presents as his fee.

The *munda* must be erected at the original home of the family or clan, even if the deceased has long since lived and died far away from this place. This is probably the reason why in new villages mundas are not to be found.

There are also certain individuals for whom no *munda* is erected. The Bhils village priest (Badwa) receive a memorial hut, called *mando* in place of munda.

The *mando* is a primitive hut, about four to six feet long and broad, on a platform which is from one to two feet high and enclosed in a wooden frame. The height of the *mando* is between three and four feet. The structure consists of wooden posts connected with cross poles; its roof is covered with grass or tiles. Usually the *mando* is built in a corner of a field, or outside the village, near the road. It may be erected even in a new village, unlike the *munda* which must be put up in the ancestral village of the family.

The *mando* stands always in a north-south direction so that the worshipper faces the east when he performs an offering before the *mando*. The floor of the *mando* which is occasionally given a coating with cow-dung contains in a row seven conic stones stuck upright into the ground. These stones are brought from the river and show no artificial carving whatever on the surface. The Bhils state that the stones represent the seven *matas,* the central and biggest stone is Sitala Mata, the goddess of small pox. Other informants maintained that the biggest stone flanked by three others on each side represents the god Bhairon, in the company of the seven *matas*. The stone at the end represents the dead *bhumka* or *parihar* in whose memory the *mando* was erected.

The erection of the *mando* is accompained by the same ceremonies as the erection of the *munda*. The son or another near relatives of the deceased lights an oil-lamp at new-moon time or on Tuesday at the *mando*; passers-by occasionally offer some tobacco before the *matas*. After some years, or if the family changes the village and moves away, the hut slowly breaks down and the memory of the deceased is obliterated by the final disappearance of the hut.

A few days before the feast is celebrated, after sunrise, the carver of the *munda* and the organiser of the ritual go with some fellow villagers to the jungle where they select a tree out of which a *munda* can be carved. It must be teak tree (*Boswellia serrata*) because of its durable wood. When the tree has been found, a red thread is tied around it. Then rice, turmeric, a coconut, lemons, *kuku* and *sindur* (vermilion) are offered at the base of the tree and a cock (of red colour) is sacrificed and a few drops of liquor are spilled in oblation. A smouldering dung cake has been taken along from home to have a fire at hand and to burn incense (*gugal*) on it. After the offering the Bhils venerate the tree by touching the ground in front of it with folded hands which they then raise to their foreheads. This offering is performed to appease the spirit of the tree which is to be cut down. The bottle of liquor is drunk by the men present; only a few drops are spilled on the ground.

After this ceremony the men cut the tree, remove all the branches and place the tree, roughly cut into block, on another tree between its branches, for it should not touch the ground.

The next day all the villagers go out and bring the block of wood with great solemnity to the village. The procession is followed by village musicians; includes drummers, flute players, and female dancers. The block of wood out of which the *munda*is to be fashioned is carried to the village on the shoulders of twelve men. It is placed in the house of the organiser of the feast, leaning against the middle post (*khamba*). Wheat cakes prepared in clarified butter are offered in front of it, also a cock, and a bottle of liquor. All the members of the family and of the wider relationship present pay obeisance.

Then the block of wood is handed over to the carver who begins to work on it on the verandah or in a corner of the house. He works continuously through the whole day and the night and stops for a while only at meal time, eats his meal and drinks half a bottle of liquor. This stimulant is to revive his spirit and to enable him to exert himself more. In the region of Petlawad, the carver does not work in the house, but in the jungle in a shady place. The Bhils of Nimar district, however, the carver of the *munda* stays in the house of the organiser of the feast.

In the afternoon of the same day the villagers again assemble and go to the jungle where they cut a bamboo. This is split and a basket-maker (*basor*) is requested to make two baskets; one a little smaller than the other so that it fits into the bigger one. The Bhils call it *solra*. Into the smaller basket the feast's organiser puts seven bamboo slivers and seven blades of the *dongria* grass. The Bhils consider these bamboo slivers and the grass blades as symbols of the bones of the deceased. Others interpret them as the seven bamboo sticks out of which the bier was made on which the corpse was carried for funeral, while the grass blades signify the grass which covered the bier.

The seven blades of grass are called *phul* means the charred bones of a burnt body. These blades of grass seem to be the most important contents of the basket, since the whole ceremony is called the 'burial of the flowers.'

The basket and its contents are taken to the nearest river or water-place of the village. There on a dry spot or on a boulder in the water they draw a *chauk* with red powder and wheat flour. Then every one present takes a leaf of the *palas*tree (Butea frondosa) and rolling it together into a cup, fills it with boiled *masur ki dal* (peas). He puts this little bag on the *chauk* which the Bhils also call *mandra*. They sprinkle liquor over it and then bring a chicken, cut off its head in sacrifice, put its liver and parts of its head on the *mandra* with other ingredients usual at an offering.

Then all the members of the family approach, one after another, take some red powder (*kuku*) mixed with water in the hollow of the hand and also the seven grass blades. Putting both hands they rub them so that the water drips on the oblations on the *mandra*. If the drops are of dark red colour, the people say that the deceased felt great affection for this particular person; if the water dripping down is of a pale red, they come to the opposite conclusion.

After the ceremony the seven bamboo slivers are tied into a bundles, and enclosed in the a basket whose two parts fit well one into another. The basket is carefully tied together with bamboo fibres and wrapped in a white cloth. This is done to prevent the bamboo slivers and grass blades from falling through the holes in the basket. Another reason for the white cloth is that the deceased's body too was covered with a white cloth when it was carried to the burial ground. A burning earthen lamp (*diya*) is placed beside the basket on a large brass plate on the *mandra*. The basket is then carried to every house of the family where a person had died during the time, since the last feast had been celebrated by that particular family. An offering is performed before the basket which is placed before the middle post of the house. This offering is performed in the name of the deceased person for whom the present feast is celebrated.

After this veneration of the contents, in the basket the inmates of the house begin to sing hymns. The female relatives of the deceased who is commemorated in that particular house begin for their kinsmen. The women jointly sing their usual dirges. These lamentations stop when the banquet which meanwhile has been prepared is served. It consists of rice and chicken meat. But before the guests begin to eat, another offering is made to the contents of the basket, in the manner as done before. Then liquor is served and also the women take a sip. Before drinking each man and woman first spills a few drops of the liquor on the ground. Then they sit down and begin to eat. This happens in every which is visited by the basket.

When the dinner is over, all return to the house of the chief organiser of the feast. They take the basket and the diya on the brass plate with them. The dinner is given usually outside on the large space between the two rows of houses. The burning light on the brass plate is anxiously protected against a blast of wind which might extinguish it.

In the house, the chief organiser of the feast sits down with his wife dressed like a groom and bride like a newly married couple on their wedding day the corner of the man's loincloth is knotted to the end of his wife's upper garment. Often in place of the host and his wife, a young boy and girl, of different clanship but both related to the host, are anointed with turmeric paste, like a bridal couple, and made to sit side by side, the boy's loincloth tied to the girl's white garment. In the attire they have to sit still till about midnight, while the others sit around them and sing wedding songs. Though both are treated like a bridal pair during the celebration, there is obligation for them to marry each other afterwards.

Next morning a crowd of young boys and girls with some elderly people march into the jungle and search for a *sauri* tree (*Bombax malabaricum*) of such a size that its stem can be cut with a single stroke. They are also particular to see that this tree has three branches in the form of trident. They cut the tree with one stroke of the axe and carry it to the spot where the carver of the *munda* is working. As soon as the carving of the *munda* is completed, one of the youths takes it on his shoulders and carries it to the village. Another youth carries the *sauri* stem. The whole crowd then returns to the host's house singing and dancing.

On arrival they are received by the sister or another near relatives of the host, dressed in a white garments and anointed with turmeric like a bride. She is requested to sit down and take the *munda* on her lap. The *munda* too is sprinkled with turmeric paste. Then the white cloth is spread in front of the house and the *munda* is placed on it. The carver of the *munda* is served some liquor so that he may hurry up and complete his work. After the last finishing touch has been laid on the carving, the *munda* is wrapped in a white sheet the ends of which are tied together.

Now the munda and the basket with the *phul* are carried into the house. As soon as this is done a woman starts trembling as if in a trance, shaking her head violently. The Bhils believe that the woman is possessed by the sprit of the deceased who is speaking through her mouth : "I am the one in whose honour the feast is celebrated."

At noon another dinner is served to the present guests. Liquor flows freely on this occasion. In some well-to-do family or who can afford expense the young men go to the nearest market and buy sweets and fruit. On their return they throw all these good things into the groups of women and children who try to catch them. Often the women throw the sweets and fruits back to the boys.

Towards evening of this third day of the feast, the host takes the *munda* on his shoulders and carries it in solemn procession under a kind of canopy to the spot where the Holi festival used to be celebrated. There a he-goat is sacrificed. It is done with a sword, according to ancient custom. As soon as the blood spurts out all the people rush at it and dip their sticks into the blood. Not even one drop of the blood is lost. Some Bhils use their weapons i.e. arrows head in place of sticks. While the ceremony goes on and the Bhils are busy dipping their weapons or sticks into the blood of the goat, an earthen pot full of germinated seeds of millet is brought. The pot is thrown on the ground and when it breaks into many pieces the crowd rushes on the spot to pick up seeds or fragments of the pot. These pieces and grains are used as hunting charms. They put the seeds and clay fragments into little bags which they hang on their weapons. They believe that it will entice the animals to approach them.

Then the basket with the *phul* is also brought to this place and hung up in a tree. Late in the evening there, or in the village, another banquet is provided for all the guests. Goat's meat, *joari-bread,* and the other usual dishes are served.

On the next morning i.e. fourth day of the feast the *munda* is brought to the spot where it is to be set up. Generally the *Badwa* is consulted to select the spot. Possessed by the spirit of the deceased in whose name the *munda* is being erected, he marks the spot where he wants to be commemorated. Usually it is a spot near the village, where *mundas* of the same family are standing. The Bhils believe that the *mundas* represent their forefather, and do not like solitary places but want company. They also wish to be seen by their descendants when they pass that way. That is also the reason why the *mundas* are so often erected near a road, outside the village. The Bhils relatives passing that way often pause a minute, offer tobacco or lemons in front of the *mundas* in their loving memory.

Whenever they intend to erect the *munda,* a hole is dug and at least one-third of the *munda* is sunk into the ground to assure a firm position. After that the basket with the *phul* is taken to the nearest river and hidden in a crab-hole under the water-level on the western side of the river, thus facing the rising sun. The basket is placed in a crab hole obviously because according to Bhil traditions it was a crab which brought the fertile soil to *bhagwan* for him to fashion man out of it. The soil is herewith returned to the crab, after that particular man had lived his span of life.

After that who carries the basket often falls into trance and tremble so vehemently that he swoons. The Badwa then go into action, recite incantations and bring him back to normal life. The whisper incantates into his ear, and invoke the moon god, and remind the deity that they had now fulfilled a good task and that the boy should not be made to suffer. In the state of trance the boy is supposed to select the spot where the *phul* finally should come to rest.

After the burial of the *phul* all return to the place where the *munda* had been set up a short while ago. There the last banquet is now prepared and served to the present guests. When the dinner is completed, all return to their respective home. But before they leave they embrace each other and beg pardon for any mistake or offence they might have committed during the course of feast.

According to Enthoven,[34] in case of the death of an important person, a year or two after his death the relations go to a stone mason and make him cut on a stone slab the figure of a man on horseback with a spear in his hand, paying him by the gift of a cow or a she-buffalo. On the first *Kalichaudas* or dark fourteenth of *Ashvin* (September-October) the stone with procession and drum beating is carried in a cart to the deceased's house, where it is washed, daubed with red powder, covered with a white cloth and again placed in a cart, and taken to the village spirit yard or *devasthan*. Then a goat is killed, its blood sprinkled on the stone and its flesh cooked and eaten with as much liquor or the party can afford.

In case of a man who killed in a fight or by a wild animal away from his home, a stone monument is erected at the spot, where he dies. A man on horseback is generally carved on the stone.[35]

On the occurrence of ultimate death of a person, Bhils perform a special rite known as *Gata Dharna*. In this rite gods are appeased by offering sacrifice of a goat and flesh is cut into pieces and the pieces are distributed among villagers as *prasad* (blessings).[36]

The Bhils erect stone tablets in memory of their male dead (never to deceased women) and as a rule, the figure of the deceased is carved on the stone. He is often represented on horseback with sword, lance or shield, sometimes on foot, but invariably clothes in the best of long clothes and armed with a sword and shield— a style of dress he was quite unaccustomed to in the flesh. Tablets are also erected to boys who have died with still minors; but instead of a figure of the deceased, a large hooded snake is carved on the stone.[37]

Notes and References

1. S. L. Doshi,*op. cit.*, 1971, p. 193.
2. T. H. Hendley, op. cit., p. 353.
3. C.S. Venkatachar, op. cit., p. 242.
4. C. S. Gupta (Ed.), *op. cit.*, p. 12.
5. Kamladevi Chattopadhyaya, op. cit., p. 76.
6. S. L. Doshi, *op. cit.*, p. 193.
7. C. S. Gupta (ed.), *op. cit.*, p. 13.
8. K. L. Bhowmik, *Tribal India, A profile in Indian Ethnology,* Calcutta, p. 72.
9. Kamladevi Chattopadhyaya, *op. cit*, p. 76.
10. C. E. Luard, *op. cit.*, p. 30.
11. C. S. Gupta (ed.), *op. cit.*, p. 19.
12. C. S. Venkatachar, op. cit., p. 242.
13. C. E. Luard, *op. cit.*, p. 31.
14. Kamladevi Chattopadhyaya, *op. cit.*, p. 77.
15. R. E. Enthoven, *op. cit.*, pp. 169-170.
16. *Ibid.*, pp. 167-188.
17. S. C. Roy, op. cit., p. 13.
18. K. L. Bhowmik, *op. cit.*, p. 72.
19. C. E. Luard, *op. cit*, p. 32.
20. R. E. Enthoven, *op. cit.*, p. 170.
21. K. L. Bhowmik, *op. cit.*, p. 72.
22. Kamladevi Chattopadhyaya, *op. cit.*, p. 78.
23. R. E. Enthoven, *op. cit.*, p. 168.
24. *Ibid.*, p. 170.
25. *Ibid.*, p. 168.
26. Kamladevi Chattopadhyaya, *op. cit.*, p. 78.
27. *Ibid.*, p. 170.
28. S. L. Doshi, *op. cit.*, p. 196.
29. S. C. Roy, op. cit., p. 14.
30. S. L. Doshi, *op. cit*, pp. 199-200.
31. C. S. Gupta (ed.), op. cit., p. 26
32. S. L. Doshi, *op. cit.*, p. 208.
33. *Census of India 1891*, p. 220.
34. R. E. Enthoven, *op. cit.*, pp. 168-169.
35. Syed Ashfaq Ali, *Tribal Demography in Madhya Pradesh* (A Socio-economic Study, 1901-1973), Bhopal, 1973, p. 28.
36. "Jhabua Ke Bhils", op. cit., p. 6.
37. W. Crook, *op. cit.*, p. 54.

Conclusion

In the preceding chapters, various Bhil rituals have been described in an ethno-historic perspective and in the geographical framework of Jhabua district. The main emphasis has been laid on birth, marriage and death rites.

The Bhils are spread over a large area. Their customs and tradition vary from area to area due to their exposure to surrounding cultures.

The Bhils are the largest group among tribal population in India. Out of 29.8 million scheduled tribes, according to 1971 census, 3.8 million are the Bhils. The Bhils stand out by certain physical features. They are distinguished by dark complexion, diminutive size, prominent cheek-bones, large nostrils. They are energetic, endowed with an astonishing power of enduring fatigue. Excellent woodmen, they know the shortest cuts over the hills, can walk the roughest paths and climb the steepest crags without slipping or feeling distressed.

The term Bhil, probably derived from the Dravidian word *Bhilla,* means bow, a characteristic weapon of the tribe. The Bhils are mentioned in the *Ramayana* and the *Mahabharata*. The noted author of the *Ramayana,* Valmiki, started his life as a Bhil bandit nemed *Walia*. Later on he became a sage through the blessings of goddess Saraswati, and his extreme grief over his dark past turned into poetry. The *Mahabharata* tells us about the famous archer, Ekalavya who was a Bhil.

Scholars are not unanimous about the racial affinity of the Bhils. Some suggest that they belong to Pre-Dravidian 'Negroid race'. Others opine that they represent a mixed race having Caucasian and Australoid elements with a touch of the Mongolian features. Considering racial data, blood group, it appears that they are the earliest settlers of India, thoroughly hybridised by contacts with alien races.

The Bhils show close racial similiarity with other aboriginal tribes. Considering derived reduced co-efficient, racially the Bhils are very close to Kadar and Chenchu tribes and they have been attributed to the same stock. However Nattu Malayan, Munda and Oraon are also close to the Bhils.

The Bhils were the rulers of Marwar or Jodhpur at the time of Aryan invasion of Rajputana. From there they were driven to the Aravali and the Vindhya hills under pressure from the invaders. The history of Rajputana mentions that Bhils were expelled from the plains by the Rajputs. They were oppressed as well as patronised by the Rajput rulers. The history during the 7th to 13th century is known as the first phase of Bhil Rajput co-operation. The prominent figure was Bappa Rawal who was bred and brought up among the Bhils. At a very early age he became their leader and put *teeka* on the forehead of the Bhil chief Ogana by his thumb's blood. Since then the tradition of *teeka* has been continuing at the time of the coronation of Rajput rulers.

Economically, the Bhils have taken to agriculture as their main occupation with some secondary sources of income which adds to the family coffers. Their concentration on this occupation has resulted in less social problembs. The rate of migration is very high which exhibit their tendency towards high earning.

The Bhils have patriarchal type of society. Their family consists of man, and his wife with their children. Grown-up sons may or may not be separated. Polygamy is prevalent among them. Polyandry is found very seldom. Widow re-marriage is commonly in practice. A younger brother can keep the widow of his elder brother but not vice versa. The kinship terms are influenced by the surrounding cultures. The term grand father is not used. Instead, the term older father or the aged father is used. The term *kaka, mamo, jiji* and *fusi* are used for persons of fathers's age, maternal uncle, all women of mother's age and father's sister respectively. Husband and wife are not permitted by customs to mention each other's name. They address each other with reference to their children's name.

In the Bhil society there is no higher or lower caste groups. The caste is divided into septs. In the Jhabua district 122 septs have been found. Each sept is represented by a totem. The head of the village is known as *Tadvi* or *Patel*. The Panchayat is a statutory body which consists of the *tadvi,* or the *patel,* the *kotwal,* the *mafidar,* occasionally the *pujari* and a few elders of the village. It is responsible for settling the disputes pertaining to petty quarrels, petty thefts and breach of tribal rules. *Badwa* is considered as a socio-religious leader. Tattooing is customary among the members of both the sexes and especially among the females.

The dance and music are the integral parts of their life. On the ceremonial occasions these displays deal with mythological subject matter, supernatural and miraculous restoration but they are more social than religious.

The fair and festivals play important role in their social and cultural life. The *Singhasan Mata Ka Mela, Bhagoria Mela, Wavni, Divasa* and *Nawai* are the important festivals. These traditional festivals are celebrated during sowing, growing and harvesting period. The worship of the village deities and offering of goat and certain materials are the characteristic features.

The Bhili dialects exhibit influences of the langauges of the surrounding areas: Rajasthani, Gujarati, Khandeshi and Marathi. The Marathi influence is only of superficial kind. About 84 per cent of the words taken from Rajputana and Mahikantha, are derived from Sanskrit, and 10 per cent are of Persian origin, and 6 per cent of uncertain origin.

Their religion has changed radically and is now nearer to Hinduism. They believe in re-birth, *karma-yoga* and *bhakti*. They revere all Hindu gods and goddesses.

The Bhils believe that they are the followers of *Mahadeva*. *Mahadeva* i.e. 'the Great God', is usually identified with the Hindu god Shiva. But it is strange that the Bhils do not worship *lingam,* which is the symbol of Shiva. The Bhils consider *Bhagwan* as the supreme god and creator of universe. They do not generally worship him, they rather fear him, especially because of the judgement which according to their belief each has to undergo after death.

During this study it has been noticed that many traits of ancient Bhils culture survive in their religious as well as social rituals. In some of the areas they show primitive type of religious practices. They do not build temples, but install stone images smeared with red lead and oil. They worship village deities, nature, animals, trees, stones and tools. Their offering of animals and liquor to the deities and lighting of a fire infront of the image point towards the survival of the primitive idea of burned sacrifice.

An old Bhil lady speculates the sex of an unborn child on the basis of certain signs visible during pregnancy viz. conditions, eating desire and the movement of expected mother. The most important means of prediction is through observation of the movement of expected mother. If a woman drags her left leg while walking, she will give birth to a male child, on the other hand if she drags her right leg a female child is expected.

For the sake of safe bearing of child the pregnant woman is looked after with great care. Charms and amulets are tied to the arms of the woman to protect the child in the womb against all evil influences, including that of spirits. There are certain taboos attached to the father of unborn child too. He is prohibited to cut anything growing, to eat any animal which had died accidently and to drive a nail or a pole into the ground.

The birth of the baby is announced by beating of a *dhol* (drum). Certain offerings of milk and liquor are made to the deities. Afterwards the *Guru* or some other person carries the news to the relatives and neighbours who assemble at the hut of the parents and present gifts according to their means or wishes.

As soon as the baby is born the umbilical cord is severed with a sharp bamboo chip or an arrow head and the part attached to the baby's body is tied up. For preventing infection, mixture of turmeric and oil is applied on the wound.

The method of disposal of placenta varies from place to place. In Rajasthan it is buried in the cattle shed outside the house. In Jhabua district it is buried in a secret palce, usually in a corner of the verandah or in the house. It is kept always under the protection of a roof.

The purificatory rite takes place generally on the fifth day (sometimes on the seventh day) of the delivery. In Alirajpur region it is performed on the 3rd day of the delivery. On that occasion, the woman and the child are bathed. Then the offerings of 'sindur' (vermillion) and coconut are given to the deities. A small feast is organised to offer *khichadi* or *rabadi* along with a small quantity of liquor to 5 children. The worship of the totemic deity on this occasion has a special significance. This is done in the hope that the deity would provide ample milk in the mother's breast.

The rites pertaining to naming of the child exhibit the primitive Bhil culture. There is no fixed day for the naming ceremony. On that occasion the *Badwa* or the local renowned person is called to perform certain rituals. The rituals are performed in a brief way by offering some coconut and red powder to the village tutelary deity. The name of the child is given by some elderly lady.

The tonsure ceremony (ear and nose piercing ceremony) performed by them seems to be influenced by the surrounding cultures. It reveals some traditional element. The worshipping of the razor and throwing of money appear to be exclusively Bhil custom.

The ceremony relating to offering solid food to a child exhibit survival culture. When the child is about 10-12 months old, this ceremony is performed. It is known as *Botan*. In this ceremony the solid food is given to the child for the first time. For this purpose special food is prepared by the child's aunt.

In Bhil's life marriage is considered as a serious matter which is performed in a long chain of rituals. The elaborate wedding ceremonies begin with search of a bride by the prospective groom's family. In this connection relatives and friends or sometimes professional match-makers help to select the right bride. After getting information about satisfactory bride, the Brahman is consulted to cast the horoscope of the boy and the girl concerned. If the constellation of their stars appears favourable the next step is followed. In case of evil chances of an unlucky horoscope are made innocuous by giving alms consisting of coconut, *Supari* (betelnut), a small coin and grain, either to the Brahman or to a poor relative or begger. The next step is followed with the settlement of *dhapa* (bride price). After settling the question of bride-price the auspicious day for bethrothal is fixed.

On the fixed day the groom's father accompanied by a few friends or relatives arrives at the bride's house with some clothes for the girl, sweets and spices, a coconut and *kuku* (red powder).

At the auspicious time things brought by the groom's father are put on a *parat* (brass plate) and are presented to the bride's father with some amount of money.

The actual wedding rituals seem to begin with the *wane* day. As a rule the *wane,* at the bride's groom house, begins one day earlier than the bride's house. It is done only to give him enough time to arrange other things. The rituals performed during *wane* period seem to be the survivals of ancient tradition. On the first of the *wane* days the village headman begins to draw certain predetermined figure of human and animal with trident on the inner wall nearest to the sleeping place.

Just after the last *wane* day proper wedding ceremonies start which comprises of more than fifty separate riltes. They are performed partly at the bridegroom's house and partly at the bride's.

The setting up of marriage booth (*Mandwo Ropwo*) is an important ritual. This ritual is performed systematically and with great care. The *Mahat* or *Boba dena* (sucking raw sugar from the mother's breast) ritual points towards the real separation of son from mother.

The full swing wedding ritual starts with a procession of the groom to the bride's home. On the groom's arrival at the bride's house, touching the Garland (*Toran Sibwun*) ritual is performed. This ritual seems to be influenced by the surrounding cultures. Moving around the ceremonial pole marks an ancient tradition. The young couple walk around the pole seven times (anti-clock wise); for first four rounds the bridegroom leads; for the last three the bride. Pulling down the marriage *Mandap* at bride's and bridegroom's house are ceremoniously performed. This is done by the bridegroom at both the houses. At the bride's house, he is allowed to pull it by his one hand and in his own house he can use his both hands.

In ancient Bhil culture marriage appears to have been essentially a contract in which a family agrees to hand over one of its young woman to another family. The bride thus switches her familial allegiance so that any children born from the union will belong to her husband's family and clan. The analysis of the wedding ritual draws attention to another aspect of the ancient Bhil society, namely the existence of patri clans.

Some ancient cultural traits have been noticed in death rites too. Except among the Muslims, cremation is practised for the disposal of the dead bodies. Persons dying of small pox and dead bodies of children upto the age of 5 years are buried. All these are buried in sleeping position. An ascetic is buried in the sitting posture. In case of the death of a woman with a four months of pregnancy, the foetus is taken out from her womb by the husband and cremated alongwith the dead body of the mother. The death is noticed by firing of guns before the deceased's house while the villagers are informed by monotonous beating of a drum. After the occurence of the death *Jogi* (traditional priest) officiates the funeral ceremony. He sits outside the door of the house and an image of a horse, and an earthen jar full of water are placed near him. Each visitor who has come to attend the ceremony gives him grain and sprinkles a little water over the image of the horse in the name of the deceased.

The procedure of bringing water for bathing the deceased seems to be ancient culture. For this purpose a woman relative goes to the stream with a new earthen pot and a sickle to which a black string is tied. On this errand, she is followed by a man carrying an axe on his shoulder. Before filling up the pot, the woman makes on the water two intersecting cuts.

As an offering to the dead a little bread, made of flour, freshly ground, care being taken that the hand in grinding always moves from left to right, is prepared. This is then mixed with *ghi* and *gur* and made into a ball, called *hamla*.

On the third day a, ceremony is performed at the side of the river. For this purpose the deceased's relatives gather and shave their moustaches and beards. On the twelfth day, death dinner is given to the guests. The *Raval* plays an active role.

The memorial feast is organised after one year or several years. This is done with the purpose to set the spirit of the dead at rest, through the final disposal of his remians. For their memory, the Bhils erect memorial post called *munda*. A magnificent feast is organised on this occasion.

Bibliography

Agrawal, B. C., "Interaction between Tribes and non Tribes" (in) *Tribal Heritage of India* (Ethnicity, Identity and Interaction), edited by S. C. Dubey, New Delhi, Vol. I, 1977, pp. 118-140.

Ahuja, Ram, *A Social Study of Bhils,* Ph.D. thesis, University of Rajasthan, Jaipur, 1964.

— "Marriage among the Bhils" *Man in India,* Vol. XXXXVI, no. 3, 1966, pp. 233-240.

— "Religion of the Bhils— A Sociological Analysis", *Sciological Bulletin,* Vol. XIV, no. 1, 1965, pp. 21-33.

Ahwa, Kalasinh F. Kishori, "The Bhils of Gujarat", *Vanyajati,* Vol. X, no. 2, 1962, 67-69.

Akhil, Viney, "Rajasthan Ke Upekshit Bhil" (in Hindi), *Vanyajati,* Vol. I, no. 3, 1953, pp. 60-62.

Ali, Syed Ashfaq, *Tribal Demography in Madhya Pradesh* (A Socio- economic Study, 1901-1973), Bhopal, 1973.

Altekar, A. S., *A History of Village Communities in Western India,* Bombay, OUP, 1927.

Anderson, J. D., "Bhil", *People of India,* Cambridge, 1913, reprint, New Delhi, 1982.

Anonymous, "Bhil or Bheel", *Census of Bombay Presidency,* part-II, General Report and Tables, 1872.

— "Bhils of Khedbrahma", *Bulletin of the Institute of Traditional Cultures,* Vol. I-II, 1965, pp. 200-209.

— "Jhabua ke Bhil" (in Hindi), *Vanyajati*, Vol. XV, no. 1, 1967, pp. 5-7.

— "Maharashtra: Bhil Movement in Dhulia", *Economic and Political Weekly*, Vol. VII, no. 5, 1972.

— "Magic Songs of the Bhils of Jhabua State", *The Encyclopaedia Americana*, reprint, New York, 1957.

— "Social work among Gujarat Bhils", *The Servant of India*, June 22, 1922.

Bacon, Elizabeth, "Bhil" *Encyclopaedia Americana*, B To Burkubg, Encyclopaedia Americana Corporation, Vol. III, 1918, reprint 1978.

Bahadur, F. (ed.), *Bulletin of the Tribal Research and Development Institute*, Bhopal, volume vii, no. 1 & 2, 1969.

Bahadur, K. P., *The Castes, Tribes and Culture of India*, New Delhi, Vol. 1977-81.

Bannerman, A. D., "Bhil", *Census of India 1901* (Rajputana), report, Lucknow, Vol. XXV, part-I, 1902.

Barbar, G. M., "Bhils and Bhil Garasias", *Tribes of India*, New Delhi, 1950.

Barnes, E., "The Bhils of Western India", *Journal of the Society of Arts*, Vol. LV, 1906-1907.

Bayti, Jamnalal, "Face to Face with Bhils", *Social Welfare*, New Delhi, Vol. XXXIV, no. 11, Feb. 1988.

Benedict, Ruth, *Pattern of Culture*, 6th edition, London, 1955.

Benthoven, R. E., "Bhil", *Tribes and Castes of Bombay*, Vol. I, 1920.

Beny, Roloff, *Rajasthan*, London, 1984.

Bhagwata Purana, Skanda 4, Chap. 14, sloka, 45.

Bhatavadekar, G. K., "Bhil", *Report on the Census of the Baroda Territories 1881*, Bombay, 1883.

Bhattacharya, J. N., "Bhil", *Hindu Castes and Sects*, Calcutta, 1896.

Bhowmik, K. L., *Tribal India: A Profile in Indian Ethnology*, Calcutta, 1971.

Bhuria, M., *Folk Songs of the Bhils,* Indore, 1979.

Biswas, P.C. and Bhattacharya, D.K., "Anthropometric Study of Bhils", *The Anthropologist,* Vol. XI, 1964.

Blair, G.W., *Station and Camp Life in the Bheel Country,* London, 1906.

Bose, Uma, "The Malwa Bhils of Dhar," Unpublished M.A. Dissertation, Cornell University, 1952.

Campbell, J. M., "Bhil", *Central Provinces District Gazetteer Nimar District* (Descriptive), Allahabad, Vol. A, 1908.

— "Bhil" (Miscellaneous), *Imperial Gazetteer of India,* Provincial series central provinces, Calcutta, Vol. VIII, 1908.

— "Bhil", *Rajputana Gazetteer,* Calcutta, Office of the superintendent of Government Printing, Vol. I, 1879.

Carstairs, G. M., *Bhil Village of Western Udaipur: A Study in Resistance to Social Change,* edited by M.N. Srinivas, Calcutta, 1955.

— "The Bhils of Kotra Bhomat", *The Eastern Anthropologist,* Lucknow, Vol. VIII, no. 3 & 4, 1954, pp. 169-181.

Chakraborti, Mukul and Mukherjee, Dipak, "Bhil", *Indian Tribes,* Calcutta, 1971.

Chattopadhyaya, Kamaladevi, "The Bhils of Gujarat and Rajasthan", (Chap. 2) *Tribalism in India,* edited by Kumar Suresh Singh, New Delhi, 1978, pp. 55-79.

Chaturvedi, D.N., "The Bhils of Rajasthan through ages", (in) *The Tribe,* Vol. V, no. 3, 1968.

Chauhan, B. M., "Tribalization (Bhil, Meena, Gond)", *The Tribe,* Vol. II, no. 1 & 2, 1966.

Chinoy, A. D., "Bhil", *Census of India 1901,* Berar report, Allahabad, Vol. VIII, part-I, 1902.

Cole, B. L., "Bhil", *Census of India 1931,* Rajputana Agency, report and tables, Meerut, Vol. XXVII, 1932.

Contractor, J. J., "Bhil", *Vikas Weekly,* October 11, 1947.

Crook, W., "Bhil", *Castes and Tribes of North West Province and*

Crook, W., "Bhil", *Castes and Tribes of North West Province and Oudh,* Calcutta, Vol. II, 1896.

— "Bhil", *North Western Provinces of India,* London, 1897.

Races of North India, Delhi, reprint 1973.

The Tribes and Castes of the North Western India, New Delhi, 1974.

Dalal, J.A., "Bhil", *Census of India 1891,* Bombay, Baroda Report, Vol. XXIV, 1894.

— "Bhil", *Census of India 1901,* Baroda report, Bombay, Vol. XVIII, part-I, 1902.

Datta, J. N., "Bhil", *Census of India 1921* (Report & Tables), Gwalior (Madhya Pradesh), Vol. XX, part-I, 1922.

Deliege, Robert, "Division and Hierarchy among the Bhils", *Man in India,* Vol. LX, no. 1-2, 1980, pp. 38-50.

— *The Bhils of Western India,* (Some Empirical and theoretical issues in Anthropology in India), New Delhi, 1985.

— "The Bhils or the Tribe as an Image", *The Eastern Anthropologist,* Vol. XXXIV, no. 2, April-June 1981, pp. 117-129.

Desai, G. H., "Bhil", *Census of India 1911,* (Baroda report), Bombay, Vol. XVI, part-1, 1911.

Doshi, J. K., *Social Structure and Social Change in a Bhil Village,* New Delhi, New Height, 1974.

Doshi, S. L., *Bhils: Between Societal Self-Awareness and Cultural Synthesis,* New Delhi, 1971.

Dracup, A. H. & Sorley, H.T., "Bhil", (Goathi), *Census of India 1931,* Bombay Presidency, General report, Bombay, Vol. III, part-I, 1933.

Drysdale, T., "Bhil", *Census of the Central Provinces 1881,* (report with appendices), Bombay, Vol. II, 1883.

Dubois, J. A., *A Description of the People of India 1817,* Madras, reprint 1879.

Egerton, B., "Bhil", *Census of India 1891,* Report on the Census of the district of Ajmer-Mewar, Calcutta, 1893.

Elliot, H.M., *The Races of the North-Western Provinces of India*, Vol. I, London, 1897.

Enthoven, R. E., "Bhil", *The Tribes and Castes of Bombay*, Bombay, Vol. I (A-G), 1920, reprint, New Delhi, 1975.

— "Bhil", *Census of India 1901* (Bombay report), 1902, Vol. IX, part-1, 1902.

Erskine, Maj. K. D., *India District Gazetteers*, (Rajputana), Udaipur, Rajasthan, 1908.

Ferreira, John V., "The Bhil", *Totemism in India*, Bombay, Oxford University Press, 1965.

Forbes, A.K., *Rasmala of Hindu Annals of the Provinces of Goozerat in Western India*, 2 Vols, London, 1856.

Forbes, James, *Oriental Memoirs Narrative of 17 Years Residence in India*, (in 4 Vols.), London, 1813.

Forsyth, Cap. J., *The Highlands of Central India*, (notes on their Forests, and Wild Tribes, Natural History and Sports), 1889, reprint, New Delhi, 1975.

Francis, W., "Bhil", *Census of India 1901* (Madras report), Vol. XV, part-I, 1902.

Frazer, Sir James George, *Aftermath: A Supplement to the Golden Bough*, London, 1963.

Fuchs, Stephen, "Bhil, Tribes in the Central India" (chapter-v), *Aboriginal Tribes of India*, New Delhi, 1973.

— *Rebellions Prophets : A Study of Messianic Movement in India*, Bombay, 1965.

— "The Marriage Rites of the Bhils in the Nimar District, C.P.", *Man in India*, Vol. XXII, nos. 2 & 3, 1942, pp. 105-139.

— "The Original Wedding Ritual of the Bhil", *Anthropos*, Vol. XXXXXXVI, 1951.

Gaffor, K. A., "Bhils in Hyderabad", *Tribes of India*, part II, New Delhi, Bhartiya Adimjati Sevak Sangh, 1951.

Ghurye, G. S., *Caste and Class in India*, Bombay, 1950.

— *The Aborigines so called and their future,* Pune, 1943.

— *The Scheduled Tribes,* Bombay, Popular Book Depot, Second edition, 1959.

Gibbs, Lieut. T.E., "Bhils in the Dangs", *The Indian Antiquary,* Vol. V, 1876.

Gibson, Alexander, "Notes on the Bheels North of the Narbudda", *Journal of the Bombay Branch of Royal Asiatic Society,* Proceedings, Official Literary and Scientific, Vol.IX, December 1866 to November 1868.

Goetz, Philip W. (ed.), "Bhil", *Encyclopaedia Britannica,* Vol.II, Chicago, 1968.

Graham, D.C., *A Brief Historical Sketch of the Bheel Tribes Inhabiting the Province of Khandesh,* London, East India College Library, 1845.

Grierson, Sir George A., "Bhili Languages including Khandeshi, Banjari or Labhani, Bahrapia", *Linguistic Survey of India,* Vol. IX, part-3, 1907, reprint, Delhi 1968.

Grigson, W. V., *The Aboriginal Problem in the C. P. and Berar,* Nagpur, 1944.

Guha, B. S., "Bhil": A Racial Affinities of the People of India, *Census of India 1931* (Ethnographical), Simla, Vol. I, part-3, 1935.

Guha, K., "Bhairon's Image on a Bhil Amulet", *Vanyajati,* Vol. VII, no. 1, 1959.

Gulati, R.K. and Srinivasan, S., "An Analysis of ABC Blood Groups of the Bhils of West Khandesh (Maharashtra)", *The Eastern Anthropologist,* Vol. XXVI, no. 1, pp. 79-85.

Gupta, C.S.(ed.), "Bhils: A Village Survey Monograph (Gagron)", *Census of India 1961,* Rajasthan, Vol. XIV, Part VI-D, New Delhi, 1969.

— "Bhils: A Village Survey Monograph (Kailashpuri)", *Census of India 1961,* Rajasthan, Vol. XIV, Part VI-C, New Delhi, 1967.

— "Bhils: A Village Survey Monograph (Khajoora)", *Census of India 1961,* Rajasthan, Vol. XIV, Part VI-A, New Delhi, 1964.

— "Bhils: A Village Survey Monograph (Panarwa)", *Census of India 1961*, Rajasthan, Vol. XIV, Part VI-B, New Delhi, 1965.

Gupta, Mangal Sain, "Glimpses of Tribal Life Mo-Hu-Janu", *The Tribe*, Vol. I, no.1, 1964.

Harit, H. L., Roy Burman, B. K. and Shekhar, A. Chandra, "Bhil", *A Preliminary Appraisal of the Scheduled Tribes of India*, New Delhi, Office of the Registrar General, India, 1961-68.

Hassan, S.S., *The Castes and Tribes of H.E.H. the Nizam Dominion*, Bombay, Vol. I, 1920.

Hasting, James (ed.), "Bhil", *Encyclopaedia of Religion and Ethics*, New York, Vol. II, 1909.

Hasting, Warren, 'Bhil', *Census of India 1891* (Berar or Hyderabad, Assigned District, Calcutta, Vol. VI, 1892.

Heber, B (ed.), "Bhil", *Gazetteer of Bombay Precidency*, (narrative), Bombay, 1825.

Hedberg, E., "The Celebration of Diwali by the Mewar Bhils", *Journal of the Anthropological Society of Bombay*, Vol. XIV, no. 3, 1929, pp. 364-400.

Hippolytus, Pere, "The Relation between Religion and Morality among the Bhils", *Primitive Man*, Vol. IV, 1931, pp. 49-53.

Hendley, T.H., "An Account of the Mewar Bhils", *Journal of the Asiatic Soceity of Bengal*, Vol. XLIV, Part-1, Calcutta, 1875.

Hooja, Rima, "Prehistoric Hunter-Gatherers: Forerunners of the "Tribal Tradition", *Tribal Movement*, edited by Ram Pande, 1984.

Hussain, Mazhar, "Bhils", *Census of India 1941*, H. E. H. Nizam's dominiond (report), Hyderabad State, Hyderabad, Vol. XX, Part-1, 1945.

Hutton, J. H., "Bhil, Tour notes of the Census Commissioner of India 1930-31", *Census of India 1931* (Ethnographical Simla), New Delhi, Vol. I, Part-3, 1935.

Jain, Bhagwati Lal, "Bhil Folk Songs as a Source of Peoples Movement", in *Tribal Movements,* edited by Ram Pande, Sodhak, Jaipur, Rajasthan, 1984.

Jain, Nemichand, *Bhil: Bhasa, Sahitya aur Sanskriti,* (The Language, Literature and Culture of the Bhils), in Hindi, Indore, 1964.

— *Bhili-Hindi Kos* (A Bhili-Hindi Dictionary), Indore, 1962.

Jain, Rajendra Kumar, "Indebtedness among the Bhils (Bhilala) of Jhabua (M.P.)", *Xth International Congress of Anthropological and Ethnological Science* (Abstract), New Delhi, Vol. II, 1978.

Jain, Santosh Kumar, *Adiwasi Bheel - Mina* (in Hindi), Jaipur, 1981.

Jethwa, Prabhat Singh Sardar, "Rajkot ni Bhil Kom" (Gujarati), Ph.D. Thesis, Ahmedabad, Gujarat University, 1965.

Jungbelt, L., *A Short Bhili Grammar of Jhabua State and Adjoining Territories,* Indore, 1937.

— "Bhil Wisdom in Proverbs and Phrases", *Primitive Man,* Vol. XVIII, 1945, pp. 56-62.

Karve, Irawati, *Kinship Organisation in India,* reprint, Calcutta, 1968,

— *The Bhils of West Khandesh* (A Socio-Economic Survey), The Anthropological Society of Bombay, Bombay, 1958, reprint 1961.

Karve, Irawati & Sankalia, *Preliminary report of the third Gujarat Expedition,* Pune, 1945.

Khan, G. Ahmed, "The Bhils of Khandesh", *Man in India,* Ranchi, Vol. XV, nos. 2 & 3, 1935, pp. 133-143.

Khan, M. M., "Bhil", *Census of India 1891,* His Highness the Nizam's Dominion (Report), Bombay, Vol. XXII, Part-2, 1894.

Khan, Mohammed, "Madhya Pradesh ki Pramukh Vanyajatian", (Principal Tribes of Madhya Pradesh), (in Hindi), *Vanyajati,* New Delhi, Vol. XVIII, no.I, 1969, pp. 3-6.

Khanapurkar, D.P., *Aboriginal Tribes of South Gujarat,* an unpublished thesis in the School of Economics and Sociology, Bombay, Bombay University.

Kincaid, Col. W., "On the Bheel Tribes of the Vindhya Range", *Journal of the Royal Anthropological Institute of Great Britain and Ireland,* Vol. IX, 1880, pp. 397-405.

Kishori, Kalasinh F., "Dang's Natives at a Glance", *Vanyajati,* New Delhi, Vol. X, no. 3, July 1962, pp. 120-123.

Kitts, E. J., *A Compendium of the Castes and Tribes found in India,* Bombay, 1885.

— "Bhil", *Report on the Census of Berar 1881,* Bombay, 1882.

Konrad, Paul, *Im Lande der Bhagoria Bhils,* Kaldenkirchen Steyler ver Langsbuchh und Lung, 1962.

Koppers, W., "Bhagwan the Supreme Deity of the Bhils", *Anthropos,* Vol. XXXV, 1940-41, pp. 265-325.

— "Buffalo and Zebu in Central India", *Anthropos,* Vol. XXXVII-XXXX, 1942-45.

— "Die Bhil in Zentralindien", Horn-Wien, Verlag Ferdinand, Berger, 1948.

— "Houshund und Wildhund in Zentral Indien", Mit Bemerkungen von Dr. U. Duerst, *Bulletin de La Societe Fribourgeoise des Sciences Naturelles,* Vol. XXXVI, 1942.

— "India and the Dual Organisation", *Acta Tropica,* (Basel), Vol. I, 1944.

Koppers, W. and Jungblut, L., "Betrothal Rites among the Bhil of North-Western Central India", *Artibus Asiae,* Vol. IX, nos. 1-4, 1946.

— "Wedding Rites among the Bhil of North-Western Central India", *Anthropos,* Vol. XXXXVI, Part I-II, 1951.

Kulkarni, D.S., "The Bhil Movement in Dhulia District (1972-74)", *Tribal Movement in India,* Vol. II, edited by Kumar Suresh Singh, New Delhi, 1982.

Kumari, Ranjna and Nath, Surendra, "Progression of Segmental Growth among Male Bhils of Udaipur", *S.A.P.,* Vol. VI, 1984.

Kurup, A. M., "Bhagoria (A Bhil Festival)", *Bulletin of the Tribal Research Institute,* Chhindwara (M.P.), Vol. II, no. 2, 1958, pp. 49-57.

— "Glimpses of Life and Culture of the Tribes of Madhya Pradesh", *Vanyajati,* New Delhi, Vol. X, no. 4, October 1962, pp. 134-145.

Lal, Hira, "Tantia Bhil", (Miscellaneous contributions), *Man in India,* Vol. V, nos. 3 & 4, 1925, pp. 250-255.

Lal, R. B., "Tribals of Gujarat (brief notes)", *Tribal Research Bulletin,* (A bi-annual Journal of Tribal Research and Training Institute), Pune, Maharashtra, Vol. II, no. 2, 1981, p. 26.

Lavania, B.K., *The Impact of Community Development and the Bhils of Southern Rajasthan,* Ph.D. thesis, Agra, University of Agra, 1969.

Law, B. C., *Tribes of Ancient India,* Pune, Bhandarkar Oriental Series, 1943.

— *Ancient Indian Tribes,* London, Luzac & co., Vol. II, 1934.

Louis, Rousselet, *India and its Native Princes,* Travels in Central India and in the Presidencies of Bombay and Bengal, London, 1875, pp. 130-155.

Luard, C. E., *Alirajpur State Gazetteer,* 1908.

— "Bhil", *Census of India 1901,* (Ethnographic appendices), Calcutta, Vol. I, 1903.

— "Bhil", *Census of India 1911,* Central India Agency, (report and tables), Calcutta, Vol. XVII, 1913.

— *Jungle Tribes of Malwa,* Lucknow, 1909.

Macfarlane, E.W.E., "Blood Grouping in the Deccan and Eastern Ghats", *Journal of the Royal Asiatic Society of Bengal,* Vol. VII, Part-1.

Macfarlane, E.W.E. and Sarkar, "Blood Groups of India", *American Journal of Physical Anthropology,* 1941, Vol. XXVIII, no. 4.

Mahalanobis, P.C., "Bhil", *Sankhya,* Vol. IX, part-2 & 3, 1949.

Maharashtra Census Office, "Scheduled Tribes in Maharashtra" (Ethnographic notes), *Census of India 1961* Maharashtra, New Delhi, Vol. X, Part V-B, 1972.

Majumdar, D. N., "Bhils", *Race Realities in Cultural Gujarat*, Gujarat, 1950.

— *Races and Culture of India*, Lucknow, 1944, reprint Bombay, 1958.

— "The Bhils of Gujarat", *Journal of the Gujarat Research Society*, Vol. IV, no. 4, 1942.

— "The Bhils of Gujarat (Preliminary Remarks on Bhil Raciology)", *Journal of Gujarat Research Society*, Bombay, Vol. IV, no. 3, 1942, pp. 220-237.

— "The Changing Canvas of Tribal Life", *The Eastern Anthropologist*, Vol. III, no. 1, Sept. 1949.

Majumdar, M. P., "The Bhils of Gujarat", *Modern Review*, Vol. XLI no. 3, 1972, pp. 296-303.

Majumdar, R. C., *The History and Culture of the Indian People: the Vedic Age*, Vol. I, London 1952.

Malcolm, John, "Essay on the Bhils", *Journal of the Royal Asiatic Society of Great Britain and Ireland*, London, Vol. I, 1827.

Mamoria, C.B., *Tribal Demography in India*, Allahabad, Kitab Mahal, 1957.

Mann, R.S., "Bhils in Historical Perspective and in Relationship with non-Tribal", (in) *Rajasthan Bhils*, jointly edited by N.N. Vyas, R.S. Mann and N. D. Chaudhary, 1978.

— "Position of Women in Tribal Rajasthan", *Tribal Women in India*, Calcutta, Indian Anthropological Society, 1978.

Master, Alfred, "On Wedding Rites among the Bhils of North West Central India", *Anthropos*, Vol. XXXXVIII, 1951.

McCurdy, David W., *A Bhil Village of Rajasthan*, Ph.D. Thesis, Ithaca, U.S.A., Cornell University, 1964.

Mead, P. J. & Macgregor, G. L., "Bhils'" *Census of India 1911*, (Bombay report), Vol. VII, Part-1, 1912, pp. 237-238.

Mehta, Balwant Singh, "Meena, Bhils, Grasias, Rawats & Merats", *Tribes of India*, New Delhi, 1950, pp. 206-214.

Mukherjee, S. V., "Bhils", *Census of India 1931*, (Baroda report), Bombay, Vol. XIX, Part-I, 1932.

Naik, D. J., *Tribes of India*, New Delhi, 1950, pp. 117-122.

Naik, T. B., "Aboriginal Festivals in Gujarat", *The Eastern Anthropologist*, Vol. II, no. 1, 1948.

— *Impact of Education on the Bhils: Cultural Change in the Tribal Life of Madhya Pradesh*, Research Programme Committee, Planning Commission, New Delhi, 1969.

Nath, Y. V. S., *Bhils of Ratanmal* (An Analysis of the Social Structure of a Western India Community), The M. S. University of Baroda, 1970.

— *Social Structure of a Bhil Tribe*, Ph.D. thesis, M. S. University, Baroda, 1956.

Navalakha, S. K., "The Authority Structure among the Bhumij and Bhil: A Study of Historical Causations", *The Eastern Anthropologist*, Vol. XIII, no. 1, 1959, pp. 27-40.

— *The Bhagat Movement among Bhils*, Delhi, 1967.

Netram, J.W., *The Bhils*, Jabalpur Mission Press, 1940.

Ojha, Deen Dayal, "Jaisalmair ke Bhil- ek Parichay" (in Hindi), *Vanyajati*, New Delhi, Vol. X, no. 1, 1962.

— "Rajasthani Bhilo ke Mrinyamaya Bhajan" (in Hindi), *Vanyajati*, New Delhi, Vol. X, no. 4, 1964, pp. 128-129.

— "Manjee Bhil" (in Hindi), *Vanyajati*, New Delhi, Vol. IX, no. 4, 1961.

Om Prakash, "Kuchh Bhili Pravartiyan" (in Hindi), *Vanyajati*, New Delhi, Vol. X, no. 4, 1962, pp. 125-127.

Oppert, G. S., *On the Original Inhabitants of Bharat Varsha or India*, West Minister, 1893.

Palmer, R., *A Little Tour in India*, London, 1913.

Pande, Ram (ed.), *Tribals Movements*, Jaipur, 1984.

Papiha, S.S. (ed.), "A Genetic Survey in the Bhil Tribe of Madhya Pradesh", Central India, *American Journal of Physical Anthropology*, Vol. XLIX, 1974.

Paul, Madan C., *Dimension of Tribal Movement in India* (A Study of Udayanchal in Assam Valley), New Delhi, 1989.

Plowden, W. C., "Bheel", report on the *Census of British India 1881*, London, Vol. I, 1883.

Ray, Sarat Chandra, "The Black Bhils of Jaisamand Lake in Rajputana" with plates, *The Journal of the Bihar and Orissa Research Society*, Vol. X, 1924, pp. 97-113.

Risley, Sir Herbert, *The People of India*, Calcutta, 1908,

Robertson, B., "Bhil", *Census of India 1891*, The Central Provinces and Feudatories, (Report), Calcutta, Vol. XI, Part-I, 1893.

Rose, Captain, "Report on the Bheel", Bombay Government Section, Bombay, Vol. X.

Rousselet, Louis, *India and Its Native Provinces*, London, 1875.

Rowney, H.B., *The Wild Tribes of India*, London, 1882, reprint 1990.

Russel, R. V. and Lal, Rai Bahadur Hira, *The Tribes and Castes of the Central Provinces of India*, Vol. II, Delhi, 1975.

Saletore, B.A., *The Wild Tribes in Indian History*, Motilal Banarasidas, Pubjab Sanskrit Book Depot, Lahore, 1935.

Sarkar, J. K., "Extent of Tribal Involvement in Rajputenisation Process: A Study in Western Madhya Pradesh", *Journal of Indian Anthropological Society*, Vol. XVI, 1981, pp. 51-58.

Sarma, Girdhari Lal (ed.), *Rahasthani Bhil Geet*, 3 Vols., Udaipur, Rajasthan, 1956.

— *Rajasthani Bhilo ke Kahavate* (in Hindi), Udaipur, 1954.

Settar, S. and Sontheimer, G.D. (eds.), *Memorial Stones*, (A Case Study of their Origin, Significance and Variety), Institute of Indian Art History, Karnataka University, Dharwad and South Asia Institute, University of Heidelberg, Germany, 1982.

Shah, P.G., "Bhils : the Original Inhabitants of Gujarat", *Journal of the Gujarat Research Society*, Vol. I, no. 4, 1939.

Shashi, S. S., *The Tribal Women of India*, Delhi, 1978.

Shyamaldas, Kaviraj, *Veer Vinod* (Mewar ka Itihas), 4 Vols., Delhi, 1886, reprint 1986.

Siddiki, M.K.A., *Bharat ke adivasi Bhil* (Bhils Tribe of India), (in Hindi), Calcutta, Anthropological Survey of India, 1984.

Singh, Bageshwar, "Bhil to Bhil, Mina to Mina: an Identity Transformation," *The Tribe,* Rajasthan, Vol. XIV, no. 1, March 1982.

— "The Bhil of Western Central India, Paper Presented at the Seminar on Environmental Anthropology", *The Anthropological Survey of India,* Dehradun, 1982.

Singh, Bageshwar and Gupta, Ramji, "The Bhils of Western Central India", *Human Science,* (Formerly Bulletin of the Anthropological Survey of India), Calcutta, Vol. XXXIII, no. 2, June 1984.

Singh, Roop, "Anatomy of Three Tribal Movements in Rajasthan", *The Eastern Anthropologist,* Vol. XXXVII, no. 2.

— "Marriage and Law among the Bhils of Rajasthan", *The Eastern Anthropologist,* Vol. XXXX, no. 2, 1987, pp. 87-99.

Soni, L. N., "Bhilala and Bhil Samooh: ek Parichey" (in Hindi), *Vanyajati,* New Delhi, Vol. XXIX, no. 1, 1981, pp. 8-11.

Srivastava, K.N., "Bhils of Mewar", *The Indian Geographical Journal,* Madras, Vol. XXI, no. 2, 1946.

Symcox, A.H.A., *A History of Khandesh Bhil Crops,* London, 1860.

— *A Memoir of the Khandesh Bhil Crops (1825-1891),* Bombay, 1912.

Terwiel, B.J., *The Tai of Assam and Ancient Tai Ritual: Life Cycle Ceremonies,* Vol. I, Gaya (India), 1980.

Thakkar, A.V., *Tribes of India,* New Delhi, 1950.

Thapar, Ramesh, *The Tribe, Caste and Religion in India,* Macmillian Company of India, Meerut, 1977.

Thompson, C. S., *Rudiments of the Bhili Language,* United Printing Press, Ahmedabad, 1895.

Tod, Col James, *Annals and Antiquities of Rajasthan,* London, 1950.

Tribal Research Institute (Chhindwara, M.P.), *Changing Tribes of Madhya Pradesh*, Indore, 1961.

Valmiki Ramayana, Ayodhya Kanda, Chap. 50, Sloka 50 and *Aranya Kanda*, Chap. 74, Slokas 17-18.

Vanikar, P.G., *Songs of the Panch Mahal Bhils*, Ahmedabad, 1946.

Varma, S., *Bhil Dialects and Khandeshi: A Linguistic Analysis*, Punjab University, 1978.

Varma, S.C., *The Bhil Kills*, Delhi, 1978.

Varshney, N.K., "Criminality among the Bhils", *Vanyajati*, Vol. XV, no. 2, 1967, pp. 81-86.

Venkatachar, C. S., "An Ethnographic Accounts of the Bhils of Central India", *Census of India 1931*, Vol. I, Part-III (Appendix 1), section A, Delhi, 1933.

Vyas, Narendra (ed.), *Adivasi Rajasthan*, Udaipur, Rajasthan, 1969.

Vyas, N. N. and Gaur, T. S., "Bhil Marriage", *The Tribe*, Vol. III, no. 1, 1966, pp. 27-43.

Walter, Yust and Others (eds.), "Bhil", *Encyclopaedia Britannica*, London, Vol. III, 1951.

Watson, J. F. (ed.), *The People of India: The Races and the Tribes of Hindustan*, Vol. VII, Delhi, 1987.

Watson, Major J.W., *Indian Antiquary*, 1874.

Webbs, H. W. T., "The Bhils of Rajputana", *Census of India 1951*, edited by Y.L.Dashora, Jodhpur, Vol. X, Part-1.

Wiesinger, Rita, "The Women's part in the Religious Life of the Bhil", *Anthropos*, Vol. LXII, 1967, pp. 497-508.

Wilson, Rev. J., *Aboriginal Tribes of the Bombay Presidency*, Bombay, 1876.

— *History of the Superssion of the Infanticide in Western India*, Bombay, 1855.

Index